M000287269

Crisis and Change in Post-Cold War Global Politics

Erica Resende · Dovilė Budrytė
Didem Buhari-Gulmez
Editors

Crisis and Change in Post-Cold War Global Politics

Ukraine in a Comparative Perspective

Editors
Erica Resende
Brazilian War College
Rio de Janeiro, Brazil

Didem Buhari-Gulmez
İzmir University of Economics
İzmir, Turkey

Dovilė Budrytė
School of Liberal Arts
Georgia Gwinnett College
Lawrenceville, GA, USA

ISBN 978-3-319-78588-2   ISBN 978-3-319-78589-9   (eBook)
https://doi.org/10.1007/978-3-319-78589-9

Library of Congress Control Number: 2018937858

© The Editor(s) (if applicable) and The Author(s), under exclusive license to Springer International Publishing AG, part of Springer Nature 2018
This work is subject to copyright. All rights are solely and exclusively licensed by the Publisher, whether the whole or part of the material is concerned, specifically the rights of translation, reprinting, reuse of illustrations, recitation, broadcasting, reproduction on microfilms or in any other physical way, and transmission or information storage and retrieval, electronic adaptation, computer software, or by similar or dissimilar methodology now known or hereafter developed.
The use of general descriptive names, registered names, trademarks, service marks, etc. in this publication does not imply, even in the absence of a specific statement, that such names are exempt from the relevant protective laws and regulations and therefore free for general use.
The publisher, the authors and the editors are safe to assume that the advice and information in this book are believed to be true and accurate at the date of publication. Neither the publisher nor the authors or the editors give a warranty, express or implied, with respect to the material contained herein or for any errors or omissions that may have been made. The publisher remains neutral with regard to jurisdictional claims in published maps and institutional affiliations.

Cover image: VINCENT MUNDY/Alamy Stock Photo
Cover design: Tjaša Krivec

Printed on acid-free paper

This Palgrave Macmillan imprint is published by the registered company Springer International Publishing AG part of Springer Nature
The registered company address is: Gewerbestrasse 11, 6330 Cham, Switzerland

PREFACE

The idea to write a book on the crises in International Relations (IR) was born during a coffee break at the 2016 International Studies Association Annual Meeting in Atlanta. A conversation between editors suggested that the crisis in Ukraine was a perfect case study, interesting not only for the changes in Ukrainian politics themselves but for what it actually meant for our field of study. We felt that writing a book about the 2013/2014 events in Ukraine opens up a sea of possibilities of research *problématiques*. Topics apparently removed from each other—regime change, corruption, social movements, nation-building, geopolitics, civil war, historical memory, democratization, economic development, genocide, civil disobedience, social media, diasporas, power politics, migration, statecraft diplomacy, international organizations—all seem to come together in Ukrainian case. In a sense, one could say that Ukraine was like a kaleidoscope of issues: depending on which way you look, you end with a different picture, a distinct perspective on things. As such, each image produced by the kaleidoscope had a unique focus, bringing out particular patterns of shapes and forms to the front. One image does not negate the other, but rather complements it and enriches the kaleidoscope experience.

It is with the kaleidoscope analogy in mind that we invite our readers to engage with the events of 2013/2014 in Ukraine and beyond. This edited volume does not aspire to provide a macro-explanation of the politics in Ukraine. Nor does it offer a clean, detailed timeline of events in a chain of logics that might lead to any kind of signs of what is to come.

In fact, this volume does not even provide to readers a clear conclusion about what happened in that time period and what might come of it in upcoming years. It does, however, bring out the multiple dimensions of the crisis in Ukraine in a labored attempt to reflect upon the events of 2013/2014 less as a crisis and more like an opportunity for social change. In this regard, the theoretical framework of crisis developed by Dirk Nabers provided us with the adequate lenses to build our Ukrainian kaleidoscope, which has ultimately yielded multi-colored, insightful images to our readers.

Furthermore, an edited volume is never a simple job of compiling chapters on a single topic. Any volume worth of its salt should transcend a mere aggregation of articles and offer readers a broad variety of images—yes, let's continue with the kaleidoscope analogy—that communicate with each other and thus construct a rich mosaic. Each chapter in this volume offers a unique perspective on Ukraine: some with a more theoretical focus, others more empirical; some explore domestic factors, other attempt to establish comparisons with other cases, be it in the region or globally. All of them, however, pose more questions than actually provide clear-cut answers to readers.

As in any publication enterprise, this has been the product of a coming-together of scholars, students, research assistants, publishers, and editors. Above all, due to the scope of the project and the diversity of contributors, they all worked in different continents and time zones, and most outside their own respective native languages. It was a network in the truest sense of the word.

As editors, we would like to thank the contributors for trusting us with their work as well as putting up with our demands of deadlines, standards, structure, references, and all those little things that make academic writing such a time-consuming task in our field. We particularly wish to thank those who were willing to step outside their comfort zone to embrace a post-structuralist framework in accordance with the proposal of this book. We appreciate your effort of un-peeling yourselves of your rationalist clothing.

Our thanks are also due to Palgrave Macmillan, especially Anca Pusca and Katelyn Zingg, for their help with the manuscript.

Erica Resende would like to personally thank her former colleagues at Candido Mendes University (UCAM) as well as new ones at the Brazilian War College, Rio de Janeiro, Brazil. This project started in mid-2016 while she was Assistant Professor at UCAM, yet the book itself will be ready when she begins in a new—and now tenured—position. She would also like to thank her co-editors, Dovile Budryte and Didem Buhari-Gulmez, who have so gracefully invited her to this fruitful collaboration. Finally, she would like to acknowledge her research grant from "Fundação Carlos Chagas Filho de Amparo à Pesquisa do Estado do Rio de Janeiro" (Faperj), for supporting her multiple times in the last 7 years, most notably through the 2016–2018 "Jovem Cientista do Nosso Estado" program.

Didem Buhari-Gulmez thanks Seçkin Barış Gülmez, Zafer and Neşe Karatay, Hakan Kırımlı, Ahmet and Meryem Buhari, and TUBITAK BIDEB 2219, for supporting her research on the Crimean Tatar community.

Dovilė Budrytė would like to thank Georgia Gwinnett College for financial support (SEED grant) and her research assistants, Charlie Marburger and Mandy Crane, for their assistance with this project.

Rio de Janeiro, Brazil   Erica Resende
Lawrenceville, USA   Dovilė Budrytė
İzmir, Turkey   Didem Buhari-Gulmez

CONTENTS

ix

EDITORS AND CONTRIBUTORS

About the Editors

Erica Resende is Assistant Professor at the Brazilian War College, Brazil, and Affiliate Lecturer at the University of Oklahoma, USA. Her research interests are IR theory, US foreign policy, identity politics, memory and trauma studies, and discourse analysis. She is US Fulbright Scholar and US State Department Alumna since 2006 and recipient of the research award "Jovem Cientista do Nosso Estado" from the Brazilian governmental grant agency, Faperj.

Dovilė Budrytė is a professor of political science at Georgia Gwinnett College, USA. Her areas of research interests include memory politics, trauma, nationalism, and gender studies. Her publications include articles and books on various topics related to minority rights and memory politics. In 2014/15, she was the recipient of the University System of Georgia Excellence in Teaching Award.

Didem Buhari-Gulmez received her Ph.D. in Politics from the London University, UK. She is Associate Professor in International Relations at the İzmir University of Economics, Turkey. Previously, she was an Early Career Researcher at Oxford Brookes University and a TUBITAK fellow at London School of Economics, UK. Her publications include: (2017) Europeanization in a Global Context, Palgrave Macmillan; (2017) Rethinking Ideology in the Age of Global Discontent, Routledge (co-edited); (2016) Global Culture: Consciousness and Connectivity (co-edited) Ashgate; (2016) "Religion and Nation-Building in Crimea" in Nation-Building and Identity in the post-Soviet Space: New Tools and Approaches, Routledge.

Contributors

Douglas Becker is Assistant Professor of International Relations at the University of Southern California, USA. His research examines the role of historical memory in foreign policy analysis and in public diplomacy. He has authored several articles, including "Memory and Trauma as Elements of Identity in Foreign Policymaking" and "Genocide, Trauma, Historical Memory and Public Diplomacy: Justifying Paul Kagame."

Aziz Burkhanov is Assistant Professor at the Graduate School of Public Policy at Nazarbayev University in Astana, Kazakhstan. His research interests include nationalism and identity theories, national identity politics, policies and practices with a special focus on identity issues and their perceptions in the public narratives in former Soviet area. He has worked in policy analysis and consulting as a Research Fellow at the IWEP, a think tank advising the Kazakhstan's government on policies, and as a Senior Associate at IHS Cambridge Energy Research Associates (CERA).

Oksana Huss is a Ph.D. candidate at the Institute for Development and Peace, University of Duisburg-Essen, Germany, and co-founder of the Interdisciplinary Corruption Research Network (ICRNetwork.org). She was a Petro Jacyk visiting fellow at the University of Toronto, Canada. She works as a lecturer at Anti-Corruption Research and Education Centre at National University of Kyiv-Mohyla Academy, Ukraine, as a consultant for international organizations. Her main areas of expertise are political corruption in hybrid regimes and theories of corruption.

Katja Lehtisaari, Ph.D. in Social Sciences, is a University Researcher at the Aleksanteri Institute, University of Helsinki, Finland, and Editor-in-Chief of "Idäntutkimus," the Finnish review for Russian and East European Studies. She is a scholar at the Finnish Centre of Excellence in Russian Studies and a member of Helsinki Media Policy Research Group. She was Visiting Research Fellow at the Reuters Institute for the Study of Journalism, University of Oxford, UK, in 2015. Her research topics have varied from changing media structures and journalism to media business and media policy, often in international, comparative setting.

Tamara Martsenyuk holds a Ph.D. in Sociology. In 2017/2018, she was a Fulbright Scholar at the Harriman Institute, Columbia University, USA. She is currently Associate Professor at the Department of Sociology, National University of Kyiv-Mohyla Academy, Ukraine. Her research interest focuses on the social structure of society and, particularly, on gender relations. Her latest research is women's activism in Ukraine, particularly in the 2013/2014 Euromaidan protests and in the war in the Donbas (the "Invisible battalion": women's participation in the military operations in the ATO).

Milana Nikolko, Ph.D. was Associate Professor of Political Science at V. Vernadsky Taurida National University, Ukraine, and Visiting Professor at Valdosta State University, USA. She is currently Adjunct Professor at the Institute of European, Russian and Eurasian Studies, Carleton University, Canada. Her areas of interests include Ukraine's national building process, conflict mediation, narratives of victimization in ethnic communities, and migration and diaspora networks.

Jukka Pietiläinen is the director of Finnish political think tank Left Forum Finland. He has worked as a senior researcher at the Aleksanteri Institute (Finnish Centre for Russian and Eastern European Studies), University of Helsinki, Finland, from 2007 to 2018, most recently heading a research project on Media and Security in Central Asia. His research interests include Russian media and journalism, Russian society and politics, quantitative audience studies, foreign news flow and Finnish society and politics.

Susanne Szkola is a Ph.D. Candidate and Teaching Assistant at the Brussels School of International Studies, University of Kent, Belgium. Her doctoral research focuses on processes of othering, ontological security seeking, and securitization in the South Caucasus vis-à-vis the EU and Russia. Her research interests include IR theory, Critical Security and Conflict Studies, Critical Geopolitics, Political and Social Psychology, EU/Eastern Europe and Central Asia/Russia relations, and the European Union, especially CSDP/ENP/Enlargement.

Iryna Troian has a B.A. in Sociology and a M.A. in Public Relations, both from the National University of Kyiv-Mohyla Academy, Ukraine. She has a Diploma of European Studies from the University of Vienna, Austria. Her areas of interest are human rights and gender.

Elira Turdubaeva is Associate Professor at the Department of Journalism and Mass Communications at American University of Central Asia, Bishkek, Kyrgyzstan. Her research focuses on media uses, political participation and media, election campaign analysis, social media uses, new media studies, ICT and youth, public relations, propaganda analysis, representations of gender, journalism education, etc.

LIST OF TABLES

CHAPTER 1

Introduction

Erica Resende, Dovilė Budrytė and Didem Buhari-Gulmez

A classic definition of crisis within International Relations (IR) comes from Charles Herman (1969, see also Herman and Brady 1972), who refers to crisis as (1) a situation that threatens high-priority goals of the decision-making unit, (2) restricts the amount of time available for response before the decision is transformed, and (3) surprises the members of the decision-making unit by its occurrence (Herman 1969: 414). As such, crisis is understood in terms of something that happens—an unexpected event—and has to be dealt with, managed. In a way, crisis is treated as an independent variable that triggers some kind of response that affects the behavior of states. It should come then as no surprise that the notion of crisis entails connotations of something that is negative, dramatic, harmful, unexpected, traumatic, unpredictable, abnormal, and undesirable that has to be put managed and put under control.

Perhaps this is why Colin Hay (1996, 2013) argues that the word "crisis" is used pejoratively and employed simultaneously to designate

E. Resende (✉)
Brazilian War College, Rio de Janeiro, Brazil

D. Budrytė
Political Science, Georgia Gwinnett College, Lawrenceville, USA

D. Buhari-Gulmez
International Relations, İzmir University of Economics, İzmir, Turkey

© The Author(s) 2018
E. Resende et al. (eds.), *Crisis and Change in Post-Cold War Global Politics*, https://doi.org/10.1007/978-3-319-78589-9_1

1

momentary emergencies, recurrent derailment, and enduring cataclysm. Crises can be conceptualized as moments in which "interventions are both possible and plausible." (Hay 1996: 425) Sometimes such moments may even be desirable, empowering actors (both domestic and international) to exercise the autonomous capacity to act upon them, contain them, solve them, and surpass them to re-impose order.

This description seems to fit an overwhelming body of literature that deals with crisis in IR (see Carr 2001 [1939]; Morgenthau 1948; McCormick 1978; Gilpin 1981; Brecher and Wilkenfeld 1982; Allison and Zelikow 1999). Indeed, most of the IR literature produced during the Cold War was very much concerned with crisis perceptions and decision-making in response to crisis[1] as well as crisis management.[2] These authors share a materialist, objectivist, rationalist approach to crisis that favors agency over structure, and which implies that crises are self-evident phenomena—like wars, financial turmoil, or natural catastrophes—that stand as "threats to basic values" (Brecher 1984: 239). Therefore, responses in terms of shifts in foreign and security policy would center around the "perceptions of the top-level decision-maker," with "high probability of involvement in military hostilities"[3] (Brecher 1984: 239).

However, a brief look at IR literature after 9/11 reveals a shift from this traditional way of conceptualizing crisis.[4] Instead of crisis being depicted and represented as "exogenous shocks" in response to policy and decision-makers react to and solve (i.e., agent-centered approaches), we observe a growing number of works that emphasize crisis as "endogenous constructions," where ontological questions about the relationship between agent and structure are integrated and thus problematized (for this distinction, see Widmaier et al. 2007: 748).

---

[1] For a review of this literature, see Stern (1999, 2003) and Boin (2004).

[2] For a review, see Kouzmin and Jarman (2004). For Nabers (2015: 19), the International Crisis Behavior Project (ICBP) promoted by the USA in 1975 epitomizes this trend of Cold War thinking in foreign policy.

[3] This approach survived the end of Cold War. See Hebron and James (1997), Brown (2004), Widmaier (2007), He (2013), and the *International Studies Review Forum* organized by Dayton (2004).

[4] Stuart Croft (2006) developed a model of crisis as a social phenomenon. He understands crises as "engines" for discursive change that have to connect with traditional narratives to become hegemonic and perceived as legitimate. Looking into the 2008 subprime crisis in the USA, Brassett and Clarke (2012) demonstrated how traumatic imagery transmitted by the media, academia, and policy-makers has produced particular subjectivities.

A recent study by Dirk Nabers offers a new and useful way to analyze crises in IR. Nabers argues that the bulk of the traditional IR crisis literature is strictly materialist and objectivist and, as such, privileges agency, decision-making, and crisis management at the expense of more structural accounts of the nature of crisis (Nabers 2015: 5). Although crisis and change are inextricably linked, they are only rarely considered jointly in the IR literature, he adds. He offers what he calls a theory of crisis and change in global politics, which is more concerned with the structural aspect of crisis and how it enables an open-ended project for global politics and social change.

For Nabers, "crisis represents a situation in which our everyday beliefs of how the world works are thoroughly disrupted by an event that is out of our control" (2015: 44). In a way, it is comparable to trauma due to its difficulty in being assimilated, domesticated, represented, and communicated (see Edkins 2003; Resende and Budryte 2013). The likely result of this disruptive process, Nabers argues, is a social change in the form of community (re)building and the construction and/or transformation of a (new) collective identity. Therefore, inherent crises of social structures as well as the disruption of all fully familiar subjectivity are at the root of any kind of social, cultural, or institutional change. Any transformation of the social, of smaller or larger extent, should then be understood as being engendered by crisis. Hence, the duality of the crisis/change nexus pointed out by Nabers (2015).

In a way, this shift in literature has been anticipated by Jutta Weldes' investigations in the late 1990s about the cultural production of crisis. Claiming that crises are always "cultural artifacts" and thus not objectively identifiable, Weldes (1999) argues that when particular events threaten the identity of a state, they become constituted as crisis which, in turn, help consolidate, reaffirm, transform, and/or appease a particular writing of a state identity. As a result, one is led to recognize that there is no ontology of crisis to be grasped beyond the practices that generate said crisis in the first place. There is no objective status of crisis that would require governmental response to it or its containment and/or management. Instead, she argues, "events that are ostensibly the same will in fact be constituted as different crises, or not as crisis at all, by and for states with different identities" (Weldes 1999: 37).

Drawing on Nabers, this book is built on the key assumption that any social inquiry into global politics should transcend the canonical emphasis on intergovernmental relations with the privileged agency conferred to the role of states. Following a not so recent trend in social theory, we conceptualize the social realm as a discursive space of infinite, endless articulations in which power attempts to transform social relations in an open process to constitute society (Laclau and Mouffe 1985).

Furthermore, it is not surprising that the study of crisis is often linked with the study of hegemonic social relations, both globally and locally. According to Friedman's (1994) thesis of "dehegemonization bringing dehomogenization," the decline of central authority paves the way for the revival of previously repressed identities, visions, and movements in the society. The events in Ukraine since the end of the Cold War mark the fall of the core visions and civic identity movement around which different groups, organizations, and individuals rallied. The decline of dominant discourses often reinforces the emergence of new, alternative ones, rendering some agents and structures more visible while disempowering others.

This growing body of literature on crises as social phenomena in IR has not yet paid enough attention to re-conceptualizing crises as social phenomena in contexts outside of the "West." Therefore, with this line of inquiry (and intent to contribute to the body of literature on crises as social phenomena), we propose to turn our lenses to Ukraine (which has been described as "classic crisis" by Menon and Rumer 2015) in order to engage with some of the assumptions prescribed above: What is the relationship between crisis and change? Is there an ontology of crisis? How are crises culturally and socially constructed? How do issues of agency and structure come into play in Ukraine? Which subjectivities were brought into existence by the Ukraine crisis discourse? How does identity come to play with the making of this crisis?

The literature describing the recent developments in Ukraine (mostly focusing on 2004 or 2013–2014) focuses on the material, tangible dimensions of economic and social developments in Ukraine, paying a lot of attention to its relations with Russia. There is an assumption that the crisis can be "fixed" (e.g., see Åslund 2015). In other cases, such as a book by Rajan Menon and Eugene Rumer, *Conflict in Ukraine: The Unwinding of the Post-Cold War Order* (2015), the focus is on the events in 2014 (that are described as a crisis) and their potential impact on the whole post-Cold War international order.

In both cases (and many other cases), the recent developments in Ukraine are conceptualized as a "prolonged" crisis, i.e., the one that cannot be easily "solved." This raises several related questions, such as:

How was the representation of Ukraine as a "prolonged crisis" made possible? Are there any dimensions other than the cultural to the events in Ukraine that allowed for its representation as a "prolonged crisis"? How did the protests in Euromaidan and armed conflict in 2014 become represented and signified as the main expressions of what became known in the global media as the "Ukrainian crisis" or "crisis in Ukraine" (often forgetting many previous crises and obscuring the transnational dimensions of these developments)?

The contributions in this volume focus on the recent developments in 2013–2014 by historically contextualizing them. Some authors such as Nikolko, Buhari-Gulmez, and Becker draw on historical material to explain the embeddedness of these developments in the previous decades, going to back to the end of the Cold War and beyond. Other authors, including Huss and Budrytė, have preferred to privilege the role of a transformative crisis—the disintegration of the Soviet Union, which distinguishes itself from more common, ordinary crises—as a starting point to better understand the Ukrainian case. In this regard, as explained by Resende in her contribution, Deleuze's concept of the "Event"—which he characterizes as "pure," "true" events in relation to ordinary, superficial, historical events—has helped us to navigate a sea of crisis discourses. For Deleuze, the issue is not events, but the "Event" with a capital E.

Deleuze's use of the imagery of scars and wounds clarifies this issue further. For him, historical events are changes in intensity and energy changed between bodies; hence, their affect is "superficial," sense-like, much like scars on the surface. True, pure Events, on the other hand, have the force to act and leave marks upon bodies. They are wounds rather than scars. As such, there is no healing or overcoming of the wound. From this, it follows that Deleuze's Event, the transcendental wound, evades domestication, management, or solving. Much like the approach, Nabers has described in regard to a new ontological understanding of the crisis. It does not allow for being overcome or "fixed."

This book aims to capture the events in Ukraine underlying multiple encounters between past legacies, alternative futures, and reformist tendencies as well as the changing individual–society–state relations in Ukrainian politics and society emerging from the event-ness of the collapse of the Soviet Union. Keeping in mind Reynolds' (2008) suggestion to seriously consider Deleuze's repeated argument that events are only effects (Deleuze 2004: 10, 29, 241) as a warning to conceive events as having double causalities involving a mixture of bodies, state of affairs and sense, that is, not to understand wound as something that accidentally and contingently befalls us, we have opted to treat the events in Ukraine not from the angle of empirics but rather of the order of the virtual, as an event-effect. The underlying challenge taken by this book will be of exploring the generative, transformative, genesis field in which the events in Ukraine are produced.

Our approach is better understood from the distinction made by Lynn Doty (1993) between "why-questions" and "how-questions." Following Hollis and Smith (1990), she argues that while the former aims to establish patterns of reoccurrence and predictability, thus producing incomplete, rationalist, and reified explanations of the social order, the latter seeks to understand how this order came into being. "How-questions" are able to problematize realities, relationships, and meanings and thus to point to the conditions of possibility of social order. By articulating "how-questions," this book will be able to stay true to both its post-structuralist influence and its Deleuzian conception of the Event.

Furthermore, we are particularly interested in the ways in which the events in Ukraine were constructed as crisis represented by social agents (mass media) not only in Ukraine, but also beyond its borders. We are especially intrigued by the "long distance" circulation of the discursive, cultural practices that constituted the events in Ukraine as a crisis and the ways in which they were communicated globally. Thus, Lehtisaari et al.'s chapter explores representations of the annexation of Crimea in 2014 and armed conflict in Eastern Ukraine in the newspapers in Kazakhstan and Kyrgyzstan, two former Soviet republics. Susanne Szkola's contribution explores collective identity formation in the EU Eastern Partnership Countries vis-à-vis the EU and Russia. Based on an analytical framework that bridges the studies of crisis with the literature on social, political, discursive, and aesthetic change, this book puts an emphasis on how crises emerge and come into being, and how they resonate and reproduce within states, societies, groups, individuals, and the global system in general.

As stated above, crisis does not necessarily imply a disabling environment for agency. The crisis discourse may end up empowering specific ideologies that were not previously part of the equation. It also provides a novel context that renders certain issues more "visible" in the global agenda while silencing others. In this regard, it is necessary to ask to what extent the developments in Ukraine have rendered different issues in the region more visible or invisible in the domestic and international arena. For example, Martsenyuk and Troian's chapter traces the participation of women during Euromaidan, arguing that this revolutionary event both disempowered and empowered women, at some points, reducing their participation to traditional roles, but also opening new spaces for egalitarianism and social criticism. Moreover, what are the implications of the changing parameters in discursive, normative, and cultural realms for minority groups, indigenous communities such as Crimean Tatars, diasporas, neighboring societies, and international community as a whole? Two chapters (Nikolko's and Buhari-Gulmez's) contribute insights into these questions.

The events and discourses that are often associated with the recent developments in Ukraine that have been labeled as "the Ukrainian crisis" or the "crisis in Ukraine"—the Euromaidan protests, the annexation of Crimea by Russia and the conflict in Eastern Ukraine—emphasize the urgent need to develop a better understanding of what constitutes an international "crisis" and what its relationship to change may be. At the same time, studying crises as social phenomena, not sudden, exogenous events, helps us to develop a more nuanced understanding of various processes and discourses, emanating from domestic and international actors, that include relations between various social and political groups, construction of myths, and (re)creation of identity groups.

As a case study, post-Soviet Ukraine is a crucial case of fragmentation between the East and the West, the past and the future, the authoritarian and the liberal dynamics, among others. It stands as a suitable example where multiple discourses clash, collapse, intensify, and evolve, transforming social relations beyond its national borders. New identities emerge and old one decline. Meanings are made and remade, and the social fabric is weaved and re-weaved.

By rejecting the prevailing tendency to resort to dichotomous analyses in the study of Ukraine based on pro-Russian versus pro-Western camps, we attempted to engage with comparative perspectives. For example, Budrytė's chapter compares memory politics in Ukraine and Lithuania. We believe that the political context in Ukraine is far from featuring unified fronts, and its complex web of social agents and structures should be reflected in the book by providing a careful analysis about the historicity, complexity, and dynamism of Ukrainian crisis after the disintegration of the Soviet Union.

Following this line of reasoning, the book is divided into three parts. Part I "Crisis and Change: Theory and Practice" starts with Erica Resende's contribution "Crisis and Change in Global Politics: A Dialogue with Deleuze and Badiou's Event to Understand the Crisis in Ukraine." Her work lays the theoretical foundation for the volume, engaging in a dialogue with Deleuze's concept of event. She argues that Deleuze's use of the imagery of scars and wounds "clarifies how he differentiates event from Event," and this is meant to provide a better understanding of the ontology of crisis and change. According to Resende, following Badiou, by recognizing events as rupture, "one is able to understand how, in an Event, the inconsistent multiplicity which always lies beneath a particular social order is able to appear subjectively. Only in an Event can the excluded part be visible. An Event succeeds in representing a part which is previously unrepresented. This unfolding of new representations from an Event produces Truths, Subjects, and new social systems. As a result, Events are intimately connected to change."

Having applied this theory to the case of Ukraine, Resende finds that Euromaidan was "particularly meaningful as a rupture to be established, dominant structures and discourses." She also finds that it was also an Event that demanded decision (What did it mean? A revolt? A power overthrown? An act of aggression by Russia?), scission (What side to take? Pro-Russia? Pro-Ukraine?), and intervention (How can we seize the moment for change?). Resende concludes by relating her theorization about the Event that created the crisis in Ukraine to "the writing and rewriting of the boundaries of both Europe and Russia." She finds that "Ukraine sits at the so-called borderland of Europe, which makes the boundaries of the conflict particularly problematic in terms of the ontology of the crisis."

Douglas Becker's chapter in this section "The Rationality and Emotion of Russian Historical Memory: The Case of Crimea" analyzes historical memory discourses by Russian President Vladimir Putin as an attempt at public diplomacy. Drawing on President Putin's speech to the Duma on the Annexation of Crimea, Becker conceptualizes the role of memory discourse as an "alternative legitimation discourse," citing historical ties between Crimea and Russia, attempting to address legal arguments against redrawing maps. Becker's analysis demonstrates how the leaders' task of legitimizing policy choices becomes easier when the discourse frames events as crises.

Memory politics plays a major role in Becker's analysis. He conceptualizes memory as a lens through which the Russians consider Crimea. The city of Sevastopol, or the "City of Glory"—to borrow Serhii Plokhy's (2000) term—is conceptualized as part of the Russian identity, almost an equivalent to Kosovo. Becker argues that even if the city had no other value than its historical importance, it could be a powerful impetus for Russian action. Becker concludes by suggesting that the memory discourses analyzed in his chapter, alternative legitimation discourses, are linked to domestic Russian politics. In his argument, "emotionalism of the memory drives" is related to "populist desires for local governance."

In "Collective Trauma, Memories and Victimization Narratives in Modern Strategies of Ethnic Consolidation: The Crimean Tatar Case," Milana Nikolko focuses on the Crimean case where the Crimean Tatar community has faced several crises, including Deportation, a difficult return to Crimea and the annexation of Crimea, among others. She emphasizes that Crimean Tatars do not constitute a unified front with a predetermined and fixed identity, referring to the multiplicity of narratives about Crimean Tatar identity and its position in the ongoing conflict between Ukraine and Russia over the peninsula.

Following poststructuralism, Nikolko discusses the role of cultural memory, trauma, and narratives of victimization underlying a constant process of reshaping the Crimean Tatar "Self" and "Other." In addition to the complex relationship between Self and Other, she benefits from the concepts of space, event, and fixity in order to explore the inclusion/exclusion dynamics of Crimean Tatar subjectivities. According to Nikolko, the victimization narratives that pave the way for new Crimean Tatar subjectivity and political mobilization have found an echo in Ukraine's post-Orange revolution and postannexation narratives about the Soviet past. Since 2014 annexation, the narratives of Deportation tend to diverge in mainland Ukraine and Crimea. While Ukraine resorts to decommunization policy and the official recognition of Deportation tragedy as an act of Genocide, Crimea's new authorities embrace an old discourse which sees Deportation as a "blurred phenomenon lacking ethno-political connotation to Crimean Tatar tragedy." Nikolko argues that both narratives lack a solid foundation in terms of detailed memory work on the Deportation.

Part II "Crisis and Social Change: Ukraine in a Comparative Perspective" starts with Oksana Huss' contribution "Corruption, Crisis, and Change: Use and Misuse of an Empty Signifier." Huss directly engages the empirical framework developed by Dirk Nabers to explore the dynamics of hegemonic processes and challenges to these processes associated with crises. Nabers thus describes the relationship between hegemony, challenges to it, and crises:

> Hegemony is understood as an articulatory practice evolving out of the interplay of the logics of equivalence and difference and based on the temporal filling of a dislocated social structure by means of empty signifiers. The dialectics of universalism and particularism is central to this process, with the former being understood as the always fruitless effort to gain a full identity. Universalism, in that sense, becomes the *pars pro toto* for this elusive fullness.

> Any *hegemonic process* can then be traced along the lines of the political ontology: Starting with the *articulation of a particular political crisis* (of lesser or greater extent), which must in some way be connected to sedimented practices to be credible, and moving to the *competition between different political forces to hegemonize the political field*, resulting in *the acceptance of a certain interpretative framework of identification (actual hegemony)* and its eventual routinization and *political institutionalization*. This final act of institutionalization causes feedback effects on the discursive articulation of the crisis, new interpretative frames start to compete, and politics continues. Theoretically, this circle never ends (Nabers 2015: 146–47).

Huss' chapter analyzes corruption in Ukraine from a post-structuralist perspective, focusing on the following question: "What meaning do the Presidents of Ukraine assign to corruption as an empty signifier and to what extent this temporarily fixed meaning unfolds potential to create social identities?" She argues that the main challenge faced by the presidents in Ukraine has been to create a dominant public discourse and frame corruption in a way that represents themselves as "non-corrupt Self" and their competitors as "corrupt Others." Presidents play a very important role in Ukraine's semi-presidential system, and their roles in shaping dominant public discourses should not be underestimated.

Huss presents two case studies exploring how Viktor Yushchenko in 2005–2010 and Viktor Yanukovych in 2010–2014 used an empty signifier of corruption, and what role the term "corruption" played for both political crisis and political change in Ukraine. According to her account, before winning the Presidency, Yushchenko drew the line between himself and then-President Kuchma, whom he portrayed as lawless. Yushchenko presented himself and society as victims of the Kuchma's regime. Furthermore, Yushchenko used a narrative of democracy and rule of law as closely connected to the "European values," attempting to portray the Kuchma's regime as the non-European "Other," autocracy with corrupt government. Trust also played a major role in Yushchenko's narrative. Yushchenko's stated priority in his early political career was trust building into political institutions through transparency and communication. Huss argues that paradoxically, Yushchenko became the victim of his own discourse on corruption when he became a president. Corruption accusations started to be used widely by the politicians, and mutual accusations of corruption became a trap for all politicians, not just the ones associated with autocracy. Furthermore, Yushchenko developed an anti-corruption strategy targeting high-level corruption in the parliament; however, the parliament could not and did not support such strategy which could have been suicidal for many politicians in the system of corruption.

Unlike Yushchenko, Yanukovych did little to assign specific meanings to corruption. Huss argues that he presented himself as a strong leader creating order in the midst of chaos associated with corruption. He presented himself as willing to control the main "villains" supposedly perpetuating corruption—that is, civil servants and bureaucrats. He identified "corrupt bureaucracy" as the main obstacle to his reforms. However, Yanukovych used the pretext of fight against the corruption to consolidate his presidential powers. While trying to achieve this goal, Yanukovych was not able to challenge the dominance of the discourse of political corruption developed under Yushchenko. The public still associated Ukrainian politics with corruption, while integration into the European Union (EU) was associated with non-corruption. Yanukovych's refusal to sign the Association Agreement with the EU (associated with non-corruption) triggered a political crisis and the Euromaidan revolution. Euromaidan created the space for identity of protestors in line with equivalences as European, democratic and non-corrupt, constituted differentially and through recourse to an antagonistic *Other* embodied in corrupt Yanukovych's "Family." According to Huss' findings, after Euromaidan, the discourse in which politics are still associated with corruption remains hegemonic; however, the identity of non-corrupt is assigned to the non-governmental institutions.

Issues related to identity are at the center of Tamara Martsenyuk and Iryna Troian's contribution on women's participation in Euromaidan protests, entitled "Gender Role Scenarios of Women's Participation in Euromaidan Protests in Ukraine." The contributors draw on Nabers' insights about the enabling potential of crises. Crisis might be seen as a source of opportunities; thus, analysis of the meanings' production and transmission through discourse helps to articulate the social changes. Applying Nabers' framework to the analysis of the Euromaidan protests, the authors show how political acts of women (such as the creation of units of women protesters) have contributed to a shift in discourse and made collective attempts to use the crisis to argue for change of gender order to make it more egalitarian.

Martsenyuk and Troian argue that at Euromaidan women were actively participating in all types of activities in the protest space. They were engaged in fighting, peacekeeping, provided information and logistics support, among other activities. In the beginning of the peaceful protests, women composed almost half of the protesters. However, by February 2014 women were excluded from the protest zone and constituted only a marginal minority among the protesters. The militarization of the protest space reinforced sexist rhetoric and gender segregation in the division of labor among protesters as well as strengthened men's privileges as warriors.

Drawing on sociological survey data and mass media analysis, Martsenyuk and Troian identified two gender-role scenarios, dividing them into "patriarchal" and "egalitarian." The patriarchal gender-role scenario consists of three main images: Mother, Ukrainian Beauty, and Victim. Women internalized traditional gendered roles and performed them during Euromaidan. These roles included cleaning, cooking, and delivering food. Women were represented as weak when compared to men, in need of defense and care. Simultaneously, the crisis opened up spaces for women to criticize sexism and create alternative initiatives. Egalitarian gender-role scenario consists of Female Warrior, Peacekeeper, and Information and Logistics Provider images. The authors of the article conclude that during Euromaidan protests, traditional gender roles were reaffirmed (expressing patriarchal gendered scenarios) as well as contested (following egalitarian scenarios). Furthermore, their research suggests that these gender-role scenarios could overlap one with another as some women's initiatives could combine features of both of them—patriarchal and egalitarian.

Similarly to Oksana Huss' contribution, Dovilė Budrytė's "Memory, War and Mnemonical In/Security: A Comparison of Lithuania and Ukraine" embraces the empirical framework developed by Nabers to explore hegemonic processes and challenges to these processes associated with crises. Budrytė explores the rise of a hegemonic discourse associated with anti-Soviet partisans in Ukraine and Lithuania. She argues that in both cases, there was a "crisis of history" that intersected with the disintegration of the Soviet Union in 1991. This was the time when new discourses challenging the legitimacy of the story about the "Great Patriotic war" were created. Powerful new discourses about anti-Soviet partisans became alternative discourses to the old discourse about the "Great Patriotic war," and eventually, these discourses about the anti-Soviet partisans became state-supported discourses, which, coupled with discourses about national genocides, rose to a hegemonic status. In Lithuania, legal acts acknowledging the legitimacy of anti-Soviet resistance were passed in 1999, and in Ukraine, the anti-Soviet resistance fighters (the Organization of Ukrainian Nationalists, or the OUN and the Ukrainian Insurgent Army, or the UPA) have increasingly received state recognition since the Orange revolution, most recently in 2015, with the decommunization laws.

Budrytė links the creation of the new powerful discourses about anti-Soviet partisans to mnemonical security. Drawing on Maria Mälksoo's (2015) work, she argues that the concept of "mnemonical security" can be used to describe securitization and consolidation of certain memory discourses that are associated with the processes of "defending" memory and can lead to security dilemmas internationally. Ukraine and Lithuania have been creating biographical narratives that include accounts of anti-Soviet resistance fighters. These biographical narratives are seen as sources of security and guides in interactions with other states. However, they are likely to be simplified stories where some memories are left out and others highlighted. No matter how carefully constructed, the narratives will include tensions and contradictions that political agents will try to hide, but these tensions and contradictions can be revealed by others, thus triggering contestation of story lines (Berenskoetter 2014: 280).

Budrytė's contribution identifies several instances when hegemonic story lines are contested. In the case of Lithuania, the participation of some of the Lithuanian anti-Soviet resistance fighters in the Holocaust is an extremely controversial and painful issue. Attacks of anti-Soviet

resistance fighters against the civilians are another painful and controversial issue. Budrytė discusses related memory wars, including public
contests over the monuments and antagonistic exchanges with Russia.
However, it appears that stories about heroism of anti-Soviet resistance
fighters appear to increase in popularity in Lithuania as insecurity has
increased after the Russian occupation of the Crimea in 2014.

Similarly, Ukraine has dealt with the contentious memories related to
the OUN and the UPA. As noticed by many analysts, these memories
have played and continue to play a negative role in Ukraine's relations
with the West. Russia often uses these discourses to "prove" that "fascism" is alive in Ukraine. Although the two organizations fought the
Soviet domination in Ukraine, their collaboration with the Nazi occupying forces and participation in the Holocaust are often obscured. As
in the case of Lithuania, the Russian occupation of the Crimea in 2014
seems to have strengthened discourses about heroism of the anti-Soviet
fighters, although regional differences still prevail.

According to Budrytė's analysis, in both cases, political developments
described as "revolutions" (a nationalist movement Sąjūdis in Lithuania,
the Orange revolution and Euromaidan in Ukraine) have coincided
with major discursive changes regarding memory politics. It is during
those times that narratives extolling the virtues of anti-Soviet partisans
and dwelling on losses associated with national tragedies, described as
genocides, have attracted more supporters willing to "defend history."
This finding is consistent with post-structuralist insights about crises and
change: Crises tend to produce new discourses; they act as engines in
the changes in discourses. Crises yield opportunities for memories to be
challenged and defended. Impulses to "defend memory" are inseparable
from the feelings of security.

Part III "International/Regional Dimensions of the Crisis in Ukraine"
starts with Katja Lehtisaari et al.'s chapter "Framing of Crimean
Annexation and Eastern Ukraine Conflict in Newspapers of Kazakhstan
and Kyrgyzstan in 2014" which explores the "external" dimension of the
crisis in Ukraine in 2014. The authors are interested in the framing of
annexation of Crimea by Russian Federation in March 2014 and conflict
in Eastern Ukraine during the spring of 2014 in newspapers of Kazakhstan
and Kyrgyzstan, two former Soviet republics. The focus of their work
is on the possible linkage of Crimean annexation to relations between
Kazakhstan, Kyrgyzstan, and Russia, including the possibility of similar
annexation of Northern Kazakhstan, which has large Russian majority.

This chapter draws on Nabers' (2015) approach by conceptualizing the crisis related to the annexation of Crimea in 2014 as a possible catalyst of social changes in these Central Asian societies. Mass media can contribute to political disagreements or even ethnic conflict. In addition, it plays a major role in the processes of democratization.

Lehtisaari and her colleagues made an attempt to understand if the security perceptions reflected in the media outlets depended on the different language or ownership of the outlet. In both Kazakhstan and Kyrgyzstan, in addition to Kazakh- and Kyrgyz-language media, outlets operating in Russian language, e.g., TV, radio stations, and newspapers, are widely available and are among nationally important news media. How did the newspapers write on the Crimea events of 2014 and how did they describe the reasons behind Russian intervention? The authors hypothesized that the situation was framed in a more "pro-Russian" way in the editions of Russian-language media outlets compared to publications printed in Kyrgyz and Kazakh languages, and that the coverage in state-owned publications was more inclined toward official statements of the state officials, thus constituting hegemonic discourses.

The authors' findings suggest a complicated picture. In both countries, the amount of coverage was rather small in official, state-published or sponsored newspapers, while in privately owned newspapers, the amount and spectrum of coverage were wider. In addition, it appears that in Kazakhstan the Kazakh-language papers were less controlled by the officials and therefore more varied in their views on the 2014 annexation than the Russian-language newspapers. In several private newspapers, the similarities of Northern Kazakhstan and Crimea were discussed, while the state media reported only the official version that the annexation was against international law but that the people of Crimea also had a right to organize a referendum. In Kyrgyzstan, the coverage had broadly the same pattern, with Kyrgyz-language privately owned newspapers being the most varied and critical in their views toward Russian policy in Ukraine.

Based on Nabers' research establishing a "missing link" between crises and transformation, Didem Buhari-Gulmez's contribution ""Crisis" and Crimean Tatars: Discourses of Self-determination in Flux" discusses how there has been a shift in the understanding of the main "crisis" that transforms the Crimean Tatar Self and its claim to self-determination. A discursive shift of emphasis from Tatar Deportation to Crimean Annexation reflects a fear of being denied political subjectivity in the postannexation Crimea. A major concern of the Crimean Tatar activists and diaspora rests on the increasing "invisibility" of Crimean Tatar self-determination claims due to the ongoing "hegemonic struggles" in Crimea. By shifting their emphasis from Deportation and the socio-economic problems they faced on their return to "the crisis" of Russian annexation of Crimea, they seek to create a new "myth" that would pave the way for a new subjectivity bridging the divides within the Crimean Tatar community.

Similarly to Nikolko, Buhari-Gulmez argues that Crimean Tatars do not embrace a unified identity, and she highlights many narratives related to the Crimean Tatar multiple complex identities. The two chapters (Nikolko's and Buhari-Gulmez's) complement each other in terms of demonstrating the "hegemonic struggles"—as Nabers call it—about who Crimean Tatars are, what the main "crisis" is, and how to deal with it. Nikolko focuses on the Ukrainian, Crimean-Russian, and Crimean Tatar narratives about the Deportation as the main "event," whereas Buhari-Gulmez examines the changing narratives of Crimean Tatars in Crimea and the Tatar diaspora in Turkey about national self-determination taking the Crimean Annexation as the main "crisis."

The broader post-Soviet space (the EU Eastern Partnership countries) is the focus of Susanne Szkola's analysis in "The Self/Other Space and Spinning the Net of Ontological Insecurities in Ukraine and Beyond: (Discursive) Reconstructions of Boundaries in the EU Eastern Partnership Countries Vis-à-Vis the EU and Russia." She argues that together with Armenia, Azerbaijan, Belarus, Georgia, and Moldova, Ukraine can be analyzed as an "in between" country, torn between the EU and Russia. Szkola is primarily interested in the "mechanisms of belonging and otherness," or discursive strategies that mark belonging to communities. In her chapter, she sets out to map a variety of others imagined by the EU Eastern Partnership countries, highlight their motivations for these conceptualizations, and "unpack" security relations involving the EU and Russia. Drawing on several bodies of literature, including identity constitution, ontological security, securitization theory, and image theory, she puts forward observations about the search for ontological security in Ukraine and beyond. Szkola incorporates crises into her analysis by conceptualizing them as "disruptive processes," as "critical situations" that include renegotiation of community boundaries and a (re)construction of collective identities. She suggests that images are instrumentalized when collective identities are (re)constructed; they (the images of othering and belonging) are used as "balancing mechanism of those relationships to security stability in 'going on (as usual)'."

The empirical section of Szkola's chapter includes an insight that the crisis in Ukraine has highlighted a case of ontological insecurity, "where the (narrated) existence and autobiography of Ukraine... [was] challenged and reconfigured." This finding is consistent with the insights into the other chapters in this volume, including Budrytė's chapter, which suggests changes in public attitudes toward the "heroes" associated with the OUN and UPA. Szkola argues that as the conflict in Eastern Ukraine and the annexation of Crimea took place, "a very specific net of ontologies, captured in enemy/amity images, emerges." She is exploring the images of amity and enmity not only in Ukraine, but also in other countries of the Eastern Partnership. Ukraine and Georgia perceive Russia as "an imperialist power whose actions range from active war promotion, violating territorial integrity and creating de facto occupied territories to limiting policy options and questioning state sovereignty." Similar image of Russia as "imperialist" is embraced by Moldova.

According to Szkola, the conflict in Ukraine has had a "profound impact on the constitution of positive/negative boundary drawings and formations" not only in the region, but domestically as well. She points out that there has been a dramatic increase in negative views of Russia in Ukraine since 2013. The peak of enmity toward Russia coincided with a strengthened positive image of the USA and the EU in 2014, together with a "net" of other friendly and unfriendly countries. The articulations of "perceived othering" have a spillover effect from Ukraine to the other countries of the EU Eastern Partnership, even in the Caucasus. Szkola concludes that the security situation in the EU Eastern Partnership countries is "discouraging," and that the countries have embraced self-conceptualizations that are "mutually exclusive," preferring to portray the "others" as imperialist or even barbarian and clearly defining intergroup boundaries. The crisis in Ukraine has not only fortified the existing images of "Self" and "Other," but also extended ontological insecurity to other actors with similar past experiences.

In sum, the contributions to this volume represent various attempts to conceptualize crisis as "a qualitative feature of the social" (Nabers 2015: 2) instead of viewing it as an attempt to deal with exogenous forces by engaging into "crisis management." As various contributions to this volume show, re-conceptualizing the crisis in Ukraine this way helps us to obtain a better understanding of what social change on different levels is all about. Focusing on crisis as "a qualitative feature of the social" has empowered us to highlight the contributions of agents that often are left out from the analyses that conceptualize crises as surprises and challenges to the elites and decision-makers. Specifically, we were able to highlight the experiences of women, minorities, and diasporas; we traced challenges to hegemonic narratives and captured the emancipatory potential of the crisis. This helped us to frame politics surrounding the crisis in Ukraine as "a practice of creation, reproduction and transformation of social relations" (Nabers 2015: 3) instead of reproducing power struggles. The processes of exclusion and inclusion on various levels (primarily societal and regional) were featured when trying to capture the practices of (re)creation of social relations and highlight relevant discourses. We believe that having conceptualized the crisis in Ukraine as a "qualitative feature of the social" (Nabers 2015: 2) helped us to transcend the inside/outside divide still plaguing IR. Our analysis captured the dynamics related to the 2013–2014 events in the broader region. Although there are still remaining questions, such as the global implications of the crisis in Ukraine and its long-term influences, we believe that this approach can enrich our understandings of issues related to hegemony, dislocations, and identity in IR.

REFERENCES

Allison, G., and P. Zelikow. 1999. *Essence of Decision: Explaining the Cuban Missile Crisis*, 2nd ed. New York: Longman.

Åslund, A. 2015. *Ukraine: What Went Wrong and How to Fix It*. Washington, DC: Peterson Institute for International Economics.

Berenskoetter, F. 2014. "Parameters of a National Biography." *European Journal of International Relations* 20 (1): 262–88.

Boin, A. 2004. "Lessons from Crisis Research." *International Studies Quarterly* 6 (1): 165–74.

Brassett, J., and C. Clarke. 2012. "Performing the Sub-prime Crisis: Trauma and the Financial Event." *International Political Sociology* 6 (1): 4–20.

Brecher, M. 1984. "International Crises and Protracted Conflicts." *International Interactions* 11 (3–4): 237–97.

Brecher, M., and J. Wilkenfeld. 1982. "Crises in World Politics." *World Politics* 24 (1): 380–417.

Brown, N. 2004. *Global Instability and Strategic Crisis*. London and New York: Routledge.

Carr, E. H. 2001 [1939]. *The Twenty Years' Crisis: 1919–1939.* New York: Perennial.

Croft, S. 2006. *Culture, Crisis, and America's War on Terror.* Cambridge: Cambridge University Press.

Dayton, B. W., ed. 2004. "Managing Crises in the Twenty-First Century." *International Studies Review* 6 (1): 165–94.

Deleuze, G. 1990. *Difference and Repetition.* New York: Columbia University Press.

Deleuze, G. 2004 [1990]. *Logic of Sense.* London: Continuum.

Edkins, J. 2003. *Trauma and the Memory of Politics.* Cambridge: Cambridge University Press.

Friedman, J. 1994. *Cultural Identity and Global Process.* London: Sage.

Gilpin, R. 1981. *War and Change in World Politics.* Cambridge: Cambridge University Press.

Hay, C. 1996. "From Crisis to Catastrophe? The Ecological Pathologies of the Liberal-Democratic State Form." *Innovation: The European Journal of Social Sciences* 9 (4): 421–34.

Hay, C. 2013. "Treating the Symptom Not the Condition: Crisis Definition, Deficit Reduction and the Search for a New British Growth Model." *British Journal of Politics and International Relations* 15 (1): 23–37.

He, Kai. 2013. "Hazard Rate Determinants of Efficient and Successful Crisis Management: An Event History Analysis of Foreign Policy Crises, 1918–2007." *Cooperation and Conflict* 48 (1): 51–79.

Hebron, L., and P. James. 1997. "Great Powers, Cycles of Relative Capability and Crises in World Politics." *International Interactions* 23 (2): 145–73.

Hermann, C. F. 1969. "International Crisis as a Situational Variable." In *International Politics and Foreign Policy*, edited by J. N. Rosenau. New York: Free Press.

Hermann, C. F., and L. P. Brady. 1972. "Alternative Models of International Crisis Behavior." In *International Crises: Insights from Behavioral Research*, edited by C. F. Hermann. New York: Free Press.

Hollis, M., and S. Smith. 1990. *Explaining and Understanding International Relations.* Oxford: Clarendon.

Kouzmin, A., and A. M. G. Jarman. 2004. "Policy Advice as Crisis: A Political Redefinition of Crisis Management." *International Studies Review* 6 (1): 182–89.

Laclau, E., and C. Mouffe. 1985. *Hegemony and Socialist Strategy: Towards a Radical Democratic Politics.* London: Verso.

Lynn Doty, R. 1993. "Foreign Policy as Social Construction: A Post-positivist Analysis of U.S. Counterinsurgency Policy in the Philippines." *International Studies Quarterly* 37 (3): 297–320.

Mälksoo, M. 2015. "'Memory Must Be Defended': Beyond the Politics of Mnemonical Security." *Security Dialogue* 46 (3): 221–37.

McCormick, J. M. 1978. "International Crises: A Note on Definition." *The Western Political Quarterly* 31 (3): 352–58.

Menon, R., and E. Rumer. 2015. *Conflict in Ukraine: The Unwinding of the Post-Cold War Order.* Cambridge, MA: MIT.

Morgenthau, H. J. 1948. *Politics Among Nations: The Struggle for Power and Peace.* New York: Alfred A. Knopf.

Nabers, D. 2015. *A Poststructuralist Discourse Theory of Global Politics.* Houndmills and New York: Palgrave Macmillan.

Plokhy, S. 2000. "The City of Glory: Sevastopol in Russian Historical Mythology." *Journal of Contemporary History* 35 (3): 369–83.

Resende, E., and D. Budryte, eds. 2013. *Memory and Trauma in International Relations: Theories, Cases, Debates.* London: Routledge.

Reynolds, J. 2008. "Wounds and Scars: Deleuze on the Time and Ethics of the Event." *Deleuze Studies* 1 (2): 144–66.

Stern, E. K. 1999. *Crisis Decisionmaking: A Cognitive Institutional Approach.* Stockholm: CRISMART/The Swedish National Defence College.

Stern, E. K. 2003. "Crisis Studies and Foreign Policy Analysis: Insights, Synergies, and Challenges." *International Studies Review* 5 (1): 183–91.

Weldes, J. 1999. "The Cultural Production of Crises: U.S. Identity and Missiles in Cuba." In *Cultures of Insecurity: States, Communities, and the Production of Danger,* edited by J. Weldes, M. Laffey, H. Gusterson, and R. Duvall. Minneapolis and London: University of Minnesota Press.

Widmaier, W. W. 2007. "Constructing Foreign Policy Crises: Interpretive Leadership in the Cold War and War on Terrorism." *International Studies Quarterly* 51 (4): 779–94.

Widmaier, W. W., M. Blyth, and L. Seabrooke. 2007. "Exogenous Shocks or Endogenous Constructions? The Meanings of Wars and Crises." *International Studies Quarterly* 51 (4): 747–59.

PART I

Crisis and Change: Theory and Practice

Crisis and Change in Global Politics: A Dialogue with Deleuze and Badiou's Event to Understand the Crisis in Ukraine

Erica Resende

INTRODUCTION

The Euromaidan Revolution, broadly called "the Ukrainian crisis" by the mainstream international media, began in February 2014, when a series of events first involving peaceful protests in Kyiv's main square—Maidan Square—escalated to violence and confrontation between protesters and riot police. Although the initial goal of the movement was to force President Viktor Yanukovych to go back in his decision of pursuing an association agreement with the European Union, protest and unrest escalated when Yanukovych signed a trade treaty with Russia (BBC 2014). As thousands of protesters took over Maidan Square and surrounding areas in a demonstration of popular disagreement with Yanukovych's policies of approximation with Russia, Ukrainian policy and security forces cracked down on the protesters, further inflaming the situation and prompting violent clashes in the streets of Kyiv. As the temperature rose, the movement called for the resignation of Yanukovych,

E. Resende (✉)
Brazilian War College, Rio de Janeiro, Brazil

© The Author(s) 2018
E. Resende et al. (eds.), *Crisis and Change in Post-Cold War Global Politics*, https://doi.org/10.1007/978-3-319-78589-9_2

who fled to Russia. A new interim government was formed, which Russia refused to recognize, calling the overthrown of Yanukovych a coup d'état. Russia military intervention soon followed as pro-Russian sentiment grew in the southeastern region of Ukraine, known as Donbas. While the new interim government signed the EU association agreement and secured a loan from the International Monetary Fund, Russia annexed Crimea and Sevastopol, in a series of actions that led to armed conflict between the Ukrainian government, pro-Russia separatists, and Russia undercover military forces passing as Russian-speaker Ukrainian militia men.

Together, these unexpected events produced an atmosphere of emergency and urgency typical of one would call a "crisis." The fast pace of developments in Ukraine as well as its repercussions throughout Eastern Europe, Russia, Western Europe, and the USA acquired not only momentum but intensity as well, warranting the classification of the worst crisis to emerge between Russia and West since the end of the Cold War (Menon and Rumer 2015: xii). Paraphrasing Ralph Waldo Emerson, those were events that are in the saddle, and riding mankind.

Indeed, the combination of urgency, emergency, momentum, and surprise expressed by the word "crisis" seemed to have proliferated in both journalistic and academic accounts of the 2013/2014 events in Ukraine, albeit in different variations in a perhaps not so conscious attempt to separate its domestic from its structural causes. While "Ukraine crisis" had broad, general use by academic authors (Åslund 2015; Menon and Rumer 2015; Laruelle 2016; Walker 2016; Huntchings and Szostek 2016), only a handful few made an open option for "Ukrainian crisis" (Trenin 2014; Wilson 2014; Sakwa 2015; Yekelchyk 2015). Most revealing was the reasons each group attributed to the crisis. While the first group stressed more domestic factors of the crisis, signaling Yanukovych's refusal to sign the trade agreement with EU as *the* turning point event for the conflict, the latter seemed to opt for a more international, structural account of the developments in Ukraine and thus stressing its links to the asymmetrical end of the Cold War.[1]

In order to avoid cheapening an already overused word such as "crisis," it might be helpful to investigate a little further the relationship

---

[1] For the specific differentiation of "Ukrainian Crisis" and "Ukraine Crisis," see Trenin (2014, footnotes).

between crisis and event in order to separate more ordinary, common occurrences from more historical, unique ones. This would also prevent us from calling different and sometimes contradictory historical discourses as "crisis." In this regard, I propose to engage the notion of crisis with Gilles Deleuze's and Alain Badiou's concept of event. The aim of this chapter is then to review the canonical literature on crisis and change, and suggest a dialogue with concept of the "Event"—which Deleuze characterizes as "pure," "true" events in relation to ordinary, superficial, historical events, while Badiou claims it a rupture in being—to help us to navigate a sea of crisis discourses. I will argue that Deleuze's use of the imagery of scars and wounds clarifies how he differentiates event from Event, which will lead us to a better understanding of the ontology of crisis and change. Furthermore, and now following Badiou, by recognizing events as rupture, one is able to understand how, in an Event, the inconsistent multiplicity which always lies beneath a particular social order is able to appear subjectively. Only in an Event can the excluded part be visible. An Event succeeds in representing a part which is previously unrepresented. This unfolding of new representations from an Event produces truths, subjects, and new social systems. As a result, Events are intimately connected to change.

In order to better develop my argument, I will use the Ukrainian case to discuss the twin concepts of crisis and change, and thus link them to the end of the Cold War, more specifically to the end of the (Russian/Soviet) Empire, which I frame as the Event. The events and discourses that are often associated with the recent developments in Ukraine, which have been labelled as "the Ukrainian crisis" or the "crisis in Ukraine"—that include the Euromaidan protests, the annexation of Crimea by Russia and the on-going conflict in Eastern Ukraine—emphasize the urgent need to develop a better understanding of what constitutes an international "crisis" and what its relationship to change may be. At the same time, studying crises as social phenomena, not sudden, exogenous events, helps us to develop a more nuanced understanding of various processes and discourses, emanating from domestic and international actors, which include relations between various social and political groups, construction of myths, and (re)creation of identity groups. The chapter is thus divided into four parts. First, I will offer a survey of the literature on crisis and change, with focus on their ontology. Second, I turn to a brief contextualization of the late 2013/early 2014 political turmoil in Ukraine linking it to the end of Russian/Soviet Empire. Next, I will explore Deleuze's and Badiou's definition of Event to reflect upon the currently unfolding dynamics in post-Soviet space to, finally, characterize the Event in Ukraine as the end of the Ages of Empire in global politics. At the end, I will offer some concluding remarks.

A SURVEY ON IR CRISIS LITERATURE

As already mentioned by the editors of this volume at the Introduction, IR literature traditionally defines crisis in terms of an unexpected event that has to be dealt with, managed. As a result, it usually brings about negative connotations of harmful, unpredictable, undesirable situations that have to be put under control. This framing leads to the general understanding that actors have the autonomous capacity to act upon them, contain them, solve them, and surpass them, thus re-imposing order.

However, the 9/11 attacks produced a shift from this traditional notion of crisis, which had been limited to agent-centered approaches, which begins to problematize the ontology of the relationship between actors and crisis. The study conducted by Dirk Nabers (2015), which is the inspiration for the theoretical framework of this volume, stands a fine example of a structuralist approach to crisis in world politics. For Nabers (2015: 44), "crisis represents a situation in which our everyday beliefs of how the world works are thoroughly disrupted by an event that is out of our control."

However, this literature on crises from a structure-centered approach has not yet paid enough attention to contexts outside of the West. The recent developments in Ukraine stand as a classic example of this difficulty. The easy way out in this case is to label such cases as "prolonged" or "permanent" crisis, i.e., one that cannot be easily solved. As a case study, post-Soviet Ukraine is a crucial case of fragmentation between the East and the West, the past and the future, the authoritarian and the liberal dynamics, among others. It stands as a suitable example where multiple discourses clash, collapse, intensify, and evolve, transforming social relations beyond its national borders. New identities emerge and old one declines. Meanings are made and remade, and the social fabric is weaved and re-weaved. As a result, one should transcend the prevailing tendency to resort to dichotomous analyses in the study of Ukraine based on pro-Russian versus pro-Western camps.

The Late 2013/Early 2014 Political Turmoil in Ukraine

On November 21, 2013, when President Viktor Yanukovych suspended negotiations for an association agreement with the European Union, Ukraine became gripped by mass protest and unrest. The main city plaza of Kyiv, Maidan Nezalezhnosti, was taken by thousands of protesters in a political movement known as "Euromaidan." After months of protests, Ukrainian protesters demanded closer relations with Europe as well as liberal reforms, thus rejecting the president's pro-Russian policy, and Yanukovych was removed from government on February 22, 2014, after which he fled Kyiv.

Yanukovych was widely disliked in Ukraine's West but had significant support in the East and in the South, especially the Donbas region, where Russian is more widely spoken. Following his ousting, political unrest spread and escalated in the largely Russophone eastern and southern provinces of Ukraine. According to Marples (2016), eastern Ukraine, most notably Donetsk and Luhansk, is the heartland of industrial development in the Russian Empire. Former Soviet lead Nikita Khrushchev began his political career in the Donbas region, where the communist party remains strong and active. Deeply Russophone, the far eastern and southern regions voted massively for Yanukovych in the previous national elections: 90% in Donbas, 81.4% in Crimea, and 88.8% in Sevastopol. This could explain why Russian-speaking Ukrainians in the Donbas/Crimea/Sevastopol areas felt that Russia necessitated to come to rescue them from a perceived Westernization from Kyiv (Marples 2016: 12–13).

In the following weeks in February to early March, as the death toll numbers grew, conflict intensified, leading to Russian military intervention in the Ukrainian autonomous region of Crimea. On March 18, 2014, after a contested referendum,[2] Crimea was annexed by Russia. Armed confrontation broke out in Donbas between the post-revolutionary Ukrainian government and pro-Russian insurgents, supported and often assisted by the Russian military forces, and paramilitary groups.

---

[2]Article 72 of the Ukrainian Constitution stipulates that only the President and the Parliament can call a referendum while Article 73 demands that any alteration in territory has to be done through an all-Ukraine referendum.

Back in Kyiv, a compromise was reached on February 21 with the help of mediators from the European Union, Poland, France, and Germany. The agreement was signed by opposition leaders and Yanukovych, and called for a restoration of the Constitution as it was between 2004 and 2010, new presidential elections, amnesty for pro-testers who had been arrested, and the surrender of public buildings under occupation by protesters. Furthermore, the Euromaidan move-ment achieved the release from prison of Yulia Tymoshenko, the repeal of the law on regional languages, which formally made Ukrainian the sole official language, as well as the removal of Soviet monu-ments throughout Ukraine. Also important to mention is the raise of Ukrainian nationalism as well as the spike in far-right organizations and militias, especially in the Donbas region. As for Russia–Ukraine relations, the status of both Crimea and Sevastopol is under dispute. While Ukraine, backed by major international actors such as the USA, Germany, France, Poland, UK, the EU, the UN, and the OSCE, consid-ers the Crimean referendum for annexation illegal, which makes Crimea an autonomous province, and Sevastopol a city with special status, Russia considers them as part of the Russian Federation.

Finally, from an analytical point of view, the 2013/2014 political tur-moil in Ukraine is far from generating academic consensus regarding its prevailing agents and structures. In fact, Ukraine's complex web of social agents and structures tends to be reflected in any analysis worthy of its salt, to the extent of even questioning dominant vocabularies in IR (see Makarychev and Yatsyk 2017). Many analysts see a singular, unique char-acter in the conflict which will bring transformation not only in post-Soviet space (including Russian relations with Eastern Europe and the European Union) but also in East–West relations as a whole (more spe-cifically, Russian relations with European Union and the USA). Others contend that Ukraine suffered a coup and that a legally elected president was removed from office due to political pressure from the West against a Russophone Ukraine. In this view, the Russian-speaking Ukrainians in the Donbas are rightfully responding and resisting to unwelcomed Western influence in borderlands of Europe. Do these interpretations radically differ and negate each other, or do they share any characteris-tic? What is the key event—if any—that underlies such all-encompassing interpretations of change? Is it even ontologically possible to pinpoint one single event as the trigger to the crisis in Ukraine? This is where

I turn to Gilles Deleuze's and Alain Badiou's contributions to the notion of event[3] to prevent us from calling different and sometimes even contradictory historical discourses as "crisis."

THE CONCEPT OF EVENT BY DELEUZE AND BADIOU (EVENT WITH A CAPITAL E!)

Deleuze's concept of the "Event"—which he characterizes as "pure," "true" events in relation to ordinary, superficial, historical events—has helped us to navigate a sea of crisis discourses regarding Ukraine. One way to think about this is understanding the difference between the singular and the ordinary in mathematics: The singular is not opposed to the universal, as it is in traditional philosophy, but to the ordinary. The singular point at which something happens is what Deleuze and Guattari (1994: 189) refer to as an event. And every singular point where something happens is related to every other singular point where something happens.

However, the issue here is not events, but the "Event" with a capital *E*. Individual, historical events are ordinary, superficial; they are mere changes in intensity, as Deleuze contends. The "Event" with a capital E, on the other hand, is the interconnection of all of the individual, historical events, hence a true, pure event. Each (singular, historical) event communicates with all others, and they all form one and the same Event, in which all events are related to each other.

Deleuze's use of the imagery of scars and wounds clarifies this issue further. For him, historical events are changes in intensity and energy changed between bodies. Their affects are thus somewhat "superficial," sense-like, much like scars on the surface.[4] True, pure Events, on the

---

[3] The primary texts in which Deleuze explicitly discusses events are "The Logic of Sense" (2004), "Difference and Repetition" (1990), and "What Is Philosophy?" (1994), co-authored with Felix Guattari. As for Badiou, the bulk of his reflections lies in "Being and Event" (2005), "Infinite Thought" (2004), and "Philosophy and Event," with Fabien Tarby (2013).

[4] As such, Deleuze conceives the historical event the affirmation of the aleatory, much like a dice throw rather than a necessary component of a providentially ordered system. Here, he is explicitly following Nietzsche, for whom the dice throw is affirms chance, producing nothing but sense (see Costache 2012).

other hand, have the force to act and leave marks upon bodies. They are wounds rather than scars. In "Logic of Sense," Deleuze (2004) treats the Event as synonymous with the wound, which is both temporal and transcendental, rather than an empirical event that happens. The Event never actually happens or is present; it is always that which has already happened, or is going to happen.

As such, Deleuze argues that the relation between wound and scar is not one of ontological antecedent or spatial succession. The Event haunts and subsists without inhabiting bodies or places. And as bodies exist in the present that spreads indefinitely in both directions of the line of time, transforming every past and every future in a past–present and future–present, the Event exists in a time that ceaselessly divides the present moment in what has already passed and what is yet to come. The time of the Event is eternity, hence constantly eluding the present, which never allows for an Event to be realized, or to definitively exist (Deleuze 2004: 64). That is why the only questions one can ask with regard to an Event are "What happened?" "What is going to happen?" but never "What is happening?"

As such, there is no healing or overcoming of the wound, i.e., the future that is perennially to come, the pure past that never was. From this, it follows that Deleuze's Event, the transcendental wound, evades domestication, management, or solving. Much like the approach Nabers (2015) has described in regard to a new ontological understanding of the crisis. For if the Event is "always and at the same time something which has just happened and something which is about to happen; never something which is happening" (Deleuze 2004: 73), it subsists rather than exists. It does not allow for being overcome or fixed.

Following Deleuze's argument, I argue that the events in Ukraine are singular, historical events (scars), while the end of the Russian/Soviet Empire is the true, real Event (the wound)—to where all other superficial events converge to and communicate with—that transforms social relations. Such conceptualization does not negate the emotional power of singular events and their perceived significance, but at the same time, it helps to conceptualize them in the crisis/change framework within the literature of crisis as social change. In a sense, Trenin's (2014) distinction between "Ukraine crisis" and "crisis over Ukraine," although reproducing the international/domestic divide to prevailing in mainstream IR, hinted on this separation between pure and historical events by role of great power rivalry after the asymmetrical collapse of the Soviet Union.

This argument aims to capture the events in Ukraine underlying multiple encounters between past legacies, alternative futures, and reformist tendencies as well as the changing individual–society–state relations in Ukrainian politics and society emerging from the eventness of the collapse of the Soviet Union.

Alain Badiou is concerned with how it is possible that something new can be seen—or employing his own grammar, how can truth emerge. In his 1996 *Théorie du Sujet*, he attempted to reconcile a notion of the subject with ontology, and in particular post-structuralist and constructivist ontologies (see Feltham and Clamens' Introduction to Badiou 2004). Indeed, a frequent criticism of post-structuralist work is that it precludes, through its fixation on semiotics and language, any notion of a subject. Badiou even admits that the purpose of his philosophy is to attempt to break out of contemporary philosophy's fixation upon language, which he sees almost as a straitjacket (Badiou 2004, especially the Introduction). This effort leads him to engage with mathematics.

As explained by Norris (2009), the title of Badiou's book expresses the two key elements of his thesis in *Being and Event*: the place of ontology, or "the science of being qua being" (being in itself), and the place of the event—which is seen as a rupture in being—through which the subject finds realization and reconciliation with truth. This situation of being and the rupture which characterizes the event are thought in terms of set theory, more specifically, to Paul J. Cohen's strategy of "condition of sets," which are conceived in terms of a domination that defines the set itself.[5]

For Badiou (2005), every discernible (nameable or constructible) set is dominated by the conditions which don't possess the property that makes it discernible as a set, thereby putting these sets in line with constructible ontology relative to one's being-in-the-world and one's being in language. As a result, one does not necessarily need to refer to language to conceive of a "set of dominations." While ontology can mark out a space for an inhabitant of the constructible situation to decide upon the indiscernible, it falls to the subject—about which the ontological situation cannot comment—to nominate this indiscernible,

---

[5] If one takes, in binary language, the set with the condition "items marked only with ones," any item marked with zero negates the property of the set. The condition which has only ones is thus dominated by any condition which has zeros in it (Badiou 2005: 367–71).

generic point and thus nominate, and give name to, the undecidable event. By enacting fidelity to the event, one performs a "generic procedure," which in its undecidability is necessarily experimental, and one potentially recasts the situation in which being takes place. Through the maintenance of fidelity, truth has the potentiality to emerge, thus allowing us to see events in a new light.[6]

When Badiou writes of an "event," he means something that disrupts the current situation. The Event represents his conception of revolution and social change, whether in politics or other domains.[7] Indeed, Badiou maintains that reality is grounded on a "void" of "inconsistent multiplicity," which is at once void and excess. An Event happens when the excluded part appears on the social scene, suddenly and drastically. It ruptures the appearance of normality and opens a space to rethink reality from the standpoint of its real basis in inconsistent multiplicity. As a result, the order of a situation—the "state of the situation," the "count-for-one," or the "dominant ideology," in Badiou's grammar—all renders the excluded part invisible, though it does not guarantee that the excluded part will remain quiet. In fact, it might—and does—erupt and revolt at any time. Thus, an Event is something akin to a rip in the fabric of being, and/or of the social order, at the same time traumatic for the mainstream but exhilaratingly transformative its participants.[8] Hence, Events are necessarily ruptural in relation to the dominant order for it declares that another world is possible.

An Event must consist both of destruction of the existing order and definition of a new order. Existing hierarchies and value statements must be destroyed, or falsified, by the Event. Such an act is taken to disrupt reality on a material level, because the formal arrangement underlies the

---

[6]Badiou identifies four domains in which a subject (who, it is important to note, *becomes* a subject through this process) can potentially witness an event: love, science, politics, and art.

[7]In line with his concept of the event, Badiou claims that politics is not about politicians, but activism based on the present situation and the "evental" rupture, which is always connected to change.

[8]According to Feltham and Clamens (see their introduction in Badiou 2004), Events have four characteristics: (1) they are radically contingent; (2) they take place at a particular locality, the Evental site, and not across a situation; (3) it is always impossible to tell whether or not an Event belongs to a situation; and (4) an Event may only be identified "reflexively"—by already having chosen to identify it.

material structure of a particular reality. It does not change the elements of the situation. Rather, it changes the structure of the situation, by forcing it to include a new element.[9]

As correctly pointed out by Robinson (2014), Badiou thinks about Events as a matter of *decision*. It involves naming the impossible. An Event is incalculable. It is incalculable because it comes from the excluded part, which is also "non-ontological" and outside the "count-for-one." As it is incalculable, it leads to a "crisis of calculation." This crisis raises a question of what to do about the Event. In Badiou, decision is also *scission*, or separation, Robinson continues. In this, to "decide" is also to carve the field, or divide the social world into different camps—those for and against the Event, as there is no space here for any middle-ground, or distanced sympathy. Robinson (2014) claims that Badiou calls for the creation of strong dualisms and absolute social antagonisms (see Mouffe 2013).

Decision is also associated with *intervention*, finalizes Robinson (2014). An intervention is a way of naming or analyzing an Event without denying its "evental" nature. For Badiou, the basic aspect of intervention is simply to decide that an Event has or hasn't taken place. It is the existence of the Event, not its meaning, which is at stake. Often, this is a decision on a *name*—to recognize or not a named Event—for example, to become the Russian Revolution rather than a power-grab by Bolsheviks in 1917. The naming of an Event is always "illegal" or unpermitted, from the viewpoint of the state of the situation and the count-for-one. In a way, it is always outside the normal structures of social control, thus interrupting the line of continuity. Events allow something completely new to come into existence, for they have no foundation, especially no legal foundation, thereby even rewriting the "social contract."

Badiou (2005) gives several historical examples of Events: the Paris Commune, the Russian Revolution, the Maoist movement in China, particularly the Chinese Cultural Revolution of the 1960s, and the revolt of May 1968 in France. Recently, he characterized the Arab Spring as an

---

[9] Using the language of mathematics, Events occur when new, previously unspeakable numbers are discovered and named. The act of naming a new number transforms the field itself, pretty much like Thomas Kuhn's idea of scientific revolutions, except that the transformative force is an act of naming rather than an anomaly in the empirical field. In this sense, political revolutions are akin to scientific revolutions in the ways their effects unfold.

Event (Badiou 2011). His concept of Event could easily be applied to recent turmoil such as the Greek popular uprising of 2008, the London insurrection of 2011, the 2013 Confederation Cup riots in Brazil, and—why not?—2014 Euromaidan Ukraine.[10] As Makarychev and Yatsyk (2017: 1) correctly point out in the introduction to their volume on crisis in Ukraine, the unexpected character of the conflict had reverberations all across the globe, producing a "rupture with the established order of things that brings structurally transformative effects" that came very close to Badiou's Event, to point of shattering the vocabulary of IR itself. I thus argue the meaning behind the Event in Ukraine is—in the sense the rupture it brings—intimately connected to the end of empires in contemporary world politics. More specifically, the end of the Russian/Soviet Empire in Europe's so-called borderlands means that this region has become increasingly contested after the eastward expansion of EU in 2004, and has since then become recognized as the new frontier for East-West power politics. As a result, any new crisis in this region is a new opportunity to contest and/or reaffirm political influence in the region.

THE FALL OF EMPIRES AS AN EVENT

As noted by Ferguson (2005: 24), empires can be traced as far back as the recorded history goes and have been the historically predominant form of order in world politics. Indeed, most history has been the history of empires, or the history of the rise and the fall of empires, I would add. Looking at a time frame of several millennia, there was no global anarchic system until the European explorations and subsequent imperial and colonial ventures connected disparate regional systems some 500 years ago. Prior to the emergence of a global-scope system of sovereign states, the pattern of world politics was characterized by regional systems. These regional systems were initially anarchic and marked by high levels of military competition. But almost universally, they tended to consolidate into regional empires. As Deudney and Ikenberry argue (2015: 7–8), it was empires—not anarchic state systems—that typically dominated the regional systems in all parts of the world. And within

---

[10]Badiou himself is reticent to enumerate long series of Events, since they are rare and exceptional, he argues. Hence, he insists that a lot of political eruptions, conflicts, and revolutions are not true Events at all, thus reinforcing my previous observation of how the word "crisis" has been overused lately.

this global pattern of regional empires, European political order was distinctly anomalous because it persisted so long as an anarchy.

If we look into the way the field of IR has been shaped, we would certainly recognize a certain fixation—fascination would be perhaps a better word—on the Westphalian state. This state-centrism has tended to obscure the multiplicity of actors in global politics and prevented the realization that it has been empires rather than states that have dominated world politics. For Ferguson and Mansbach (2006), a distorted narrative of the Westphalian era that has been reproduced in the field undermined the fact that it was always at least as much about empires as it was states. Indeed, no sooner the emerging European states began to consolidate that they were off on campaigns of conquest and commerce to the farthest reaches of the globe.

By comparison, the nation-state "appears as a blip on the historical horizon," a human invention that emerged recently from the ashes of empires and "whose hold on the world's political imagination may well prove partial or transitory." This might explain why the persistence of empires challenges the common place idea that "the nation-state is natural, necessary, and inevitable" (Burbank and Cooper 2010: 2–3). In his masterpiece on world politics, Hedley Bull wrote that "in the broad sweep of human history...the form of states system has been the exception rather than the rule" (Bull 1977: 21). Working from a distinct theoretical stand, Robert Gilpin reaches the same conclusion about empires.

> The history of interstate relations was largely that of successive great empires. The pattern of international political change during the millennia of the pre-modern era has been described as an imperial cycle... World politics was characterized by the rise and decline of powerful empires, each of which in turn unified and ordered its respective international system. The recurrent pattern in every civilization we know was for one state to unify the system under its imperial domination. The propensity toward universal empire was the principal feature of pre-modern politics. (Gilpin 1981: 110–16)

In his critique of Michael Hardt and Antonio Negri's Empire (2000), Akif Okur (2007) argues that since 9/11 the world's balance of power has shifted substantially. One of the changes has to do with an intellectual trend toward looking at the contemporary political order under the logics of re-territorialization of the political space. One consequence of this logic is the resurface of classical imperialist practices based on discourses impregnated with the inside/outside duality identified by Walker (1993) and the self/other dichotomy highlighted by Neumann (1996). As a result, one can identify the deliberate weakening of international organizations, the decline of transnational solidarism and norms such as human rights, the resurface of protectionism practices in world economy, the return of nationalism in its multiple versions, the reactive stand against globalization, and, above all, the politics of identity emphasizing a state's subjective perception of a special place in the world (mostly recognized as the "my nation first" discourse). For Akif Okur, these changes point a dawn of new age: the "Age of Nation Empires," as global power blocs as the USA are dislocated by regional power blocs centered upon a regional great power, such as China and Russia. As a result, this new form of nation-empire regionalism claims sovereignty over its respective regional political, economic, social, cultural, ideological, and military spheres. As demonstrated by my colleagues in this edited volume (see especially Becker's chapter), this sounds very much like Putin's Novorossiya discourse about Ukraine.

Going back to the notion of empire, one has to keep in mind that in 1866 the Russian Empire was the second largest contiguous empire to have ever existed. Its rise happened in times of decline of neighboring rival powers: the Swedish empire, the Polish-Lithuanian Commonwealth, the Persian and the Ottoman Empire. Stretching over three continents, the Russian Empire was surpassed in landmass only by the British and Mongol empires. It extended from the Arctic Ocean in the North to the Black Sea in the South, from the Baltic Sea in the West to the Pacific Ocean, and into Alaska in the East. With 125.6 million subjects registered in 1897, it had the third-largest population in the world at the time, after China and India. Although smaller in extension, its successor, the Soviet Union, also functioned like an empire.

Indeed, in a region that lived under loose arrangements of empires—Polish-Lithuanian, Austro-Hungarian, Swedish, Russian, and Ottoman—nations have been mostly defined by cultural aspects such as language, religion, and common history. As a result, in order to accommodate such diversity, national politics in the Soviet Union had to choice but to be "fundamentally ambivalent," argues Kiryukhin (2016: 59). Therefore, while Russian national traditions—most notably the imposition of the Russian language—were perceived as the main representative of the Soviet culture, they had to coexist with the ideology of the "new Soviet person" in all Soviet Republics, whereby regional identities had to be somehow accommodated. Following the collapse of the Soviet Union in 1991, former Soviet Republics became independent[11] but are still struggling with their national projects.

In case of Ukraine, it is at heart "bilingual and bicultural," according to Petro (2016: 31). Its Eastern region—which includes Crimea, Dnipropetrovsk, Donetsk, Kharkov, Kherson, Lugansk, Odessa, Nikolayeevsk, and Zaporozhye—forms a relatively compact community of ethnic and cultural Russian-speakers, representing one third of the national population in Ukraine. While on the West, ethnic Ukrainians made of Ukrainian speakers constitute a majority—especially in urban areas—that have adopted a strong nationalistic position since the 1992 Ukrainian independence (Marples 2016), thus actively participating at Euromaidan. The events of 2015 point to the emergence of a post-Soviet Ukraine as a truncated state, split between regions that literally speak different languages (Beissinger 2014), and stuck in an unfinished, polarized process of nation-building following the decline of the Russian/Soviet Empire (1721–1991).

Concluding Remarks

Crisis does not necessarily imply a disabling environment for agency. The crisis discourse may end up empowering specific ideologies that were not previously part of the equation. It also provides a novel context that renders certain issues more "visible" in the global agenda while silencing others. In this regard, it is necessary to ask to what extent the developments in Ukraine have rendered different issues in the region more visible or invisible in the domestic and international arena. For example, it is meaningful to trace the process through which pro-Russian, anti-Russian, pro-Western (including, e.g., those who seek EU and/or NATO membership), and anti-Western forces within and without Ukraine clash

---

[11]While Russia was more easily internationally recognized as the lawfully successor of USSR after the official dissolution of the Soviet Union in December 1991, the remaining 14 post-Soviet states struggled for recognition as independent states. The three Baltic states were the first to declare their independence, between March and May 1990, claiming continuity from their 1918 to 1939 independent status prior to their annexation by the Soviet Union in 1940. The remaining 11 states (Armenia, Azerbaijan, Belarus, Kazakhstan, Kyrgyzstan, Moldova, Tajikistan, Uzbekistan, Turkmenistan, Georgia, and Ukraine) initially formed the Commonwealth of Independent States and then eventually gained independence (see Arbatov et al. 1997).

with one another during the Euromaidan event. Moreover, what are the implications of the changing parameters in discursive, normative, and cultural realms for minority groups, indigenous communities (such as Crimean Tatars), diasporas, neighboring societies, and international community as a whole?

Keeping in mind Reynolds' (2008) suggestion to seriously consider Deleuze's argument that events are only effects (Deleuze 2004: 10, 29, 241) as a warning to conceive events as having double causalities involving a mixture of bodies, state of affairs and sense, that is, not to understand wound as something that accidentally and contingently befalls us, I have opted to treat the events in Ukraine not from the angle of empirics but rather of the order of the virtual, as an event effect. The challenge then becomes the exploration of generative, transformative, genesis field in which the events in Ukraine are produced and reproduced.

Following Deleuze's distinction between historical and pure events, I developed the argument that the events in Ukraine are singular, historical events (scars), while the collapse of the Russian/Soviet Empire is the true, real Event, with capital E (the wound)—to where all other superficial events converge to and communicate with—that currently remakes and transforms the social order in Eastern Europe and beyond. Euromaidan was particularly meaningful as a rupture to established, dominant structures and discourses. And following Badiou's philosophy, it was also an Event that demanded decision (What did it mean? A revolt? A power overthrown? An act of aggression by Russia?), scission (What side to take? Pro-Russia? Pro-Ukraine?), and intervention (How can we seize the moment for change?).

The Event that created the Ukrainian crisis also comes from the writing and rewriting of the boundaries of both Europe and Russia, a region that historically lived many experiences of the rise and the fall of empires. Ukraine sits at the so-called borderland of Europe, which makes the boundaries of the conflict particularly problematic in terms of the ontology of the crisis. While most Russians believe that the conflict is a domestic Ukrainian problem caused by conflicts between Russian-speaking Ukrainians and Ukrainian-speaking Ukrainians over a national project (pro-Russia versus pro-West), Ukrainians view the conflict as directly fueled by a foreign state: Russia. As a result, an acute othering process between those groups is dislocating identities, weakening societal cohesion, challenging dominant discourses about Ukraine and Ukrainians, thus pushing the region into a spiral of tension and violence.

REFERENCES

Akif Okur, M. 2007. "Rethinking Empire After 9/11: Towards a New Ontological Image of World Order." *Perceptions, Journal of International Affairs* XII (1): 61–93.

Arbatov, A., A. Chayes, A. Handler Chayes, and L. Olson, eds. 1997. *Managing Conflict in the Former Soviet Union: Russian and American Perspectives.* Cambridge: MIT Press.

Åslund, A. 2015. *Ukraine: What Went Wrong and How to Fix It.* Washington, DC: Peterson Institute for International Economics.

Badiou, A. 2004. *Infinite Thought: Truth and the Return to Philosophy.* New York: Continuum.

Badiou, A. 2005. *Being and Event.* New York: Continuum.

Badiou, A. 2011. "Tunisie, Egypte: quand un vent d'est balaie l'arrogance de l'Occident." *Le Monde.* http://www.lemonde.fr/idees/article/2011/02/18/tunisie-egypte-quand-un-vent-d-est-balaie-l-arrogance-de-l-occident_1481712_3232.html. Accessed January 18, 2018.

Badiou, A., and F. Tarby. 2013. *Philosophy and the Event.* Malden: Polity.

BBC. 2014. "Ukraine Crisis Timeline." http://www.bbc.com/news/world-middle-east-26248275. Accessed January 18, 2018.

Beissinger, M. 2014. "Why We Should Be Sober About the Long-Term Prospects of Stable Democracy in Ukraine." *The Washington Post*, March 11. https://www.washingtonpost.com/news/monkey-cage/wp/2014/03/11/why-we-should-be-sober-about-the-long-term-prospects-of-stable-democracy-in-ukraine/?utm_term=.115d1df98851. Accessed January 18, 2018.

Bull, H. 1977. *The Anarchical Society: A Study of Order in World Politics.* London: Macmillan.

Burbank, J., and F. Cooper. 2010. *Empires in World History: Power and the Politics of Difference.* Princeton: Princeton University Press.

Costache, A. 2012. "Real Events-Ideal Events: A Deleuzian Approach to the Concept of Historical Event." *European Journal of Science and Theology* 8 (3): 91–101.

Deleuze, G. 1990. *Difference and Repetition.* New York: Columbia University Press.

Deleuze, G. 2004. *Logic of Sense.* London: Continuum.

Deleuze, G., and F. Guattari. 1994. *What Is Philosophy?* London: Verso.

Deudney, D., and J. Ikenberry. 2015. "America's Impact: The End of Empire and the Globalization of the Westphalian System." Working Paper, Princeton University, Princeton. http://www.scholar.princeton.edu/sites/.../am-impact-dd-gji-final-1-august-2015.pdf. Accessed January 18, 2018.

Ferguson, N. 2005. "The Unconscious Colossus: Limits of (Alternatives to) American Empire." *Daedalus* 134 (2): 18–33.

Ferguson, Y. H., and R. W. Mansbach. 2006. "Superpower, Hegemony, Empire." Annual Meeting Paper, The International Studies Association, San Diego, March 22–26.

Gilpin, R. 1981. *War and Change in World Politics.* Cambridge: Cambridge University Press.

Hardt, M., and A. Negri. 2000. *Empire.* Cambridge: Harvard University Press.

Hutchings, S., and J. Szostek. 2016. "Dominant Narratives in Russian Political and Media Discourse During the Ukraine Crisis." In *Ukraine and Russia: People, Politics, Propaganda and Perspectives,* edited by A. Pikulicka-Wilczewska and R. Swaka. Bristol: E-International Relations Publishing.

Kiryukhin, D. 2016. "Roots and Features of Modern Ukrainian National Identity and Nationalism." In *Ukraine and Russia: People, Politics, Propaganda and Perspectives,* edited by A. Pikulicka-Wilczewska and R. Swaka. Bristol: E-International Relations Publishing.

Laruelle, M. 2016. "The Ukrainian Crisis and Its Impact on Transforming Russian Nationalism Landscape." In *Ukraine and Russia: People, Politics, Propaganda and Perspectives,* edited by A. Pikulicka-Wilczewska and R. Swaka. Bristol: E-International Relations Publishing.

Makarychev, A., and A. Yatsyk, eds. 2017. *Vocabularies of International Relations After the Crisis in Ukraine.* London: Routledge.

Marples, D. 2016. "Ethnic and Social Composition of Ukraine's Regions and Voting Patterns." In *Ukraine and Russia: People, Politics, Propaganda and Perspectives,* edited by A. Pikulicka-Wilczewska and R. Swaka. Bristol: E-International Relations Publishing.

Menon, R., and E. Rumer. 2015. *Conflict in Ukraine: The Unwinding of the Post-Cold War Order.* Cambridge: MIT Press.

Mouffe, C. 2013. *Antagonistic: Thinking the World Politically.* London: Verso.

Nabers, D. 2015. *A Poststructuralist Discourse Theory of Global Politics.* Houndsmills and New York: Palgrave Macmillan.

Neumann, I. 1996. "Self and Other in International Relations." *European Journal of International Relations* 2 (2): 139–74.

Norris, C. 2009. *Badiou's Being and Event: A Reader's Guide.* London: Continuum.

Petro, N. N. 2016. "Understanding the Other Ukraine: Identity and Allegiance in Russophone Ukraine." In *Ukraine and Russia: People, Politics, Propaganda and Perspectives,* edited by A. Pikulicka-Wilczewska and R. Swaka. Bristol: E-International Relations Publishing.

Reynolds, J. 2008. "Wounds and Scars: Deleuze on the Time and Ethics of the Event." *Deleuze Studies* 1 (2): 144–66.

Robinson, A. 2014. "An A to Z Theory: Alain Badiou: The Event." https://ceasefiremagazine.co.uk/alain-badiou-event/. Accessed January 18, 2018.

Sakwa, R. 2015. *Frontline Ukraine: Crisis in the Borderlands*. London: I.B. Tauris.

Trenin, Dmitri. 2014. *The Ukraine Crisis and the Resumption of Great-Power Rivalry*. Moscow: Carnegie Moscow Center.

Walker, R. B. J. 1993. *Inside/Outside: International Relations as Political Theory*. Cambridge: Cambridge University Press.

Walker, E. W. 2016. "Between East and West: NATO Enlargement and the Geopolitics of the Ukraine Crisis." In *Ukraine and Russia: People, Politics, Propaganda and Perspectives*, edited by A. Pikulicka-Wilczewska and R. Swaka. Bristol: E-International Relations Publishing.

Wilson, A. 2014. *Ukraine Crisis: What It Means for the West*. New Haven: Yale University Press.

Yekelchyk, S. 2015. *The Conflict in Ukraine*. Oxford: Oxford University Press.

CHAPTER 3

The Rationality and Emotion of Russian Historical Memory: The Case of Crimea

Douglas Becker

INTRODUCTION

On March 18, 2014, Russia annexed the Crimean peninsula, seizing the territory from neighboring Ukraine. Citing the long tradition of Russian/Crimean relations, arguing that the territory had been seized from Russia illegally under Soviet rule, and citing the popularity of the decision among the residents of Crimea, Putin legitimated the annexation in direct opposition to the United Nations Charter. What motivated this decision? How seriously should researchers take his historical arguments as an alternative legitimation discourse from international legal grounds? When Putin laid out his justification, who was the intended audience? And how can we take this action and the justifications attached to it as a guide for future Russian foreign policy?

This essay will examine the motivations behind the Russian act of aggression and compare them to the stated reasons by the Russian

D. Becker (✉)
School of International Relations, University of Southern California,
Los Angeles, USA

© The Author(s) 2018
E. Resende et al. (eds.), *Crisis and Change in Post-Cold War Global Politics*, https://doi.org/10.1007/978-3-319-78589-9_3

President for this policy. It will examine in particular the historical arguments, rooted in the concept of historical memory (defined here as the use of history for contemporary political purposes), as a guide to understand Russian interests. It will conclude as a guide to the relationship between the emotion of historical perceptions of injustice and cultural affinities and the rational motivations for increasing resources, power, security, and population. As such, it is intended as a case study in the ongoing conversations about emotion, rationality, historical memory, and realism as guides for both foreign policy analysis and general public diplomacy.

The nature of the "crisis" as it unfolds within Crimea is a feature of post-Soviet politics, particularly as an element of Russian nationalism and foreign policy. International Relations (IR) theory has typically conceptualized crisis as a discrete event, where a challenger seeks to upset and existing status quo. Crisis is defined in this context by the features of commitment of the challenger, power martialed against the challenge, and a limited time frame where decisions must be considered and implemented without delay. In some ways, the Crimea annexation and ongoing intervention in Ukraine's civil war fits this description, with Russia serving as the challenger.

According to Nabers' post-structuralist account of crisis, political intervention to counter crisis appears to be always enabled (Nabers 2015: 45). His own work cites the responses to the 9/11 attacks in the USA, where then President George W. Bush stated a nearly perpetual war in the global war on terror (and mirrored by an open-ended authorization of the use of force under opaque definition that continues to this date—the so-called Authorization of the Use of Military Force and constant invocation of Article 51 of the UN Charter, on self-defense). This notion of crisis, with endless opportunities for intervention that challenge the contemporary norms that seemingly govern crisis behavior (and crisis as defined in part by a relaxation of norms and normal behavior), grants a nearly unchecked ability of political actors to intervene.

This model of crisis and perpetual intervention though is not a particularly post 9/11 development. Both the USA and the Soviet Union manipulated the notion of crisis during the Cold War to create space for intervention based on their own perceptions of threat and notably a merely advancement of their own preferences. "Manufactured" crises used to justify direct overthrowing of governments throughout Latin America and East Asia for the USA and Eastern Europe for the Soviet Union demonstrate that this crisis/intervention nexus with perpetual and unchecked opportunity for intervention is not a new development. Therefore, the notion of crisis itself is built into a system and the conditions of crisis remain relatively unchecked, or at least not as a positive definition that is fixed across cases. It is a loosening of intervention that calls the whole notion of crisis into question.

Nabers, taking the post-structuralist lines of constructivism and extending them, then highlights that this loosening of language and social phenomena attached to the language calls even what we might call "reality" into question (Nabers 2015: 57). This structure allows for definitions of norms within international law to serve with a degree of fluidity depending on the structure. The examples of Cold War interventions and then post-9/11 interventions demonstrate the nature of the structure that at least becomes permissive of intervention. The post-Soviet space constitutes another of these structures, aided by the loosened definitions of nation, sovereignty, space, protection, and guided by the memory of history. In short, historical claims constituting a form of historical memory create a potential fluidity of nation; of border; and a potential alternative legitimation discourse that considers the crisis to enable intervention. While protection of co-nationals serves as a more traditional legitimation (a common theme in post-Russian legitimation of intervention, as discussed later in the chapter), the return of historical lands and the unification of the abstracted nation, with its sacred and historical spaces, offer a potential of a loosening of the norms of sovereignty as embodied in international law, specifically Article 2 (4), as a conservative notion of peacekeeping through maintaining of borders. Therefore, the historical discourse poses a potential challenge, using the language of crisis to justify intervention, aggression, and revision of borders. It is to this technique, enabled by the structure but demanding some form of public justification, to which I now turn.

MEMORY AS PUBLIC DIPLOMACY VS MEMORY AS FOREIGN POLICY ANALYSIS

Are references to historical memory a tool of public diplomacy or an insight into the foreign policy preferences of the state leader? Traditional IR (as a field of study) tends to discount the actual discourse of leaders when explaining motivations for foreign policy choices. Interests, rather than discourse, guide state leaders in foreign policy preferences.

Skeptical of justifications serving as fig leafs for military action, foreign policy analysts have tended to discount the legal and political arguments leaders make (particularly when justifying aggressive military action).

IR theory has traditionally privileged the study of power, interests, norms, and strategic interactions. IR scholars have only recently started to focus on the importance of identity as a fundamental influence on state action. More specifically, the field of foreign policy analysis has largely focused on either state interests, or elite preference formation, or decision-making processes, or domestic political alliances, or even perhaps public opinion in analyzing how foreign policy is formulated. Constructivism, fortunately, has begun to address this omission of identity within foreign policy analysis. As Wendt (1992) writes, "identities are the basis of interests." Meanwhile, Cynthia Weber (2010) states that "what states do depends on what states' identities and interests are, and identities and interests change." And Ernst Renan (1990) has proclaimed that nations both possess in common a rich legacy of memories and, at the same time, will forget certain things. Nations, particularly in the context of Benedict Anderson's imagined communities, share these common memories and forge a common identity through them. The constructivist paradigm within IR makes a series of claims about foreign policy analysis. It claims that interests and identity matter. This, in contrast with the simpler realist conception that states act according to interests, is—to borrow an analogy by John Lewis Gaddis (2001)—used in a similar vein, rather like arguing that fish must swim in water: It is true, yet theoretically uninteresting. (His assertion is about states seeking security in a self-help system, but is apropos here.) The concept of interests often becomes so elastic that the term ceases to have meaning. But for most realists state action is guided either by the structure of the system or by opportunities to change the system. There is nothing unique about any individual state interest—only its capabilities and the capabilities of its potential rivals. Constructivists reject the simple construction of state interests in the realist paradigm. Instead, they argue that interests are fundamentally a component both of state identity and of strategic and meaningful international interactions. As Hopf argues, "[m]eaningful behavior or action is possible only within an intersubjective social context" (Hopf 1998: 173). Through the lens of identity, durable expectations about state behavior ensure predictable patterns (Hopf 1998: 174). Hence, as stated, constructivists assume nothing about the generalizability of state identity, but instead treat it as an essential line of analysis.

The use of image helps policymakers to craft their arguments based on teleological rather than ontological descriptions of state interests and motivations (Edkins and Zehfuss 2005). Image becomes the lens through which state leaders invite external analysis to view any policy. States are defined therefore by their image rather than objectively through their actions. Australia's intervention in Indonesian domestic politics—crafted as a version of the Responsibility to Protect (R2P), coupled with an eventual recognition of East Timorese sovereignty—is therefore not to be characterized as an invasion. Australia's image, particularly reinforced through the apology to the "Stolen Generation" of indigenous persons in that nation for atrocities that many describe as a genocide, provides the lens of humanitarianism necessary to justify its support for East Timor's independence. American policymakers have sought to make similar arguments concerning the potential for empire-building in the aftermath of the terrorist attacks of 9/11 and the announcement of the Bush Doctrine. The role of identity in foreign policy formation is considered an element of the "public psyche" in much of the literature. Roger Morgan considers this concept to run deeper than simple public opinion, which is a common theme within foreign policy analysis. It is a deeper, emotional connection that the general public has to their image of what their nation represents (Morgan 2003). In other formulations, identity becomes a vehicle by which a nation can define its historical existence. It is a lens through which international interactions are viewed. Information on potential international interactions is filtered through this lens of image, so that threats are perceived as they relate to historical threats to the nation.

In addition, even when considering the role of security, it is not clear that physical security can override the interests of a state's identity-security, or what Brent Steele calls ontological security. Steele indicates a state will go to great lengths to protect its own image and conception of itself, even potentially to the detriment of its own physical security. Utilizing the work of Giddens, Steele indicates that well-ordered and constructed language can identify a state's sense of image and security of self—even more so than slips of the tongue or comments off the cuff. These are the constructed notions of action and justification, intended to protect the actor's own identity (Steele 2008: 14). As such, the stated reasons for action are to be taken seriously, in particular when they are thoughtful constructions or arguments and justifications. As such, Presidential statements, for example Putin's speech, provide even greater insight than a simple discourse analysis of any statement, precisely because they are the reasoned statements of purpose.

This need to protect the Russian state identity is contrasted with the increasing use of Ukrainian historical discourse to contrast it with the Russian narrative of the two states. Ilya Nuzov (2017) details the memory discourses, with a particular eye toward institutional shift that embodied a new Ukrainian European (that is, a western-looking Ukraine toward Central Europe) approach to contrast the previous Ukrainian Russian ("Little Russia," eastern-looking Ukraine) that embodies a great deal of the partisan contestations in the nation. The urgency of the Russian move appears motivated by these precise memory discourse shifts that accompanied the political changes in 2014.

In contrast to this notion of image as guiding actual foreign policy and interests is the argument that justification and legitimation are just meant to build public support for the policy. The field of Public Diplomacy is a rapidly growing field with a particular salience in the USA following the 9/11 terrorist attacks. Diplomatic studies as a subfield grew during the Cold War, specifically as a general disinterest in IR theory (with a preferred emphasis on history). Yet, this field has generally been marginalized in US IR classrooms (Wiseman 2015). Nevertheless, the field grew as an interdisciplinary field in the USA as a joint venture in communications and IR (Wiseman 2015). It melds media studies, public relations, even product branding, with the more traditional study of IR.

According to Nicholas Cull, public diplomacy "refers to the government-sponsored programs intended to inform or influence public opinion in other countries" (Cull 2009). Contrast this with traditional diplomacy, which is the diplomacy between official diplomatic sources, largely government to government contacts. In essence, public diplomacy is intended to extend beyond governments and engage foreign publics. Altering public opinion, as well as broadly informing the foreign public about the society, culture, political positions, of history of the foreign state is the key. Historical memory is a particularly powerful tool of public diplomacy. The key distinction in memory as public diplomacy compared to public diplomacy as a lens through which to understand state interest is the intended audience of the memory discourse. Public diplomacy presumes the audience is the foreign public. However, as I will demonstrate throughout this analysis, the intended audience may well be the domestic audience at the expense of foreign publics.

Differentiating between what parts of the discourse and legitimation of the Russian annexation of Crimea are the actual lens through which to view Russian motivation and which are a mere form of public diplomacy and perhaps a fig leaf to cover realist interests is methodologically difficult if not impossible. In part, the researcher would be required to understand what was in the heart and mind of Russian leaders—and in particular Vladimir Putin—in determining his interests. At one level, the best any analysis can hope to accomplish it to lay out the multi-motivational approach and demonstrate how these motivations influence the actual decisions and actions.

In doing so, I will take the actual legitimation discourse—the speech the Russian President delivered to the Duma to justify the annexation, at its face value. It will serve as the primary source for understanding his motivation, in particular with its references to memory discourses and cultural maps. I will break down passages from the speech and outline a more detailed discussion of its references and meanings. Then I will evaluate the realist interests the Russians should desire, based on security and power considerations. In this, I will outline the short-term and long-term interests. In concluding whether Russian emotional (memory) interests seem to have outweighed their rational (security) interests, I will attempt to evaluate each motivation, particularly when comparing outcomes. I will address, in those areas where Russian security interests may not be served by this aggression, whether this lack of "rational" behavior is due to the emotionalism of the issue; of misperception of interests and responses; of short-term gains at the expense of long-term security; or of gambles and bluffs that were ineffective. The analysis, by its very nature, will be speculative.

Multiplicity of Audiences and Memory Discourses

Dovilė Budrytė (2013) has highlighted the multiplicity of audience who could be the target of a memory discourse. While memory may well be intended for the domestic audience, it can also give rise to contestations and alterations based on external actors. Japan, in constructing a memory of the Second World War, alters its historical textbooks accordingly. This brings it into conflict with Chinese and Korean activists who insist this is a whitewashing of Japanese atrocities during the war. Remembrances of the dropping of the atomic bombs in Hiroshima and Nagasaki bring similar responses in the USA and Japan. Duncan Bell (2009) references these discourses and contestations in his discussion of trans-national memory, a multi-actor commemoration field when considering certain memories have both a multi-national and super-national element to them.

Throughout their histories both extended and recent, Ukrainians and Russians have seen these memory contestations lend themselves to dramatic and significant conflicts. How much of the Crimea annexation is given to these competing memories and identities? These range from the decision of Ukraine to join the Russian Empire (or be swept into it, as the contestations of the Treaty of Pereiaslav indicate) to the experiences of the Soviet state (the famine, the Second World War, and other related issues) and the cultural importance of the Crimean peninsula. The contestations themselves have led the two countries into conflict. But perhaps even more problematic is determining when a political actor (in this case Russian President Putin) is referencing historical memory, who exactly is his intended audience? Is the speech laying out a historical justification for the annexation intended to serve as public diplomacy, convincing foreign publics either in Ukraine or perhaps in the West of the legitimacy of his decision? Or is the intended audience the Russian public? Indeed, what resonates with Russians might precisely draw the state into conflict with its neighbors. Pithily, is this memory discourse a matter of IR or comparative politics? Does it speak with a Russian accent or with an international one?

THE ANNEXATION OF CRIMEA: COMPETING EXPLANATIONS

There are a multitude of competing explanations for why Russia chose to annex Crimea in 2014. Some of these explanations focus on the timing of the decision; others take a broader scope and examine the general motivations for the decision. This analysis tends to the latter—the timing itself is a bit beyond the scope of my analysis, although the question is particularly interesting. First, Hill and Gaddy's psychological examination of Putin begins with the suggestion that the decision to annex Crimea was a break with Putin's past pattern of behavior. Specifically, unlike previous interventions that Putin either ordered or oversaw (specifically the invasion of Georgia or the support for the independence of Transdniester), this was a very specific landgrab. There was much less of a reference to governmental actions against Russophones as a human rights justification for the intervention. Instead, he cited historical injustices and the memory of Russian culture and experiences in Crimea as his justification. Hill and Gaddy (2016) further suggest this break with the past pattern of behavior serves as an important insight into his true character. How much of this decision is rooted in Putin's own personality; in Russian historical desires for empire; in specific responses to changes in the regional balance of power; or in the perception that a historical injustice needed correction?

Hill and Gaddy (2016) lay out four different arguments as to the motivation for Russian aggression. The first is the importance of the recognition of the greatness of Russian power (*derzhavnost*) and even perhaps rising to the importance of a "secular religion"—and how it may well undermine the notion of equality of sovereignty. Ukraine, following the Orange Revolution and the Presidency of Viktor Yushchenko (and the Russian continued domination of Ukraine despite anti-Russian rhetoric), had challenged this notion. The EU has reached out to the former Soviet non-Russian Republics in its campaign of the "Eastern Partnership." Now, is this challenging principle in IR (sovereignty) in the case of Ukraine simply becomes equal with the ability of the EU to serve as a counterweight to the Russian domination? Wayne Merry emphasizes the argument that Russians view Ukrainian sovereignty as fundamentally unnatural (Wood et al. 2016).

The centrality here of the "Association Agreement" which would have formalized Ukrainian/EU partnerships needs to be noted. Viktor Yanukovych has chosen not to sign the agreement in 2013, due to a financial counteroffer from the Russians. This decision created instability and compelled protests on the part of the Ukrainians, demanding a change in government. In February 2014, in what is called either the Euromaidan Revolution or the Revolution of Dignity, Yanukovych is overthrown, and he flees to Russia. He then requests, while in hiding but still claiming legitimacy over the government of Ukraine, which Russian troops occupy Crimea to bring about law and order—this is done on March 2, 2014. It sets the stage for the vote and annexation. The current President of Ukraine is Petro Poroshenko, who helped lead the Maidan Revolution. Clearly, the nation's rejection of Russian influence continues to be apparent (Wood et al. 2016).

Next, William Pomeranz argues that it was a trade dispute driven by Putin's zero-sum strategies vis-à-vis Kyiv. In 2012, Russia creates the Eurasian Economic Union, with Belarus, Kazakhstan, Armenia, and Kyrgyzstan, but Ukraine does not join. This is in part to the original trade deficits Russia runs when it joins the WTO in 2012 (estimated at $13 billion). Ukraine did not want to join the EEC, and Yushchenko—on the backs of a Ukraine that was absolutely bankrupt by early 2013—decides on a "winner take all" trade strategy pitting the EU against the EEU in the hopes of getting a bailout. The Russians suffered as a result of the trade disruptions with Ukraine. Ukraine was Russia's #1 trade partner, and pursuing this agenda has hurt the Russians economically. Interestingly, this economic downturn has compelled most Russians to blame the limited sanctions, and in particular US President Barack Obama, for their fates (Wood et al. 2016).

Focusing more directly on Russian power, the core question may be whether this annexation is this a part of Russia's Grand Design—shall it be a Superpower that other countries fear or be economically prosperous as a nation? Maxim Trudolyubov argues that this is a false dichotomy, and that greatness normative is tied to economic prosperity. But it is tied very much to this notion of superpower status, and that domination over Ukraine and the ability to simply seize territory demonstrate the fear it had lost as a result of the breakup and exacerbated by the ongoing conflict in Chechnya. Russia was awash with cash and was confident there would not be economic consequences (Wood et al. 2016). So is this a failure to anticipate future developments or even potentially matching the American conservative critic position on Obama's foreign policy that he was seen to be feckless and weak?

Another potential explanation is that the annexation and aggression is closely tied to the symbolic politics of Vladimir Putin, who wanted a win in a small war as a way to bolster his own position. In a documentary called "Crimea: Path to a Homeland," produced in 2015, Putin himself explained he was reacting to a spontaneous demonstration and was simply asserting the rights of Russians in Crimea at a time where they were threatened. Additionally, if Ukraine joined NATO or denied Russia access to the Black Fleet, it threatened Russian security.

Elizabeth Wood ties these symbols to the masculinist image Putin has created and how Crimea personifies this image. She goes so far as to argue that Putin has fomented image over ideology or strategy, allowing there to be an ideological and ideas vacuum within Russia filled by right-wing ideologues and oligarchs. In 2011–2012, Putin suffers some real image denigration, with protests. August 2011 is when Pussy Riot was formed, as a point of reference. His political party sees its vote totals drop from the mid-60s to 49% in the 2012 elections (Wood et al. 2016). She highlights the Sochi Olympics meant to demonstrate Russian power and prestige but they had been marred by allegations of corruption and mismanagement. Putin had a lot of personal prestige at stake for the Olympics—did he choose the end of the Olympics to change to the discourse and instead emphasize the return of Russian power?

Putin then also draws contacts with Russian activists on behalf of Crimea—the most famous of which was a motorcycle gang called the Night Wolves. This group had fostered close relations with the Russian President as part of a calculated move in 2009, when Obama comes to Moscow but lets it be known he was to meet with then President Medvedev, not the Prime Minister. Putin then meets the Night Wolves, and this dominated Russian television, not the Obama visit. They patrol Crimea in advance of the Russian troops and serve as a sort of paramilitary presence—this image of Hell's Angels working with Putin to protect Russians help to build his image of strength.

Russian "Compatriots"

Adopting a realist tone in her interpretation of Putin's public discourse and foreign policy, Agnia Grigas argues that the rights of ethnic Russians and Russophones is the foundation of Russian neoimperialism. The protection of the rights of what he calls "Russian compatriots" serves as the theoretical underpinning of Putin's expansionist justifications (Grigas 2016). This has certainly inspired allegations of mistreatment of Russians in the former Soviet Republics, direct interventions, and support for rebel groups aligned with the Russians. Several conflicts, both directly leading to military aggression and those which rely on threat, intimidation and blackmail, have cited the rights of Russians at the core. On the former, the two obvious examples are the invasion of Georgia to ostensibly support the independence drives of Abkhazia and South Ossetia and the military support for rebel groups in Moldova in the division of the nation and support for the independence of Transdniester. The latter has numerous examples, notably the 2007 Russian cyber-attack on Estonia in protest of the removal of Russian statues and removal of Russian graves dating to the Second World War.

President Putin references this point directly in the speech he delivers to justify the annexation of Crimea. He cites the referendum he called to determine the popular support for Russian annexation in the region. Then, citing the results, he argued that:

> More than 82 percent of the electorate took part in the vote. Over 96 percent of them spoke out in favour of reuniting with Russia. These numbers speak for themselves... we expected Ukraine to remain our good neighbor, we hoped that Russian citizens and Russian speakers in Ukraine,

especially its southeast and Crimea, would live in a friendly, democratic and civilised state that would protect their rights in line with the norms of international law. However, this is not how the situation developed. Time and time again attempts were made to deprive Russians of their historical memory, even of their language and to subject them to forced assimilation. (Address of the President of Russian Federation 2014)

Therefore, it was the protection of Russophone communities, at least in this sense of legitimation, which motivated Russian aggression. The move is both democratic and preserves human rights, in this estimation.

Each case of Russian intervention based on protection of the rights of Russian peoples is distinct and deserve their own analysis. Nevertheless, they can be grouped as cases where Russia had either supported the division of its neighbor in support of Russophones (or Russian Compatriots) or threatened direct aggression and forced the state to back down. In each case, the decision to intervene was intensely popular in Russia, and invited outside resistance and often political and economic sanction. Yet despite the political and economic ramifications, the Russians pursued their aggression. A realist interpretation would suggest Russian motivation in these cases were the seizure of territory and the weakening of their neighbors because of relative power considerations. In short, Russia was more powerful and hence took what it wanted. In the conclusion we will consider the long-term and short-term interests and question whether this actually has enhanced Russian power. The legitimation the Russians used in each case was the protection of Russians (even claiming a planned Georgian genocide against Russians at one point) (Grigas 2016). Internationally the legitimation has fallen on deaf ears. Yet, legitimation discourses remain popular domestically.

Crimea though is different than Georgia or Moldova. Crimea is an escalation in that Russia actually annexed territory. Did it escalate because Russia had been testing the West and was determined that they could get away with this escalation? Was it the relative value of the territory, including the port and the access to the Black Sea fleet? Or was it the intensity of the historical memory and the significance of these sites as parts of the Russian cultural map? The speech suggests the latter, but the enduring sense of "crisis" as justification for intervention for other purposes, as Nabers conceptualizes, suggests the Russians are using this sense of risk as a justification for a land grab.

Domestic Politics of Russia

Turning attention to domestic politics, the annexation of Crimea is driven by Putin's desire to build support for this government. The popularity of the Russian moves within the Russian population, coupled with the perception of Ukraine as being criminal and lawless (or even "Nazi," with Russian references to Stepan Bandera—for a more detailed account of Ukrainian corruption and lawlessness see Wilson 2014), make the Russian moves quite popular. Putin's citation of these statistics in his speech, coupled with sagging approval ratings before the annexation— reported as low as in the 40% range in 2012—compelled his action. This returns us to the multiplicity of audience observations about historical memory. While the public diplomacy component of the campaign has been largely ineffective, it has made Putin quite popular in Russia. In fact, he cites his own approval ratings around that 86% range mirroring those who believe Crimea is Russian. That Russians view Crimea as a part of their cultural map and historically a part of the Russian state is quite clear.

President Putin certainly had Russian domestic politics in mind when he justified the annexation of Crimea. He cites specific polls in his speech to the Duma:

> The most recent public opinion surveys conducted here in Russia show that 95 percent of people think that Russia should protect the interests of Russians and members of other ethnic groups living in Crimea—95 percent of our citizens. More than 83 percent think that Russia should do this even if it will complicate our relations with some other countries. A total of 86 percent of our people see Crimea as still being Russian territory and part of our country's lands. And one particularly important figure, which corresponds exactly with the result in Crimea's referendum: almost 92 percent of our people support Crimea's reunification with Russia. (Address of the President of Russian Federation 2014)

The disregard Putin has shown for international protestation against the aggression is countered here by the support with the Russian nation. His citation of its popularity helps to position him as a defender of Russian interests despite the potential reaction internationally.

UKRAINE AND THE WEST

Indeed, President Putin countered the international reaction by laying the threat to Russia directly at the feet of Ukrainians turning their backs on Russian compatriots. The Ukrainian turn to the West was orchestrated by the West in the traditional policy and strategy of containment. Ukrainians turned west and compelled the Russians to act in their annexation of Crimea. To this end, the Russian President stated:

> In short, we have every reason to assume that the infamous policy of containment, led in the 18th, 19th and 20th centuries, continues today. They are constantly trying to sweep us into a corner because we have an independent position, because we maintain it and because we call things like they are and do not engage in hypocrisy. But there is a limit to everything. And with Ukraine, our western partners have crossed the line, playing the bear and acting irresponsibly and unprofessionally. (Address of the President of Russian Federation 2014)

This portrays the annexation as a defensive move to counter Western assertion of power. Ukraine, flirting with the West, seeks to encircle and weaken Russia.

Echoing this argument, Pomeranz, as stated early, laid the roots of the conflict at the feet of the Ukrainian decision to pivot west economically. The negotiations of a trade agreement, where Ukraine was actively choosing to back away from Russian economic ties and invite European investment and trade, was a clear motivation for Russian aggression. Putin lays the blame at the feet of the Europeans. Is this a realist motivation, with a fear of a neighbor aligning with the West and the potential continued re-adjustment of the NATO presence even more fully on Russia's borders? Or is this rooted in identity issues, discussed in the next section? In any case, this is one of the most intriguing elements of the decision to annex Crimea.

Nothing has advanced the Ukrainian case to join NATO more than their suffering Russian aggression in the annexation of Crimea. While it is still relatively unlikely that Ukraine would join the western alliance in the near future, their application was generally disregarded before the crisis. This is an embodiment of the Hobbesian security paradox. Russian insecurity about NATO compels the nation to seize the most valuable military resource—the port at Sevastopol. In doing so and demonstrating their threat to Ukraine, it invites Kyiv to more seriously pursue a Western alliance with which they were merely flirting in 2014. While Putin might have determined that Ukrainian entry into NATO is inevitable, I would maintain that is a miscalculation. But he is enabling the outcome he most wishes to avoid.

The evidence necessary to understand the shifts from an eastern-looking to a western-looking Ukraine is best viewed in this lens of historical memory contestation. Nuzov (2017) identifies two particular political camps within Ukraine that demonstrate this cleft. The liberals, as champions of a Ukraine civic-nation that is increasingly European, Western, and more aggressive form this cleft with contestation from the more passive, Eastern-looking elites. The latter look to state paternalism, as clients of the Russian state, benefitting from closer ties to their historic partner, and a post-Soviet space that identifies Russian domination in exchange for protection (Nuzov 2017). The key variable here is corruption. The liberals have argued that the paternalists are particularly corrupt, with ties to the Russian oligarchy and the use of the state as a vehicle for their own enrichment. That was at the core of the grievance as advanced by the 2014 Euromaidan Revolution. Pro-Russian identity corresponds therefore to corruption and a loss of state power, sovereignty, and even identity. The use of identity through memory discourses, therefore, undermines the corruption of the pro-Russian state. Putin and the Russians understood this and therefore moved to blunt the Ukrainian power, seizing not only Crimea but also fomenting revolution in Eastern Ukraine.

This leads to what Nuzov refers to as the securitization of memory. Decommunization laws are intended to purge the nation of its Russian influences by emphasizing Soviet crimes (often with no reference to German or indigenous Nazi crimes during World War II). This lays atrocity in Ukraine during the Soviet period firmly at the feet of a communist party headquartered in Moscow. Russia, by emphasizing its own nationalism, has resisted the accrual of memory onto its own record. Its emphasis is on Ukrainian atrocities headed by Nazi sympathizers. In emphasizing Ukrainian/Central European collaboration in the commission of atrocities, Russia seeks to both delegitimize the Ukrainian drive westward as well as expunge its own culpability. Hence, transitional justice questions—who was responsible for the previous atrocities, lead to conflict and remain at the heart of the identity clashes between Ukraine and Russia (Nuzov 2017).

DISCOURSES ON LEGITIMATION—INTERNATIONAL
LAW AND ALTERNATIVE DISCOURSES

Goddard and Krebs (2015) highlight the importance of legitimation in the constructivist estimations on discourse for political action. Legitimacy has always been viewed as an important variable in the exercise of power in politics. Dating a century back, Max Weber argued that the state as community claims "the monopoly of the legitimate use of physical force within a given territory" as the logic of sovereignty (Weber 1918/1946). This desire for legitimacy leads states' leaders to assert their legitimacy in the exercise of power internationally as well. This legitimation discourse creates potential precedent and norms for other states to cite in their own desires for legitimation (Goddard and Krebs 2015).

Legitimation often cites international law, and in particular the assertions of legality under the UN Charter. Liberals often argue the importance of international law, but have cited the "marketplace of institutions" challenging the UN in a sole role of legitimation. Specifically, the US decision to ignore the UN Security Council and instead seek legitimation through a NATO operation in the air campaign over Yugoslavia addressing violence in Kosovo and the rejection of the Rambouillet proposal to demonstrate the multitude of legitimation options under international law. Collective self-defense—usually cited as a stronger case than unilateral self-defense—responsibility to protect, global collection action against a stated threat such as terrorism, and opposition to genocide are often cited as norms at the state's disposal when legitimizing its military actions. But even under this consideration, the legality of the action is often unclear, even with a strong normative claim.

Goddard and Krebs view legitimation as more than just a citation of legality, and open the door to the idea of alternative forms of legitimation. In the Crimea case, Putin cited a series of legal and normative claims as legitimation. He stated the holding of the referendum as a legal justification for annexation—though he was quite limited in the use of referenda to determine borders, with his unwillingness to consider a referendum for instance in Chechnya. Perhaps the most passionate, and more clearly cited, alternative legitimation discourse was rooted in historical memory. Goddard and Krebs do not cite memory as an alternative legitimation discourse, but it clearly fits their criteria for legitimation.

President Putin engages international law explicitly in justifying the annexation of Crimea, stating that:

> Pursuant to Article 2, Chapter 1 of the United Nations Charter, the UN International Court agreed with this approach and made the following comment in its ruling of July 22, 2010, and I quote: *"No general prohibition may be inferred from the practice of the Security Council with regard to declarations of independence,"* and *"General international law contains no prohibition on declarations of independence."* Crystal clear, as they say... the Written Statement of the United States America of April 17, 2009, submitted to the same UN International Court in connection with the hearings on Kosovo. Again, I quote: *"Declarations of independence may, and often do, violate domestic legislation. However, this does not make them violations of international law."* (Address of the President of Russian Federation 2014)

And while the case he is making is based in international law, it is best to describe it as an alternative discourse to the dominant argument that Article 2 (4) of the UN Charter clearly states the seizure of territory of another sovereign nation is a violation of international law.

In this case, the Russians advance arguments about human rights, state sovereignty, and national identity that can best be described as alternative yet not discredited approaches to international law. Mälksoo (2015) indicates that the Russian interest in the protection of human rights—defined not as individual rights but as collective rights in the protection of the identity of Russian populations) is a selective yet uniquely Russian approach to international law. In essence, Russia takes R2P-type arguments as justification for military action to protect human rights and appropriate them as a means to defend aggression on their part to protect Russian rights. The particularist approach, applying only to their own intervention rather than a universal intervention and specifically about identity, is best described as a melding of human rights discourses and Steele's notion of ontological security.

CONSTRUCTION OF IDENTITY OF NEW STATES

Whether Crimea has always been a part of Russia obscures a much more interest and significant historical cultural map—have Ukrainians always been Russians? Plokhy argues this is the distinction between the notion of Ukraine as a nation and a nationality, or whether Ukrainians are merely "Little Russians." Is Russia as a concept more expansive to include nationalities such as Ukrainians as well as Belorussians, often included in this discussion? Or is "Russian" a largely Muscovite construction?

Russian identity, particularly in the post-communist world, is coupled with the Russophone arguments cited in the earlier section. President Putin makes an appeal to the sense of Russian identity in justifying the annexation, stating:

> In people's hearts and minds, Crimea has always been an inseparable part of Russia. This firm conviction is based on truth and justice and was passed from generation to generation, over time, under any circumstances, despite all the dramatic changes our country went through during the entire 20th century. (Address of the President of Russian Federation 2014)

The popular sentiment "in the people's hearts and minds," the historical memory component "from generation to generation" and a harkening to the traditional identity of Crimea as Russian, all feature heavily in the speech.

New states often seek new identities as unifying principles to build support for the government, for social institution, and in general for national identity. Ukraine is a fascinating case in this instance, because while it is a new state, it is far from a new identity. For generations, Ukrainians have struggled with its identity tied to Russian identity; tied to Central European promises of protection from Russia; and straddling the East and West in a delicate balancing act. In many ways, Ukrainian identity varies little from the Hetmanate leading to the Treaty of Pereiaslav, when Ukraine had to choose between a Western-focuses alliance with Poland and Lithuania or to the East to its Russian neighbor from protection. The historiography of memory recovery—of Ukrainian history independent of its more dominant neighbor to the East, is embodied in the work of Mikhail Hrushevsky.

As a historian, Mikhail Hrushevsky authored the first detailed scholarly synthesis of Ukrainian history, his ten-volume History of Ukraine-Rus', which was published in the Ukrainian language and covered the period from pre-history to the 1660s. In this work, he balanced a commitment to the common Ukrainian people with an appreciation for native Ukrainian political entities, autonomous polities and such, which steadily increased in the final volumes of this, his master work.

In general, Hrushevsky's approach combined rationalist enlightenment principles with a romantic commitment to the cause of the nation and positivist methodology to produce a highly authoritative history of his native land and people. Hrushevsky also wrote a multi-volume *History of Ukrainian Literature*, an *Outline History of the Ukrainian People* in Russian, and a very popular *Illustrated History of Ukraine* which appeared in both Ukrainian and Russian editions. In addition to these major works, he wrote numerous specialized studies in which he displayed a very acute critical acumen. His personal bibliography lists over 2000 separate titles (Plokhy 2008).

In Hrushevsky's varied historical writings certain basic ideas come to the fore. Firstly, Hrushevsky saw continuity in Ukrainian history from ancient times to his own. Thus he claimed the ancient Ukrainian Steppe cultures from Scythia, through Kievan Rus' to the Cossacks as part of the Ukrainian heritage. He viewed the Principality of Galicia–Volhynia as the sole legitimate heir of Kievan Rus'. This is opposed to the official scheme of Russian history which claimed Kievan Rus' for the Vladimir-Suzdal Principality and Imperial Russia.) Secondly, to give real depth to this continuity, Hrushevsky stressed the role of the common people, the "popular masses" as he called them, throughout all these eras. Thus popular revolts against the various foreign states that ruled Ukraine were also a major theme. Thirdly, Hrushevsky always put the accent upon native Ukrainian factors rather than international ones as the causes of various phenomena. Thus he was an anti-Normanist who stressed the Slavic origins of Rus', put the emphasis upon internal discord as the primary reason for the fall of Kievan Rus', and emphasized the native Ukrainian ethnic makeup and origins of the Ukrainian Cossacks. He thought run-away serfs as especially important in this regard. Also, he stressed the national aspect to the Ukrainian renaissance of the sixteenth and seventeenth centuries and thought the great revolt of Bohdan Khmelnytsky and the Cossacks against the Polish-Lithuanian Commonwealth was largely a national and social rather than simply a religious phenomenon. Thus continuity, nativism, and populism characterized his general histories (Plokhy 2008).

With regard to the role of statehood in Hrushevsky's historical thought, contemporary scholars are still not in agreement. Some believe that Hrushevsky retained a populist mistrust of the state throughout his career and his deep democratic convictions reflected this, while others believe that Hrushevsky gradually became more and more of a partisan of Ukrainian statehood in his various writings and that this is reflected in his political work on the construction of a Ukrainian national state during the revolution of 1917–1918 (Plokhy 2008).

Embodying this memory contestation between the Ukrainians and Russians is the concern over commemoration of the 350th Anniversary of the Treaty of Pereiaslav in 2004. Russians view this Treaty, signed in 1654, as the foundation for the unification of Ukraine and Russia. The Ukrainian Hetmanate in this period, leading the Cossack nation, had been a part of Polish rule. Cossack uprisings over Polish rule culiminated in the 1648 revolt let by Hetman Bohdan Khmelnytsky. Poland's desire to crush this uprising will eventually lead to the Treaty in 1654. Was the Treaty a mutual assistance pact, where the Hetman chose the Russians to aid in their defense but with a promise of a free hand to govern the territory? Or was this the decision Ukrainians chose to join the Russian Empire, cementing their brotherhood in a unified rule? This is the birthing of Ukrainian/Russian relations, and its interpretation carries a significant cultural weight.

Pereiaslav did eventually divide Ukraine along the Dnipro River. Russians moved largely to the east of the river, while Ukrainians remained west. This roughly corresponds to the ongoing civil war (or war of Russian aggression) in Ukraine today. Ukrainians charged the Russians with a quasi-colonial policy of seizing traditional Ukrainian lands over the course of the 5 or so decades following Pereiaslav. In response to the growing unease at the loss of independence, in 1708 Hetman Ivan Mazepa tries to reverse the loss of power with the help of Sweden. They failed. This defeat at the hands of Peter I leads to a continued loss of Ukrainian autonomy and further cements the nation as a junior partner in the Russian Empire (Plokhy 2008).

Ukrainians continued to resist the loss of national identity through the poetry and history as well as political activism of figures such as Taras Shevchenko who became such a significant figure that the national university is named after him. Ukrainian resistance to Russian aggression took the form of this nineteenth-century figure and the celebration of the Cossack identity and greatness. Ukrainians re-enact Cossack military victories and celebrate the Cossack military identity. Ukrainian identity and Cossack identity's wedding is largely due to the work of Shevchenko.

In 2004, then Ukrainian President Leonid Kuchma had a difficult decision: How should the Treaty of Pereiaslav be remembered?

The muted commemorations, intended to demonstrate a level of iciness without a direct challenge to the Russians, serves as a predictor for further conflict. Ukraine did not antagonize the Russians into the annexation of Crimea, but they certainly chafe at the notion that they are essentially Russian. Putin's oft-cited references to Ukraine as "Little Russia" have a historical context that dates back to the seventeenth century (Plokhy 2008). His references to the nation as "the" Ukraine (indicating it as a region and a part of the Russian Empire—without the word "the" Ukraine is recognized as an independent nation) are intended to remind the Ukrainians as well as Russians of Ukraine's junior partner alliance. It should come as no shock then that the economic negotiations between the EU and Ukraine were interpreted as seeking a balancing of Russian power against its neighbor.

"City of Glory"

There is a particular importance paid to the role of the city of Sevastopol, the cultural center of Crimea and historic site of so many of Russia's battles with both the West and with the Ottoman Empire. President Putin makes explicit reference to the city when he stated that "This is also Sevastopol—a legendary city with an outstanding history, a fortress that serves as the birthplace of Russia's Black Sea Fleet" (Address of the President of Russian Federation 2014). From the Russian perspective, this is an essential part of its history and culture, and perhaps even alone would justify the annexation of the province.

Challenging the Ukrainian historical narrative, Russians have cited the importance of Crimea and in particular the city of Sevastopol as a part of their own identity. Plokhy writes:

> When the independent Ukraine left the USSR, it effectively took a number of the major imperial "sacred places" prominently present on the Russian cultural map. They included traditional "all-Russian" places of religious worship and pilgrimage, such as the Caves Monastery an St Sophia Cathedral in Kiev, and places associated with the history of the Russian empire during its "golden age" of the eighteenth and nineteenth centuries, like Poltava and Sevastopol...as the Soviet authorities awarded them the status of "hero-cities" to commemorate the heroism of their defenders during the second world war. (Plokhy 2000: 370–71)

The issue of control of Sevastopol was reported in the immediate aftermath of the breakup of the USSR, with the contestations over the Black Sea fleet in 1992. Interestingly, this was often reported as merely a question of military control of the fleet itself, echoing a realist interpretation of the conflict. Plokhy, however, cites the importance of the fleet in the historical memory and cultural imagination of Russians, in their insistence on its return. It was, in essence, a mask for the historical importance of Sevastopol specifically and Crimea in general in historical memory (Plokhy 2000).

Sevastopol has clear importance religiously and historically, as cited throughout Putin's speech. But the "fortress" that served as the foundation for Russian resistance to British and French aggression in the appropriately named Crimean War demonstrates its importance (in particular to nineteenth-century Russia). This is an ascendant Russia, both considered a threat to European security and an essential partner to European peace under the auspices of the Concert of Europe. The graves Putin references in Sevastopol are the fallen Russian heroes, but also to the grave of Russian expansion cut off by the West but potentially in Russia's sites again. This "City of Glory" is considered almost a Russian Kosovo in the eyes of authors like Plokhy (2008). If the city had no other value than its historical importance, it could compel Russian action. That it serves as a modern port in the Black Sea region enhances its importance all the more.

STRATEGY VS EMOTION: IS HISTORICAL MEMORY COMPELLING RUSSIA TO ACT AGAINST ITS INTERESTS?

What tool might evaluate whether Russia was acting against their material or strategic interests in its aggression against its neighbors? I propose outlining a realist scenario as a thought experiment analyzing material interests to serve as a guide, and then evaluate Russia's material changes as a result of its foreign policy. This will show that, while Russia may appear to make material gains in the short run, its long-term interests are poorly served by its acts of aggression. Whether this is a general failure of long-term strategic thinking or a weddedness to its emotional ties to its compatriots or land it believes is historically Russian is the more difficult issue to unpack.

First, Russia has in fact gotten away with the annexation. Crimea remains Russian, and it is unlikely to change status in the near or even medium future. Largely shielded by Europe's energy dependence on the

Russians, the sanctions have been far from decisive. The war in Eastern Ukraine continues, and Kyiv has remained chastened as a result of Russian aggression.

Additionally, Putin's own approval ratings have grown, although the actual level of support is difficult to gauge. Russians overwhelmingly supported his decision, as stated above. His reported approval ratings have grown from 49% in 2012 to an astronomical (and likely inflated) 86% recently. While it is reasonable to suggest that the approval rating he has cited is inflated, it is reasonable to believe his approval rating is higher now than before the aggression. This increase in support is in spite of the economic downturn Russia has experienced. In the multiplicity of audiences, if the Russian public was the intended audience, the citation of historical memory has been quite popular.

Yet the economic downturn is in part because of the sanctions, and in part because of ongoing economic trends which are both a response to the Russian aggression and undermine its ability to avoid the next round of sanctions. European dependence on Russian energy has been decreased. This is in part due to a research drive to ensure greener and more domestic sources of energy. It would be foolish to lay this drive solely at the feet of Russian aggression, but it was definitely one of the motivations. It has undermined Russia's ability to act without fear of deeper sanctions, as interdependence is less apparent.

Russia's ties with NATO have also suffered as a result of its aggression. Indeed, this predates the Crimea annexation. The most significant political sanctions were a reaction of Russia's invasion of Georgia. As a result, many of the consultation arrangements between Russia and NATO were ended, and Russia was removed from the G-8. Additionally, European states and the USA have cemented ties with NATO partners in the Baltics region as a result of the aggression. Ukraine's desire to join NATO is now taken more seriously. If Russia's main desire is to improve relations with the West (and in particular with the USA), and enhance its soft power (typically through propagandistic means—see Van Herpen 2015), the ongoing aggression undermines this drive. The local aggression against its neighbors is undermining its larger global drive. Is this an example of emotional and memory motivations undermining largely rational goals, or simply a miscalculation of long-term goals at the expense of short-term gains?

Concluding Remarks: Role of Memory
and Legitimation in International Relations

In 2016, the Russian public diplomacy campaign directed toward the American public was one of the most successful in modern history. In 2012, during the US Presidential campaign, Americans held a broad negative view toward the Russian leader. Both political parties' candidates for President expressed concern over Putin's aggression, while debating whether the Russian leader was the most significant threat to US interests and global peace and prosperity. Republican candidate Mitt Romney adopted an even harsher tone against the Russian leader than did President Barack Obama, citing Putin as the greatest threat to global peace.

American attitudes about Putin drew even more unfavorable in 2014, the year of Russia's annexation of Crimea and support for Russophones in Eastern Ukraine in the ongoing civil war. The net favorability rating (favorable minus unfavorable) of the Russian leader averaged an alarming—60% in 2014 polls. By November, 2016, those net favorability ratings among all Americans had risen for the Russian to around 30% averaged. It appears that the Russian President was being rehabilitated in the eyes of the American public, a clear victory in the Russian public diplomacy campaign.

However, a closer examination of trends shows that there is a clear partisan divide in the net favorability ratings among the American public. Democrats, who had fairly consistently held unfavorable views of Putin at roughly a—50%, slipped to an even greater—70% by November of 2016. Republicans, on the other hand, had seen net unfavorability of Putin drop, from an average of 60% to a mere 10%. In essence, the rise in Putin's general favorability is a definitive partisan issue in the USA.

What accounts for this shift? If the historical memory discourse justifying the annexation of Crimea caused this shift (and hence a successful legitimation discourse), it would be reasonable to observe either an ideological or legal shift in American attitudes about Russian aggression. However, pollsters usually cite the combination of Putin's increasing social conservatism and his support for their candidate for President (and the President's reciprocal support for the Russian President) as the cause. US President Donald Trump has remained remarkably silent about the annexation. His position appears to be a desire to improve relations with the Russians without any reciprocal change in Russian foreign policy or its position vis-à-vis its neighbor Ukraine. In fact, the annexation of Crimea is often the second most cited cause of the continued weakening relations between the two nations, despite improvements in the Russian leader's favorability—the first being the suspicion that the actual cause of the improvements in public perceptions about Putin was election interference in 2016. So I remain skeptical that the historical memory legitimation discourses outlined by Putin have been very effective as tools of public diplomacy.

So in conclusion, are these memory discourses alternative legitimation discourses intended for an international public, or are they intended for a domestic audience to build a populist support? Are they a lens through which to understand Russian foreign policy or a tool to build support for what is essentially a realist drive for power, resources, and a weakening of forces on Russia's borders? I maintain that the local audience discourse and the lens through which to view interests are closely linked as to serve the same variable—domestic Russian politics. While many of these campaigns have negligible material effects—particularly in Georgia and Moldova—even the material benefits of Crimea pale in comparison to the long-term damage Putin is doing to Russian power. Either the Russians have terribly little interest in diplomatic advance, economic integration, and political cooperation or they believe they can "fix" these long-term threats while realizing their short-term goals. So we are left with either concluding Russian miscalculation of international response or a tone-deafness to this international response because of populist desires for local governance. The emotionalism of the memory drives is too compelling to dismiss the latter. It portends to future aggression against neighbors based on historical ties and perceptions of space and place that remain an essential component of the Russian cultural map.

References

Address of the President of Russian Federation. 2014. March 18. Kremlin, Moscow. http://en.special.kremlin.ru/events/president/news/20603. Accessed January 27, 2018.

Bell, D. 2009. "Introduction: Violence and Memory." *Millennium: Journal of International Studies* 38 (2): 345–60.

Budryte, D. 2013. "Traumatic Memory and Its Production in Political Life: A Survey of Approaches and a Case Study." Presented at the International Studies Association Annual Conference, San Francisco, USA.

Cull, N. 2009. *Public Diplomacy: Lessons from the Past.* Los Angeles: University of Southern California Press.

Edkins, J., and M. Zehfuss. 2005. "Generalising the International." *Review of International Studies* 31 (3): 451–72.

Gaddis, J. L. 2001. "In Defense of Particular Generalization: Rewriting Cold War History, Rethinking International Relations Theory." In *Bridges and Boundaries: Historians, Political Scientists, and the Study of International Relations*, edited by C. Elman and M. F. Elman. Cambridge: MIT Press.

Goddard, S. E., and R. Krebs. 2015. "Rhetoric, Legitimation, and Grand Strategy." *Security Studies* 24 (1): 5–36.

Grigas, A. 2016. *Beyond Crimea: The New Russian Empire*. New Haven: Yale University Press.

Hill, F., and C. G. Gaddy. 2016. *Mr. Putin: Operative in the Kremlin*. Washington, DC: Brookings Institution Press.

Hopf, T. 1998. "The Promise of Constructivism in International Relations Theory." *International Security* 23 (1): 171–200.

Mälksoo, L. 2015. *Russian Approaches to International Law*. Oxford: Oxford University Press.

Morgan, R. 2003. "Images, Identities, and Foreign Policy." *Government and Opposition* 36 (4): 583–90.

Nabers, D. 2015. *A Poststructuralist Discourse Theory of Global Politics*. Houndsmills and New York: Palgrave.

Nuzov, I. 2017. "The Dynamics of Collective Memory in the Ukraine Crisis: A Transitional Justice Perspective." *International Journal of Transitional Justice* 11 (1): 132–53.

Plokhy, S. 2000. "The City of Glory: Sevastopol in Russian Historical Mythology." *Journal of Contemporary History* 35 (3): 369–83.

Plokhy, S. 2008. *Ukraine and Russia: Representations of the Past*. Toronto: University of Toronto Press.

Renan, E. 1990. "What Is a Nation?" In *Nation and Narration*, edited by H. K. Bhabha. London and New York: Routledge.

Steele, B. 2008. *Ontological Security and International Relations: Self Identity and the IR State*. Oxon: Routledge.

Van Herpen, M. 2015. *Putin's Propaganda Machine: Soft Power and Russian Foreign Policy*. New York: Rowman and Littlefield.

Weber, M. 1918/1946. "Politics as a Vocation Lecture." In *Essays in Sociology*, translated and edited by H. H. Gerth and C. Wright Mills. Fair Lawn, NJ: Oxford University Press.

Weber, C. 2010. *International Relations Theory: A Critical Introduction*. London: Routledge Press.

Wendt, A. 1992. "Anarchy Is What States Make of It." *International Organization* 46 (2): 391–425.

Wilson, A. 2014. *Ukraine Crisis: What It Means for the West*. New Haven: Yale University Press.

Wiseman, G. 2015. "Introduction." In *Isolate or Engage: Adversarial States, US Foreign Policy, and Public Diplomacy*, edited by G. Wiseman. Stanford: Stanford University Press.

Wood, E., W. E. Pomeranz, E. W. Merry, and M. Trudolyubov. 2016. *Roots of Russia's War in Ukraine*. New York: Columbia University Press.

CHAPTER 4

Collective Trauma, Memories, and Victimization Narratives in Modern Strategies of Ethnic Consolidation: The Crimean Tatar Case

Milana Nikolko

INTRODUCTION

The identity of an ethnic group is a sophisticated combination of different, not necessarily compatible, discourse practices regarding the group's past, present, and future (Assmann 2014). The moments of national glory and pride are often accompanied by dramatic narratives, memories of tragic past, and fears for the collective future. In this research I will study the consolidative role of the traumatic cultural memory for the ethnic group in a multi-ethnic society. The scholarship will be devoted to detailed study of political narratives in Crimean and Ukrainian mass media. The work is structured around three major parts: first, I will draw the methodological outline between identity,

M. Nikolko (✉)
Institute of European, Russian and Eurasian Studies,
Carleton University, Ottawa, Canada

© The Author(s) 2018
E. Resende et al. (eds.), *Crisis and Change in Post-Cold War
Global Politics*, https://doi.org/10.1007/978-3-319-78589-9_4

trauma, and victimhood; second, I will apply this research methodology to the period of independent Ukraine 1991–2014; and last, I will compare dominant narratives of deportation in mainland Ukraine and annexed Crimea after 2014.

According to Dirk Nabers, the process of reconstructing an identity manifests in the acts of developing differences between "Self" and "Other"[1] (Nabers 2015: 95). I will consider the collective identity as a mosaic of shared narratives involving various categories in relation to space and time. I also want to emphasize that collective identity is highly responsive to external factors as much as to internal (intra-group) challenges, and it is in a constant process of reshaping its dominant categories. Hence, the process of substantiation of recognition of "Who we (as an ethnic group) really are?" is ongoing and inevitable.

In the post-Cold War era of International Relations (IR), ethnic identity is considered as one of the core characteristics of intercommunication, where most issues surrounding ethnic identities and national conflicts lie in the sphere of the process of differentiation. The notion of "difference" constructed the "Other," provided "Self" with the "the normative implications of exclusion, and it's questioning the foundations of interactions."[2] The threat of existence of "Other" could be found in many ongoing ethnic tensions: "It is clear that the separation between 'Self' and 'Other' goes hand in hand with a modernist agenda that tends to categorize the world into binaries, including inside/outside, mind/world, subject/object, domestic/international, good/evil, realist/constructivist (or institutionalist), and so forth" (Nabers 2015: 96). All the processes of inclusion/exclusion, deeply based on this interpretation of differences between "Self" and "Other," reveal the basic fear of breach of security in the most generic sense of this term. The process of political construction of "Other" (which could be a particular ethnic group, or nation) usually starts with objectification. Objectification of an ethnic group denies its active role as communicative subject and puts it in an object (i.e., non-subject) state. Hence, the political process of alienation of

---

[1] The dichotomy "Self"/"Other" will be used to describing both individual and collective actors.

[2] The "Other" may become a close friend or partner, but on another side of the spectrum the "Other" represents absolutely alien, unknown and dangerous subject.

any particular group could be characterized through the change of the communication position from subjectivity "who" to objectivity of discourse "what."

In this case, the "Otherness" and objectification identify the same process, and it is realized in everyday practices through the following:

- act of creating the homogeneity of the "Other" ethnic group (narratives "they are all the same"),
- simplification of the complex issue (deliberate illumination of complexity is often found in this process) and,
- production of easy readable texts promoting antagonism, based on contrast "Us" versus "Them."

In order to develop better understanding of traumatic memories of Crimean Tatars, we need to introduce the core element of our research. I will engage the concept of "Event," legitimized in social discourse by Gilles Deleuze (1990, 1994) and Alain Badiou (2015). Deleuze characterizes Event as a "true" unique happening of personal or collective existence. He applies this category to the micro (personal) and macro (collective) events in a broad sense (Beck and Gleyzon 2016). For Badiou, Event is something of great magnitude for a large group of people, which is capable of shaking up the identities and discourses and reshape collective memory of the group. In this large happening, often each singular event communicates with all others, and they all form one and the same Event, in which all events are related to each other (Robinson 2015). The Event has a special relation with space, so the major question "what is happening?" is deeply related to "where is it happening?" We also want to take another methodological turn, and find out how Event is interpreted by a victim, i.e., someone, who was denied subjectivity as a result of a happening. In this case, the Event will be studied as a chain of small occasions, gradually "growing" from starting point of trauma to the open public discussion, search for justice and reconciliation. Due to the trauma of Event, the discursive practices and their effect on community may reappear over time. This research will draw compelling connections between the concept of space (Crimea), the act of terror (deportation), and future work of collective memories.

Another methodological tool involved in the study will be the "narrative fixation" (Bhabha 1994), which is an important feature of the mechanism of ideological construction of "Otherness." "Fixation is a form of stereotypical knowledge and identification that vacillates between what is always in place, already known, and something that must be anxiously repeated" (Bhabha 1999: 17) it presents itself in large discourse formations, and survives in the course of different political epochs. Paradoxically, the fixation is not necessarily located in the topic of narrative, but in the mechanisms of the presentations. The fixation mechanism may be found not only in dominant narratives of majority, but also in the narratives, produced by repressed group.[3]

In this research, we are going to see the ongoing repetition of the official Soviet historical narrative about the Crimean Tatars' collaboration with the Germans during the Second World War in many different ways, and at least in three different temporal episodes: during the Soviet time (which is not surprising), during the first decade after the collapse of USSR, and again after the annexation of Crimea in 2014. The mechanism of simplification, homogeneity, and fixation is used together to justify the deportation of Crimean Tatar people.

The identity of Crimean Tatars was shaken by acquisition and the ensuing trauma of deportation. During the deportation, the objectivity of Crimean Tatar group (performed as a denial of Subjectivity) was dominant. In circulated narratives, Crimean Tatar ethos was present openly or silently as a traitor. As the time goes on, we can evidence the subjectivity of ethnic group becomes more and more visible through the political actions, demonstration, and Samizdat literature. The collective effort of Crimean Tatar activists was focused on return to Crimea, but in repressed society, the narratives of trauma and victimhood of *Sürgün* were very much oppressed.

COLLECTIVE TRAUMA OF DEPORTATION/*SÜRGÜN* 1944

Zygmunt Bauman identified strong connection between modernity and massive atrocities in the modern history of Europe. The tragic history of the twentieth century has proved capability of political nationalism

---

[3] Group self-blaming or degeneracy is often presented as convicted narratives in colonial cultures. Together with public ignorance of traumatic narratives and silence about injustice and wrongdoing by both parties, the degeneracy is an important mechanism of preserving repressed nature of colonial system.

to rationalize and build up sophisticated legitimate construction for the oppression of a targeted group, based on racial or ethnic "Otherness" (Bauman 1989: 29). The history of oppression in the Soviet Union yields evidence of this subaltern relation and provides countless evidence of reprisals, massacres, and violent deportations. Toward the end of World War II, hundreds of thousands of Crimean people were deported from the newly liberated Crimea following Stalin's decision. All these people were deported within just three days in May 1944, based on the State Defense Committee Decree No. 5859ss, which alleged that the Crimean Tatars (mostly) had "actively collaborated with the German occupation authorities and Wehrmacht" (for details, see Roman'ko 2000, 2004a, b; Williams 1997: 235).

In fact, the population deported from Crimea totalled 225,009 people, of which 183,155 were ethnic Crimean Tatars (Williams 2001). Essentially, the NKVD completely cleansed the Crimean peninsula of its non-Slavic population. Those non-Tatars who survived the cleansing were obliged to stay in designated areas of deportation until 1956, when they were allowed to leave those areas. The regime of "Spetsposelenija" (special settlements) was lifted by two decrees of Presidium of the Supreme Council of the USSR: the Decree "On lifting restrictions in the legal situation of Greeks, Bulgarians, Armenians and members of their families on special settlement" of March 27, 1956, and by the Decree "On lifting restrictions on special settlements with the Crimean Tatars, Balkars, Turks are citizens of the USSR, Kurds, Hemshins, Armenians and members of their families, evicted during the Great Patriotic War" of April 28, 1956. Thus, the Crimean Tatars were rehabilitated in civil rights, except the right to repatriation and restitution, i.e., the right to return and reclaim their property, homes, and land. However, the ban to return to their homeland was not lifted yet, and they were forced to live and settle anywhere but in Crimea. In 1967, the Supreme Soviet (the Parliament of the Soviet Union) officially recognized the injustice of the deportation of Crimean Tatars by Stalin's orders, but nonetheless prevented Crimean Tatars from returning to their homeland.

The movement for the return of Crimean Tatars to their motherland originates from the nationwide campaign of petitions in 1956. In 1966, the protest rallies for home return took places in most post-deportation settlements of Crimean Tatars in Kirgizstan, Kazakhstan, and Uzbekistan. The initiative group of Crimean Tatar activists ("group of 400") went to Moscow[4] to present their collective petitions (more than thousand letters and hundreds of telegrams) regarding the Crimean Tatars' return (Williams 1997: 239). But the Kremlin's reaction left the activists disappointed, and the general discussion ended without any commitment on its part. It was only after another massive demonstration in Tashkent (Uzbekistan) in September the same year that the Soviet government revised the original decree signed by Stalin in 1944 (Bekirova 2017). The blame of collaboration was partly washed out, but the process of home return was postponed for decades, in accordance with the current legislation on employment and the compulsory residence and passport registration ("propyska"). This apparently technical issue became a major obstacle in the process of return of the Crimean Tatars back to Crimea. Control and oppression were scattered in small mechanisms. The first Crimean returnees faced reluctance of Crimean authorities to cooperate, and after failed attempts to register, many of them settled in areas close to Crimea—in Kherson, Mykolaiv, Zaporizhia, Melitopol, etc.

The first mass migration of Crimean Tatars (about 5 thousand people) back to Crimea took place in 1977–1979. In the following ten years, the number of Crimean Tatars increased to 2% of the population of the peninsula (approximately 38,000 Crimean Tatars were then living in Crimea according to the Soviet Census of 1989). In 1987, the State Commission on Crimean Tatar People Issues was established, but its activities were limited to recommendations in the area of social and cultural life. With ongoing democratization of the Soviet system, but also pressured by international community, the Soviets finally started to develop a plan of Crimean Tatars' return. In their approach to orchestrate massive return home, the Soviet authorities established a government program for the return of the Crimean Tatars to Crimea in 1990, which declared recognition of their right to return to Crimea but provided a protracted plan: the first wave to go in 1996, and the next in 1998. However, with the collapse of the Soviet Union in

---

[4]Intriguing new documents and archive materials could be found here: https://ru.krymr.com/a/28633585.html, https://ru.krymr.com/a/28626977.html.

1991, the practice of return was implemented by newly independent Ukraine.

Thirty-three years passed until the declaration of the Supreme Council of November 14, 1989 (Recognition as Illegal and Criminal, the Forced deportation and Repressive Measures against Displaced Peoples and Provisions for Their Rights) restored the rights of all deported peoples. This declaration finalized all formal procedures for the return of Crimean Tatars to their homeland. Since then, there has been an influx of more than 260,000 deportees back to Crimea, among whom about 250,000 were Crimean Tatars. The process of re-establishing social, political, and economic connections took long, and over the entire period, reintegration was facing challenges from the dominant Russian-speaking community (Kullberg 2004; Williams 2001).

To a large extent, the return of the Tatars was spontaneous and unpremeditated. In 1991, an unprepared government of the newly independent Ukraine lacked the capacity to handle the issue. The research of Abdultairova (2016) lists such economic factors as a high rate of unemployment (up to 25% in 1992–1993), limited access to social services in newly developed settlements, ongoing difficulties with property ownership and general economic decline, all of which made the returnees' life more difficult. In 1995, up to 60,000 of them did not have Ukrainian passports yet, which completely deprived them of the social services (Williams 2001: 248) and the right to vote. Deportees, who were supposed to obtain reparations and reimbursement of damages, were in fact facing difficulties obtaining both housing and jobs due to economic privatization. High inflation reduced their savings and the income obtained from sales of their previous residences.

To complicate the matters, Crimea's production decreased rapidly, and the tourist industry, which underpinned the Crimean economy, declined when the borders between the former republics of the Soviet Union were established and ethnic conflicts transformed into open warfare in the Caucasus. Difficulties in obtaining the Ukrainian citizenship endangered the political and economic rights of the Tatars in particular (e.g., the right for land, to vote and to participate in privatization). While other diasporas in Crimea (e.g., the Armenians, Bulgarians, Greeks, and Germans) relied heavily on support and assistance from their homelands, the Crimean Tatars, being indigenous peoples of Crimea, could only expect support from each other or seek assistance from the international community (Allworth 1998). As a result, the massive return of the deported people weighed heavily on the economically weak Crimea, which was unprepared to handle such a substantial and hasty migratory incursion (Shevel 2000, 2001). Moreover, negative stereotypes and prejudices concerning the Crimean Tatars, artificially nurtured during the Soviet time over several generations, returned with vengeance (Nikolko and Carment 2010: 375). Despite the international attention to the problem of return, the adaptation to the new Crimean reality was going very slow. People continue to suffer from economic and social inequality, along with limited political mobility. The devastating economic crises and the long stagnation of 1990s affected the most vulnerable strata and the returnees in particular.

Despite all the obstacles, the ethnic group managed to preserve its culture and memory of Crimea as their Fatherland ("Vatan"), the land to which they continue to dream of returning (Bezverkha 2015: 127). As Uehling argues, the tragic memory of deportation is closely interwoven with the idea of the Crimean land and constitutes a central pillar of the Crimean Tatars' ethnic identity. For the Crimean Tatars, she argues, the past is of particular importance as it emphasizes the centrality of the drive to return to Crimea from exile: "The need to reclaim the past is vital both for construction of the historical continuity of their [the Crimean Tatars] homeland loss and for negotiation about their future" (Uehling 2004: 6).

Surrounded by the harsh economic reality, Crimean Tatars found themselves in the society with powerful narratives of justification of Stalin's act. "Slavic and Tatar views of the past compete for attention, suggesting that collective processes of interpretation have a significant role to play, and that the past has become a valuable commodity in the chaos of restructuring" (Uehling 2004: 8). Soviet narratives of deportation as a deserved punishment of the Crimean Tatar for the wrongdoing committed during World War II are still widely accepted in the Russian-speaking community.

THE THEORY OF VICTIMHOOD AND VICTIMIZATION

To understand the mechanism of political mobilization of the Crimean Tatar people during the Soviet time, but particularly after 1991, we will introduce the theory of victimhood. For the purpose of this research, we are placing the Event, *Sürgün*, as a core trauma, one of the most important episode of Crimean Tatar ethnic identity in the twentieth century. This collective trauma provoked creation of new discourses and significantly influenced self-representation of the group and reshaped the ethnic entity of the Crimean Tatars. Although the event of deportation was aimed to dismiss political subjectivity of the Crimean Tatars, de facto it provoked the rise of new Subjectivity, a new "Self," where victimization narratives formed leading stories, and search for justice became a new source for unification.

We draw on the theory of political mobilization through the focal point of victimization of the nation in order to find a link between the act of national trauma and the group's positionality. According to Bouris, a victim identity is "the identity of the one who suffered injustice, the one who needs to see the perpetrator accept full responsibility for the wrongs that have occurred" (Bouris 2007: 21). The victimization will provide a specific identity construct: "a simple dichotomy victim- perpetrator relationship" (Bouris 2007: 15). We consider victimhood to be a post-factum process of interpretation of collective trauma, involving interpretation, reflection, and comparison of original traumatic event. The victimhood is a collection of histories, personal and collective memories, arranged in the collective action, driven by search for retribution of truth (Bouris 2007; Jacoby 2014). The victimhood as a mechanism for political mobilization is "alive," when victimization narratives and evidences of the crime are circulated within the group. The totalitarian oppression created a fear of punishment for revealing the truth spreading self-blaming narratives among Crimean Tatar community. Elena Veleshko (2007) detected a significant number of self-blaming testimonies among the Tatars regarding the deportation. Recognizing the deportation as a major people's tragedy, some of the Crimean Tatar activists justified the Soviets and have continued to reproduce the myth about massive episodes of collaboration.

For the victimization narratives, the fixation on the deportation has provided Crimean Tatars a distinctive place within the cultural landscape of Ukraine's ethnic communities. Similarly, seeking justice within the international community, involving diaspora groups (see Buhari-Gulmez's chapter in this book), and changing the international agenda regarding the Soviets crimes became the primary agenda of leading political groups of Crimean Tatars after 1991. On the one hand, the battle for moral support, truth, fairness, rectitude, and future retribution has not only helped to soften differences among people in Ukraine, but also awoke the Soviet narratives and nostalgia among certain part of population.

Group solidarity, which has manifested itself through the pursuit of truths about *Sürgün*, puts Crimean Tatars on the same path as Jewish diasporas in recognition of the Holocaust, and Ukrainians from all over the world in recognition of Holodomor tragedy (Nikolko 2016b).

During the first decade after the collapse of the Soviet Union, the society's interest to the past tragedies was sporadic, and this period could be characterized by lack of memory work, and limited professional attention to the subject (Etkind 2013). This might apply to the most of post-Soviet countries with the exclusion of Baltic states (see Assmann 2014). The absence of free discussions and deep research of deportation provided with the wide range of possibilities for the political speculations.

NARRATIVES OF VICTIMIZATION AND POLITICAL MOBILIZATION

The major connection between political mobilization and victimhood will be explained using Tami Jacoby's idea of "victimization/victimhood" relation (Jacoby 2014). She argues that a "political theory of victimhood is driven by distinction between victimization as an act of harm perpetrated against a person or group, and victimhood as a form of collective identity based on that harm." The act and the identity are neither linear nor even causally related, but rather fluid and open-ended. Jacoby provides us with the clear development of victim-based identity: At the very first stage, the structural conduciveness could be identified; then, political consciousness would become a phenomenon. The following stage occurs when this political phenomenon enters the ideological concurrence, demonstrated in political mobilization, and finally ends up in political recognition (Jacoby 2014: 513).

Jacoby argues that while victimization is more frequent in repressive states where violence occurs with impunity, victimhood is more common in democracies that allow grievance-based identities to emerge. Jacoby points out that the paradox is that a victim-based identity is only possible in political structures that promise a possibility of justice, and thus where actual victimization is less common (i.e., a peaceful society). In other words, victim-based identities are more common in democracies precisely because these have greater opportunities for political expression, freedoms, and higher expectations of political effectiveness than authoritarian regimes in crisis or transitional societies (512–4). Presumably, all of the following three factors—diaspora, international community, and the collapse of totalitarian regime—formed the bridge between victimization and victimhood.

The brought out by political dissidents and ethnic intelligentsia, trauma memories cemented the ethnic conciseness and provided victimized group with strong motivation to the democratic changes. With democratic transformation of political institution, the new interpretation of Soviet past provoked the completion of discourses regarding the past and with ongoing social and political reforms more and more possibilities to discuss the past and achieve some recognition has appeared. Thus far, my assessment of mobilization is consistent with Jacoby's framing of victimization and justice in a democratic society. Indeed, it may well be a perfect example. Below, we examine that process in detail. Throughout this period, there emerges the formation of "stable" narratives of collective trauma and descriptions of similar experiences of group members. These include especially the desire to talk about physical and mental suffering, to convict and punish the offender. These narratives also speak of the desire for justice, retribution, and revenge. The borderline between a victim and a perpetrator vanishes. Political manipulation with victimization may again return to the dual narratives about exclusion/inclusion with a stable image of the antagonist, or the "Other" as the source of the crime.

Public discussion and hence search for justice of past collective traumas couldn't possibly have happened during the Soviet Union era, because of the totalitarian character of the regime. Hence, wide discussions and intercultural communication regarding the deportation of Crimean Tatar people could be considered as a democratic shift that occurred in the Ukrainian and Crimean society particularly after the Orange Revolution in 2004/2005, simply because "that morality and justice can only be practised within a shared discourse" (Nabers 2015: 100).

Analyses of Discursive Formation of Victimization Narratives (1991–2014)

Despite the apparent complexity of the issue within the Ukrainian-Crimean political discourse between 1991 and 2014, deportation narratives were always present in the Crimean political agenda as one of the central themes. During this period, we evidenced the mobilization of Crimean Tatars around this shared trauma, particularly around the commemoration of deportation on May 18. Starting in 1993, this day was marked on the calendar not only as a commemoration date of the Event, but also as an occasion to exchange political ideas and express economic concerns. On May 18, thousands of Crimean Tatars marched to Simferopol (the administrative capital of Crimea) to express their political and economic needs, and to reunite with people from different parts of Crimea. The memory of physical and emotional injury gave a powerful impetus to the consolidation.

The shared trauma memories could be found in political activism as well. In early 2000s, the regional political elite of Crimea was constituted by parties with strong pro-Russian stance, Communists (also affiliated with the pro-Russian agenda), situational pro-Ukrainian parties, and the ethnic bloc of Mejlis. The latter, being an informal assembly representing the Crimean Tatar interests, has never been registered as a political party in Ukraine. Although formally Mejlis position was not clear, its influence on the Crimean Tatar community was tremendous. Based on ethnic principle, Mejlis sustains the executive mechanism of Qurultay (all people assembly of Crimean Tatar) and projected the decisions of Qurultay in political activism. A special role in the strong political mobilization of Mejlis has been played by Mustafa Dzhemilev, who headed the organization from the very beginning till 2013. Dzhemilev is a veteran of democratic movement from the late USSR; he has been an open critic of the Soviet system and a political prisoner for his persuasions of Crimean Tatars to return to Crimea. Even after Russian authorities declined his entrance to Crimea (2014), he continued to be the principal figure in the ongoing discussion regarding the wrongdoing of deportation.

A Crimean academic Elena Veleshko studied the impact of 1944 deportation on modern political behavior of the Crimean Tatar returnees through the prism of victimhood. She reflected on victimization of ethnic lobbyism in Crimea at the end of the twentieth century, and her findings will be discussed and analyzed next. In her research, Veleshko emphasizes the ambivalent nature of victimhood, with tendency of political narratives to become predominant in a particular period of the democratic development (Veleshko 2007: 6). She states that the Orange Revolution and the victory of Victor Yushchenko in the president rally provided Ukraine with broad spectrum of national democratic narratives, where revision of the Ukrainian Soviet past was among the central issues on the agenda. Yushchenko actively supported developing research on Ukrainian Holodomor 1932–1933, which resulted in November 2006 positive vote in Verkhovna Rada on the recognition of Holodomor. Being provided with evidence and scientific research, the Ukrainian parliament passed a law recognizing the Holodomor as an act of genocide against Ukrainian people. Veleshko has conducted analysis of the same year's issues of the Crimean Tatar national newspaper "Golos Kryma" ("Voice of Crimea"), and her research shows the growing domination of victimization narratives[5] in the national press, particularly in 2006 (Veleshko 2007: 148).

We can find evidence for the continuation of this trend in Crimean research of 2012 (Muratova 2014; Kouts and Muratova 2014), based on a collection of interviews with Crimean Muslim groups. The research shows strong fixation among Crimean Muslim communities (mostly of Crimean Tatar ethnicity) on past national traumas, particularly on repeated traumas of forced migration.[6] This research also spotted some alternative discourses in the Crimean Muslim community regarding the national politics and future of Crimea. According to Elmira Muratova, the active participation of SAMC[7] representatives in the discussion on

---

[5] In the political landscape of Crimea some significant changes took place: first, during the Orange revolution and all the time after, Mejlis bent itself with all-Ukrainian national democratic movement. Second, in the first years of the twenty-first century, most of "pro-Russian" Crimean political groups were "absorbed" by regional and all-Ukrainian political blocs.

[6] This research also studied perceptions of first Russian annexation of Crimea in 1792, which created a few waves of Crimean Tatar migration to the territory of Turkey and developed a Crimean Tatar diaspora. This event was echoing the deportation 1944 much more closely.

[7] Spiritual Administration of the Muslims of the Crimea (SAMC) is religion organization, which has a strong affiliation with Mejlis.

people's political situation can be explained by their more active involvement compared to other Islamic organizations (*M.N.*—e.g., Spiritual Center of Muslims of Crimea, SCMC, and Alraid[8]), in the political processes of Crimea, or they mentioned that they do not share the political goals and methods of the Mejlis and therefore do not participate in its political actions (Muratova 2014: 22). Alternative discourses could be found in the Crimean Tatar community about the current situation and the common future, but the perception of the past traumas remains unified.

Fixation on the trauma of forced migration and deportation in this particular episode of the Russian/Soviet/colonial past has led to a forming of the sustainable "victimization" narratives. For the Crimean Tatars, the fixation on the Oppressor (in this case the Russia/Soviet regime) has become one of the primary motivation factors for their active political involvement. Thus, the battle for truth, fairness rectitude, and future retribution has helped overcome the differences among repatriates. Group solidarity has manifested itself through the pursuit of truths and shared information about *Sürgün*.

In the 1990s, the Russian-speaking majority of Crimean population were mostly following Soviet narratives regarding the deportation, and the divergence of collective memories continued to divide society. The post-Soviet sentiments and legacy of the Soviet historical meta-narrative, shared by the Russian-speaking Slavic majority of Crimea, dominated in the mainstream media discourse of Crimea, imposing its meanings and patterns of representation of the Crimean Tatars' deportation, its character and reasons behind it. We agree with Berezhna's summary of that period: "Historical delineation between the dominant and alternative versions of the collective memory draws social borders between the ethnic groups within Crimea."

The situation started to change slowly with growing processes of democratization of the Ukrainian society. During the first decade of twenty-first century, Ukraine experienced growing interests and public awareness of the Communism and national movement in Ukraine. The turning point in domestic discourse regarding the past occurred with the Orange Revolution of 2004/2005. The strong interest for revision of

---

[8] Association of Islamic Cultural Centres and Social Organizations Alraid is an all-Ukrainian organization.

the Communist past came with the changing political agenda in Kyiv. In 2005, the newly elected president Yushchenko reintroduced discourse on Holodomor, and the discourse of deportation was complemented with the victimhood national narratives regarding the Soviet past.

THE CRIMEAN TATARS NOWADAYS: SURVIVING STRATEGIES OF AN ETHNIC GROUP

The crises that erupted in Ukraine in 2013–2014 shook dramatically interethnic interactions, tore apart the entire existing fabric of political communications, particularly in Crimea and Eastern Ukraine. For the situation of high-peak crises, Nabers stated "the limit between internal and external structure, between 'Self' and 'Other,' would become impossible to identify, and it becomes clear that in processes of crisis and change, mechanisms of inclusion and exclusion are purely artificial" (Nabers 2015: 99), which is hard to argue with. The annexation of Crimea, and in particular, the artificially created DNR and LNR,[9] the idea of "Novorossiya" (the New Russia) and a short-lived project of renaming Donbas (The Donetsk Basin) into "Malorossiya" (the Little Russia, summer 2017) constitute together a perfect proof of how artificial borders between group identities may be in reality. In a tragic way, all of these new entities are "living proofs" of victoriousness of the post-structural approach to the contemporary idea of "Nation." The new narratives and new versions of old stories show the ability to neglect borders and institutions by creating new political reality. By reapplying borders of exclusion and by rethinking the past in favor of some particular events and threads of the history, these new narratives were able to build up a new "alternative" vision of the future.

In the last part, we will study the two different formations of discourse regarding *Sürgün*: One of these formations is taking place in the territory of Ukraine, and the second one developing in the territory of the annexed Crimea.

After the first shock of the hasty Crimean referendum and the ensuing annexation of the peninsula by Russia in March 2014, the Ukrainian elites were scrambling to provide various audiences in Ukraine and

[9]Donetsk People's Republic (Donetskaya Narodnaya Respublika) and Luhansk People's Republic (Luganskaya Narodnaya Respublika), respectively.

abroad with a clear discourse regarding the future of Crimea and the people living in that territory.

During the first twenty years of independence, reflection on the role of the "Soviet otherness" has never been carried through to its conclusion, and the result has been the emergence of an extraordinary mix of national, Soviet, and global narratives in Ukraine (Nikolko 2016: 44). Now that the country has been involved in a dramatic conflict and afflicted by various kinds of social, political, and physical trauma, the Ukrainian society initiated comprehensive revision of basic discourses of national identity. The accent on "Other" in the guise of Russia/the Soviet Union has become the dominant narrative in political and social communications. Under the influence of this "Otherness," a political nation is being forged; boundaries of both a physical and a symbolic kind are being repositioned, engendering uniqueness and fuelling differing notions of national sovereignty.

The cardinal revision of the past began with the adoption, by Ukraine's Verkhovna Rada, of a package commonly dubbed as "de-communization" laws.[10] Law no. 2558, "On Condemning the Communist and National Socialist (Nazi) Totalitarian Regimes and Prohibiting the Propagation of their Symbols." The latter is entirely toponymic in content, targeting the symbols of the country's former communist regime—place names, street names, and company names evoking political figures or parties. The Ukrainian Institute of National Memory issued a list of just under 900 towns and villages earmarked for renaming.[11]

With this package of laws, the government is effectively decreeing what does and does not constitute "true knowledge" about "the Ukrainian nation." Once again, politicians are attempting to gain control over political reality by gaining control over dominant symbols and narratives. This is a struggle that seems to wax and wane with internal political opposition. The gamble of rejecting the past in order

---

[10] Interview with Serhiy Yekelchyk "You can't provide Ukraine with the only one view on the 'Heroic UPA'—Canadian Historian," http://www.radiosvoboda.org/content/article/27024469.html?utm_medium=email; Kulik, Volodimir. "About low quality laws and their arrogant critics." http://krytyka.com/ua/solutions/opinions/pro-neyakisni-zakony-ta-nechutlyvykh-krytykiv.

[11] De-Sovietization in Ukraine: 871 cities, towns and villages freeing their names from the Soviet legacy, http://euromaidanpress.com/2015/06/12/de-sovietization-in-ukraine-871-cities-towns-and-villages-freeing-their-names-from-the-soviet-legacy/.

to embrace an uncertain future may well prove successful for Kyiv but will entail squaring up to, or indeed denying, Ukraine's uneasy twentieth-century past. This law met strong critique from different camps, but the critics can be summarized in two major arguments. The first is Ukraine's adherence to the kind of highly politicized approach to history adopted during the Soviet era, when the government mandated a single correct interpretation of history, decided who were the heroes and who the villains, and reduced historical complexities to black-and-white notions of the ideologically good "Self" versus the ideologically bad "Other." The second is the legislation's failure to match up to European standards of commemoration, in which civilian victims of political violence hold the center stage, and the murder and brutalization of civilian populations is condemned, regardless of reasons behind it (Shevel 2016).

Crimean Tatars in Ukraine

In a polemic between two ex-Crimeans, Kazarin (2016) and Kostynskyi (2016), the competitive political discourses (or myths), produced in Crimea after 1991, were discussed. Kazarin pointed out that recent "success" of Russian myth, which resulted in the referendum and continues to be actively present in Crimea,[12] is based on the inclusive model, where Crimea is represented as a combination of regional, heroic, and international models (the latter being used in the Soviet version of internationalism with domination of Russian ethnicity). His reflection on the Crimean Tatar myth emphasized the idea of exclusiveness of Crimean Tatars and their sacral relation to the land of Krym (Crimea). For them, as Crimea's indigenous population, the peninsula is the only land they have, so exclusivity of this myth becomes a major factor for the Tatars, while for the non-Tatar population "it is difficult to be part of it (*Myth, M.N.*), if you are not a Crimean Tatar" (Kazarin 2016: 22). And what about the Ukrainian discursive formation for Crimea? Over all these years of Ukrainian independence, the mutual ignorance will be the best characteristics of Crimea-Kyiv elite relations.

Working on this methodology of three competing myths of Crimea, Kostynskyi supported the Crimean Tatar interpretation as the only one

---

[12] Please see result of most recent survey conducted by ZoiS (Sasse 2017).

useful for Ukraine under current circumstances: "Because it is the only one that has inner strength and the only one that brings Ukraine into Crimea's symbolic space. It is also the only one that has been consistently on offer to Ukrainian politics over a long period. The Crimean Tatars, who make up 13 percent of the population of Crimea, have not only created a myth of their own; they have fed that myth into Ukraine's political 'black box'" Kostynskyi (2016: 27). And as a matter of fact, the Ukrainian political elite has followed this formation. Significantly, the legislation restoring the rights of people deported on ethnic grounds, kept in abeyance by the Ukrainian parliament for many years, was only adopted on April 17, 2014, just one month after the annexation of Crimea.

The year of 2015 was the most productive period of implementation of the Crimean Tatar discourse in Ukraine's political agenda. In November, Verkhovna Rada voted in favor of recognition of 1944 deportation of Crimean Tatars as an act of genocide against Crimean Tatar people (Decree #2493a).[13] It thus extended the narrative of oppression to the modern situation: It characterized the current situation in Crimea as "ethnocide" against Crimean Tatars. The same Decree established the National Day of Remembrance and Mourning of Victims of the Genocide of the Crimean Tatar People. Detailed analysis of this Decree provided us with very little information regarding its implementation, as it did not assign any budget funds or establish any further political and legal projects. Declarative nature of this decree was widely discussed in both Ukrainian and Crimean Tatar communities. Recently, Verkhovna Rada registered a bill "On the Status of the Crimean Tatar people." As this project is supposed to establish a national-territorial autonomy of the Crimean Tatars in the territory of Crimea, it is essential for Crimean Tatar activists in Ukraine.[14] Although the bill

---

[13]The Decree could be found here: http://w1.c1.rada.gov.ua/pls/zweb2/webproc4_1?pf3511=56254 and further discussion: https://www.unian.net/politics/1181372-rada-priznala-genotsid-kryimskih-tatar-i-nazvala-politiku-rossii-v-otnoshenii-nih-etnotsidom.html.

[14]After the annexation of Crimea 2014, the immigration to Ukraine increased. Between 20,000 and 30,000 migrants flee Crimea since 2014, and half of them are Crimean Tatars. Please see alternative numbers regarding the Crimean immigration to Ukraine here: http://www.msp.gov.ua/news/14445.html and http://www.sobytiya.info/public/kiev-otdaet-krym-krymskim-tataram.

states that such an autonomy will exist "within the unitary Ukraine",[15] it provoked massive debates in the parliament and among experts regarding the minority rights and problems with its implementation (Shapoval 2017).

The Crimean Tatar theme is gaining popularity in the Ukrainian mass culture. In 2013, a movie "Haytarma" was released. It was the first full-scale feature film about the deportation of 1944. The film was acclaimed by critics, but most importantly, it provided the artistic interpretation to the collection of personal stories of deported people. The cinematography about *Sürgün* gave a basic, but so much needed knowledge about 1944 event to the millions Ukrainians.

Jamala, a Ukrainian singer of Crimean Tatar origin, entered the Eurovision singing contest in 2016 with her song "1944" dedicated to the Crimean Tatar deportation. This song presented the tragic story of *Sürgün* to a broad European audience. Surprisingly, the message was heard, and Jamala secured the first prize.

The 2014 political crisis triggered accelerated revision of Soviet political narratives and resulted in rapid decommunization and continues to realize itself in growing narratives of victimhood.

THE MEMORY WORK IN CRIMEA UNDER RUSSIA

To better understand the situation with collective memory of the deportation in Crimea nowadays, we have to analyze the official discursive formation regarding this event. The Mejlis of Crimean Tatar people, having actively supported Euromaidan and the new Ukrainian state authorities, de facto became a center of pro-Ukrainian activism in Crimea. A day prior to the referendum orchestrated by Russians, the leaders of Mejlis openly criticized it and addressed their concerns to the international community. The Crimean Tatar elite was actively working on the issue of securing national-territorial autonomy for Crimean Tatar people; however, the hastily written new Constitution passed by the Crimean parliament less than a month after the referendum contains no reference to that. The new constitution of the Republic of Crimea aimed to

---

[15] Full text in Ukrainian can be found here: https://dt.ua/internal/avtonomiya-v-krimu-u-poshukah-arhitekturnih-rishen-252869_.html.

harmonize the Crimean institutions with the Russian political system, and to provide secure position of the Crimean Tatar language (Article 10) and national religious holidays, but did not go any further.[16] Soon after, on April 21, 2014, Russia's President Vladimir Putin signed a decree "On Measures for the Rehabilitation of the Armenian, Bulgarian, Greek, Crimean Tatar and German Peoples and State Support in Their Recovery and Development" with an ostensible aim to provide rehabilitation, social and financial support to the victims of past reprisals. This date was assigned as a new memorial day, "The renaissance day of repressed people of Crimea." Although there were a few attempts of a dialog between Mejlis and the new authorities, the situation worsened after the official denial of entrance to Crimea for the leader of Mejlis, Mustafa Dzhemilev. Having not found a reliable partner in Mejlis, the Russian authorities began a systematic work on its exclusion from the Crimean political system.

The commemoration on the 70th anniversary of the Crimean Tatars' deportation from Crimea was originally planned as a political manifestation and all people mourning activities. Under new rulers the commemoration of deportation became localized (we can see segmentation, realized in number of singular meetings in some municipalities), and it was denied its political agenda. In his recent comment on commemoration practice, the head of the pro-Russian movement of the Crimean Tatar people "Kyrym," Remzi Ilyasov said: "The memorial day for the victims of deportation should be placed outside of political interests… this tragic day over the years was used for a 'show'…and incitement to hatred."[17]

Depolitization together with generalization of the memorial dates and events is followed by unification of memorial practices. All these trends can be found in Crimea today. The events of the "Crimean Spring" have exacerbated ethnic divisions between the Russians and the Crimean Tatars. For example, this is reflected by the decline of the number of interethnic marriages and the increase of divorces in this category (Muratova 2016b).

---

[16]Crimean Constitution, April 12, 2014. http://crimea.gov.ru/content/uploads/files/Constituciya.pdf.

[17]See http://crimea.ria.ru/radio/20160518/1105076413.html?inj=1.

The repressive trends developing in Crimea make it hard to stay positive about interethnic communications and open discussion of past traumas. The growing number of political prisoners (a large number of them are Crimean Tatars) together with ongoing processes of liquidation or replacement of ethnic civil and political organizations with the "quasi" equivalents provided us with a very little hope for fair research and public discussions of the traumatic past in Crimea. The Mejlis, for example, formerly a representative body elected by the Council of the Crimean Tatar People (Qurultai), has been forced to change its leadership and register as a regular public (civil society) organization. The Crimean Tatars, who had a long record of strong organization and an established set of public institutions, now find themselves in a position of having every public activity subject to approval by the authorities. Gradually, the Crimean Tatar movement was channeled into religious and cultural practices. The Crimean Tatars narratives in mass media lost their civic and political "colors." Now their community is represented in the Crimean media by spiritual leaders and is thus positioned as a Muslim community, not much as an indigenous group, or a politically motivated group. The Crimean SAMC, as well as the newly established Taurida Muftiyat, is seeking to earn trust among the Crimean Tatar population, particularly as Mejlis were dismissed from political stage.

The dramatic transformation has also affected narratives of memories and remembering practices of deportation. The new authorities returned to the 1994 interpretation of the event, when May 18 was set as day of commemoration of the deportation's victims without any particular ethnic connotation. The Soviet discourse of ignorance of the trauma of a particular indigenous ethnic group was revitalized once again.

Concluding Remarks

In provided scholarship of traumatic narratives of the past and their influence on the ethnic group during the crises, we identify that the collective trauma of deportation provoked creation of a new discursive formation of victimization and intensified collective attempts to proceed with justice. It has also significantly influenced self-representation of the group and reshaped the ethnic entity of the Crimean Tatars.

Although the Event of deportation aimed to dismiss political subjectivity of the Crimean Tatars, de facto it provoked the rise of a new Subjectivity, a new "Self," where victimization narratives become leading stories. Due to the repressive nature of the Soviet system, the political mobilization of ethnic group was suppressed, but a new impetus to the traumatic narratives emerged during the democratic transformation in Ukraine 1991–2014, where subjectivity of the Crimean Tatar nation was growing together with democratic initiatives and general attempts to revise the Soviet past.

We were able to trace the fixation of the victimhood narratives in discursive formation (following Jacoby's methodology), from the early stage of political consciousness of Crimean Tatar activism in 1960s and 1970s, through the epoch of incipient ideological concurrence in early 1990s to the crucial point of the annexation of Crimea in 2014. Since the latter, the narratives of the traumatic past of deportation are represented in two alternative versions: in mainland Ukraine, we can see the continued political recognition of the deportation tragedy, formally implemented through the Decree of recognition of deportation as an act of Genocide (2015), while in Crimea new authorities rolled back to the discourse of 1994, where deportation is presented as a blurred phenomenon lacking ethno-political connotation to Crimean Tatar tragedy. What could be found in both cases is the absence of detailed memory work regarding the Event of deportation and continuation of political prevalence in traumatic narratives.

REFERENCES

Allworth, E. A. 1998. *The Tatars of Crimea: Return to the Homeland*. Durham and London: Duke University Press.
Assmann, A. 2014. "Transnational Memories." *European Review* 22 (4): 546–56.
Badiou, A. 2015. "Ethics and Politics." *Philosophy Today* 59 (3): 401–7.
Bauman, Z. 1989. *Modernity and the Holocaust*. Cambridge: Polity Press.
Beck, C., and F. Gleyzon. 2016. "Deleuze and the Event(s)." *Journal for Cultural Research* 20 (4): 329–33.
Bekirova, G. 2017. "My obyazatelno vernemsya v Krym." *Krym.Realii*, July 24. https://ru.krymr.com/a/28633585.html. Accessed January 20, 2018.
Bezverkha, A. 2015. "Reinstating Social Borders Between the Slavic Majority and the Tatar Population of Crimea: Media Representation of the Contested Memory of the Crimean Tatars' Deportation." *Journal of Borderlands Studies* 32 (2): 127–213.
Bhabha, H. K. 1994. *The Location of Culture*. New York: Routledge.

Bhabha, H. K. 1999. "The Other Question: Difference, Discrimination and the Discourse of Colonialism." In *Out There: Marginalization and Contemporary Cultures*, edited by Russell Ferguson. New York: New Museum of Contemporary Art.

Bouris, E. 2007. *Complex Political Victims*. Bloomfield: Kumarian Press.

Deleuze, G. 1990. *Logic of Sense*. New York: Columbia University Press.

Deleuze, G. 1994. *Difference and Repetition*. New York: Columbia University Press.

Etkind, A. 2013. *Warped Mourning: Stories of the Undead in the Land of Unburied*. Stanford: Stanford University Press.

Ilyna, J. 2014. "The Evolution of the Crimean Tatar National Identity Through Deportation and Repatriation." Unpublished dissertation, Leiden University Repository, Leiden. https://openaccess.leidenuniv.nl/handle/1887/28649. Accessed January 27, 2018.

Jacoby, T. A. 2014. "A Theory of Victimhood: Politics, Conflict and the Construction of Victim-Based Identity." *Millennium: Journal of International Studies* 43 (2): 511–30.

Kazarin, P. 2016. "Three Myths of Crimea." In *Engaging Crimea and Beyond: Perspectives on Conflict, Cooperation and Civil Society Development*, edited by David Carment and Milana Nikolko, Global Dialogues 11, Duisburg. http://www.gcr21.org/publications/global-dialogues/. Accessed January 27, 2018.

Kostynskyi, S. 2016. "The Quest for the Political Mythology: Ukraine and the Crimean Tatar Story." In *Engaging Crimea and Beyond: Perspectives on Conflict, Cooperation and Civil Society Development*, edited by David Carment and Milana Nikolko, Global Dialogues 11, Duisburg. http://www.gcr21.org/publications/global-dialogues/. Accessed January 27, 2018.

Kouts, N., and E. Muratova. 2014. "The Past, Present, and Future of the Crimean Tatars in the Discourse of the Muslim Community of Crimea." *Anthropology & Archeology of Eurasia* 53 (3): 25–65.

Kullberg, A. 2004. *The Crimean Tatars. Victims of Geopolitics Returning to Existence*. Helsinki: East-West Books.

Muratova, E. 2014. "Islamic Groups of Crimea: Discourses and Politics." *Anthropology & Archeology of Eurasia* 53 (3): 9–24.

Muratova, E. 2016a. "Crimean Muslims in New Political Realities." *Oriens* 5 (1): 163–71.

Muratova, E. 2016b. "Future of Crimea: Crimean Tatar Perspective." In *Engaging Crimea and Beyond: Perspectives on Conflict, Cooperation and Civil Society Development*, edited by David Carment and Milana Nikolko, Global Dialogues 11, Duisburg. http://www.gcr21.org/publications/global-dialogues/. Accessed January 27, 2018.

Nabers, D. 2015. *Poststructuralist Discourse Theory of Global Politics.* Houdsmills and New York: Palgrave Macmillan.

Nikolko, M. 2016a. "Phantom Pain Syndrome: The Ukrainian Nation One Year after the Annexation of Crimea." In *Engaging Crimea and Beyond: Perspectives on Conflict, Cooperation and Civil Society Development,* edited by David Carment and Milana Nikolko, Global Dialogues 11, New York. http://www.gcr21.org/publications/global-dialogues/. Accessed January 27, 2018.

Nikolko, M. 2016b. "Political Narratives of Victimization Among Ukrainian Canadian Diaspora." In *Diaspora as Cultures of Cooperation: Global and Local Perspectives,* ed. Arianne Sayed and David Carment. Basingstoke: Palgrave Macmillan.

Nikolko, M. V. and D. B. Carment. 2010. "Social Capital Development in Multiethnic Crimea: Global, Regional and Local Constraints and Opportunities." *Caucasian Review of International Affairs* 4 (4): 368–85.

Robinson, A. 2015. "Alain Badiou: The Event." *Ceasefire.* https://ceasefiremagazine.co.uk/alain-badiou-event/. Accessed January 27, 2018.

Roman'ko, O. V. 2000. *Musul'manskiye legiony tret'yego reykha. Musul'manskiye dobrovol'cheskiye formirovaniya v germanskikh vooruzhennykh silakh (1939–1945).* Simferopol: Tavriya-Plyus.

Roman'ko, O. V. 2004a. *Musul'manskiye legiony vo Vtoroy Mirovoy Voyne.* Moscow: AST.

Roman'ko, O. V. 2004b. *Krym, 1941–1944 gg. Okkupatsiya i kollaboratsionizm.* Sb. statey i materialov. Simferopol: Antikva.

Sasse, G. 2017. "What Is the Public Mood Like in Crimea?" Carnegie Europe, November 6. http://carnegieeurope.eu/strategiceurope/74635. Accessed January 27, 2018.

Shapoval, V. 2017. "Autonomy in Crimea: In Search for Architectural Solutions." *Dzerkalo Tyjnya,* September 4. https://dt.ua/internal/avtonomiya-v-krimu-u-poshukah-arhitekturnih-rishen-252869_.html. Accessed January 27, 2018.

Shevel, O. 2000. "Crimean Tatars in Ukraine: The Politics of Inclusion and Exclusion." *Analysis of Current Events* 12 (1–2): 9–11.

Shevel, O. 2001. "Crimean Tatars and the Ukrainian State: The Challenge of Politics, the Use of Law, and the Meaning of Rhetoric." International Committee for Crimea. http://www.iccrimea.org/scholarly/oshevel. Accessed January 27, 2018.

Shevel, O. 2016. "No Way Out? Memory Wars in Post-Soviet Ukraine in Comparative Perspective." In *Beyond the Euromaidan: Comparative Lessons of Reform for Ukraine,* edited by H. Hale and R. Orttung. Stanford, CA: Stanford University Press.

Uehling, G. L. 2004. *Beyond Memory: The Crimean Tatars' Deportation and Return.* New York: Palgrave Macmillan.

Veleshko, E. 2007. "Vliyanie victimnyh factorov na povedenie krymsko-tatarskih repatriantov." PhD dissertation, V.I. Vernadsky University Press, Simferopol.

Williams, B. G. 1997. "A Community Reimagined. The Role of "Homeland" in the Forging of National Identity: The Case of the Crimean Tatars." *Journal of Muslim Minority Affairs* 17 (2): 225–52.

Williams, B. G. 2001. *The Crimean Tatars.* Leiden, Boston and Cologne: Brill.

PART II

Crisis and Social Change: Ukraine in Comparative Perspective

CHAPTER 5

Corruption, Crisis, and Change: Use and Misuse of an Empty Signifier

Oksana Huss

INTRODUCTION

The problem of persistent corruption in Ukraine became a puzzling topic for many scholars. Most of them are taking either agency—or structure-oriented approach to analyse corruption. On the one hand, the agency-oriented approach explores corruption as an actors' problem, looking at oligarchs and political institutions, their properties and (inter-) action (Darden 2008; Pleines 2009; Melnykovska 2015; Halling and Stewart 2016). On the other hand, the structure-oriented approach explores corruption as a problem of the context actors act in, looking at actors' environment and institutions as a set of formal and informal rules, culture and the society (Miller et al. 2001; Way 2005; Hale 2015; Huss 2016a). These perspectives lead to an assumption that either actors and their decision-making or the institutional context should be changed in order to solve the problem.

An alternative, post-structuralist approach, allows conceptualizing corruption as an empty signifier—"a symbolic nodal point [in the

O. Huss (✉)
Institute for Development and Peace,
University of Duisburg-Essen, Duisburg, Germany

© The Author(s) 2018
E. Resende et al. (eds.), *Crisis and Change in Post-Cold War Global Politics*, https://doi.org/10.1007/978-3-319-78589-9_5

construction of discourse] through which different political contestations, identities and demands can be articulated" (Koechlin 2013: 23).
Thus, instead of looking at institutions, actors and decision-making that
possibly influence persistence of corruption, the main focus of post-
structuralist perspective is the meaning, assigned to the empty signifier
of corruption. Post-structuralist logic allows to critique that actor—and
structure-centred approaches to corruption analysis are an attempt to
hit a moving target, since the meaning of corruption can vary in time
and context, for the main feature of an empty signifier is that it is always
reversible and the meaning is fixed only temporally.[1]

Applying the post-structuralist approach to corruption, the aim of
this chapter is twofold: First, this chapter explores how the Presidents
of Ukraine use an empty signifier of corruption, and second, what
role the term "corruption" plays for both, political crisis and political
change in Ukraine. Accordingly, the main question is: *What meaning do
the Presidents of Ukraine assign to corruption as an empty signifier and
to what extent this temporarily fixed meaning unfolds potential to create
social identities?* The main challenge the Presidents face with this respect
is creating a dominant public discourse and framing corruption in a way
that represents themselves as "non-corrupt Self" and their competitors as
"corrupt Others".

I narrow the analysis to the framing of corruption that two Presidents
of Ukraine—Viktor Yushchenko in 2005–2010 and Viktor Yanukovych
in 2010–2014—use in the public discourse.[2] The reason for this focus is
the decisive role that the President has due to Ukraine's semi-presidential
political system and to the perceptions of the citizens.[3] Methodologically,
I conducted content analysis of the presidential speeches and citations of

[1] "Empty signifiers enable both the articulation of dissent as well as the production of
consensus in society. Hence, they play a constitutive role for the possibility of society as
such; they are a necessary condition for the (re)organization of political order. Oscillating
within this tension between plural and potentially antagonistic views on the one hand, and
the potential of socially acknowledged, universalized representations on the other hand,
empty signifiers are always reversible" (Koechlin 2013: 23–24).

[2] This chapter is a part of my Ph.D. research, where I also elaborate the case of Kuchma's
presidency.

[3] According to the sociological polls, conducted by the Razumkov Centre 30 September
2010–05 October 2010, in the answer to the question "How strong do following institutions influence decision-making in Ukraine?" 44.2% indicated that the President of Ukraine
is the most influential institution http://old.razumkov.org.ua/ukr/poll.php?poll_id=579.

presidential comments and press conferences in the press, mentioning corruption between 1999 and 2014. The data covers about 900 news articles, from the databases of Factiva and Integrum, documents with speeches and autobiographic books. For data analysis, I used an inductive coding approach with the software MaxQDA.[4]

This chapter has following structure: In the theoretical part, I elaborate the post-structuralist perspective on corruption, where corruption is conceptualized as an empty signifier. Afterwards, I apply the discourse theory of crisis and change, developed by Dirk Nabers, to the analysis of corruption. The empirical part contains the analysis of meanings that the presidents assign to the empty signifier of corruption and change of these meanings due to political crisis the presidents face.

Post-structuralist Perspective: Corruption as an Empty Signifier

The connection between corruption and politics in a post-structuralist perspective is based on conceptualization of corruption as an empty signifier within the *hegemonic struggle*.[5] Here, the concepts of hegemony and discourse are closely interwoven. Dirk Nabers puts their interrelation as follows: "Different discourses compete for hegemony, that is, they constantly struggle to fix particular meanings in a way that makes them look like universal ones". (Nabers 2015: 104). Importantly, *discourse* is defined as a structure, created around nodal points—what Laclau and Mouffe call "the temporary fixation of meanings" (Nabers 2015: 115). For the articulation of nodal points, use of an empty signifier seems most suitable tool.

> *Empty signifiers* are characterized by an indistinct or non-existent signified, that is, terms that can have different meanings and can thereby serve to unite disparate social movements. They have *no fixed content* and can embrace an open series of demands...

---

[4]The code system includes analysis of the following code groups with regard to corruption: "types", "causes", "consequences", "description of the problem", "Corrupt spheres and institutions", "Role of the West", "Responsibility for Anti-Corruption", "Anti-corruption Activities", "Accusations in Corruption" and "Reaction to Accusation".

[5]"*Hegemony* is understood as an articulatory practice evolving out of the interplay of the logics of equivalence and difference and based on the temporal filling of a dislocated social structure by means of empty signifiers" (Nabers 2015: 146).

Empty signifiers have three interrelated purposes: First, *they signify the universal*; second, they *provide a name for the chain of equivalences*; and third, by embodying the ideal of universality, they *keep the equivalential sequence indefinitely open*. (Nabers 2015: 116–17)

"Corruption" is the phenomenon that corresponds to all these purposes and thus fulfils perfectly the requirements to become a powerful medium in the competition for hegemony:

First, the term "corruption" has *no fixed content*. International organizations such as the United Nations (United Nations Convention against Corruption 2003) or Transparency International (TI) either refrain from defining corruption (the first example) or use a broad definition—"corruption as abuse of (public) power for private gain" (the second example)—that is also full of ambiguous terms that change their meaning depending on context.[6] Some scholars define corruption as an "umbrella term" for many other associated practices, such as clientelism, patronage, state capture (Varraich 2014; Rothstein and Varraich 2014, 2017), or fraud, bribery, extortion (Langseth 2002: 3), but also moral decay (Franziskus and Sievernich 2014).

Second, "corruption" is perfectly suitable to *provide a name for chain of equivalences*. The "umbrella function" of the corruption term shows that no empty signifier is completely empty. Corruption raises powerful, mostly negative associations,[7] when mentioned. Research of corruption as an empty signifier in Africa shows:

---

[6] The term "power" is extremely problematic, because both its meaning and its latitude differ between public office power, decision-making power in private sector, discursive power, etc. The relationship between public and private is also very ambiguous, since not many societies have a clear, formal line separating public and private. The word "misuse" can indicate either violation of the formal rules (illegal behaviour) or violation of public trust (illegitimate behaviour) and can differ according to different nations/cultures. Finally, both dimensions—legality and legitimacy—depend highly on local and temporal context (Debiel and Pech 2010: 54).

[7] Rothstein and Tannenberg argue: "Within the development community, combating corruption has become one of the key pillars of good governance policy" (2015: 45). The authors list many negative effects of corruption, some of them are: increasing inequality (Gupta et al. 2002); undermining the legitimacy of the state (Dahlberg and Holmberg 2014); reducing education attainment (Kaufmann 2006); decreasing social trust and social capital (Rothstein 2005, 2011).

> The difficulty of defining corruption on the one hand, and the threatening image it evokes on the other hand seems to lend itself to metaphorical language. Speaking of corruption frequently means speaking in terms of decay and illness. The 'rotten society' noted above invokes a society deteriorating physically and morally. (Koechlin 2013: 14)

Third, corruption *signifies not only normativity but also the universality*. In general, the public associates corruption with the notion of bad governance in the opposite to the quality of government or good governance (Rothstein 2014; Rothstein and Tannenberg 2015). Rothstein argues: "Terms like of 'good' or 'quality' are inherently normative (as is corruption)" (Rothstein 2014: 739). If corruption is a normative term, the question of universality of this norm is in place: Is the norm valid and legitimate on a global scale (universal) or does this norm defer by society and culture (relative)? (Rothstein 2014: 740). On the one hand, a smaller part of the scholarship raises critique that "the international anti-corruption agenda represents a specific Western liberal ideal that cannot be applied to countries outside that part of the world" (Heidenheimer 2002, quoted in Rothstein 2014: 740; Gephart 2009). On the other hand, the scholarship relies on "public goods theory of corruption" (Rothstein 2014: 741) claiming that all societies produce some kind of public goods and "when those who are responsible for managing the public goods convert them into private goods, people generally see this as morally wrong", which stresses very similar understanding of what is corruption independently of cultural context. This argument makes the widespread claim for the universal use of corruption as normatively bad.

In summary, central function of "corruption" is its universality in terms of negative normative perception but at the same time another function of "corruption" is that one can assign different meanings to corruption as an empty signifier. Due to these two functions, corruption becomes highly political, since it provides a platform for competing discourses in hegemonic struggles and herewith for process of crisis and change.

DIFFERENT CONCEPTUALIZATION APPROACHES

Theoretically, it is possible to differentiate two broad approaches on how to define and interpret the problem of corruption: principal–agent approach and collective action/institutional approach. The principal–agent approach (Klitgaard 1988; Rose-Ackerman 1978) is based on three assumptions: First, corruption is a deviant action of individuals, so the focus is on agency and not institutions. Second, corruption is a crime of calculation, not passion (Klitgaard 1998: 4). Third, the focus is mostly on monetary forms of corruption, such as bribery or economic schemes, which allow obtain profit. Following the principal–agent logic, the implications for anti-corruption are obvious: The "honest" principal is willing and able (has necessary power) to impose following measures (Klitgaard 2009: 75): collect information about the agent; remove corrupt agents and appoint/elect the honest ones; introduce institutions (laws) of rewards and penalties; change the "costs" of being corrupt.

In comparison, the system of corruption approach explains corruption as a failure of institutional context and collective actors, such as the parliament and the government for instance. Accordingly, not only monetary forms of corruption, but also its social forms, such as cronyism, clientelism, patronage and nepotism, are of relevance. The anti-corruption measures cannot be reduced to the laws only, but a much broader institutional change of formal and informal rules is needed. Thus, anti-corruption measures are broader than countering monetary forms of corruption.

In order to test which of these approaches different presidents use, the concept of *framing*[8] seems to be appropriate. Robert M. Entman defines framing as follows:

> To frame is to select some aspects of a perceived reality and make them more salient in a communicating text, in such a way as to promote a particular problem *definition, causal interpretation, moral evaluation, and/or treatment recommendation* for the item described. (Entman 1993: 52)

In line with this concept, the framing analysis of corruption will include the questions, how Yushchenko and Yanukovych defined corruption, describe its causes and evaluate its consequences as well as what remedies for the problem do they suggest.

---

[8] On analysis of the corruption framing strategies (see Wickberg 2016).

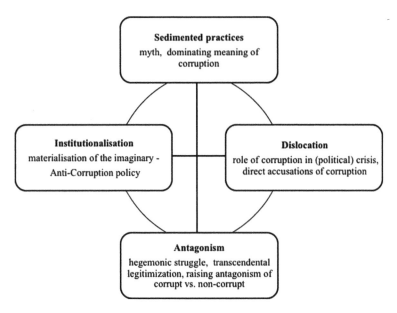

Fig. 5.1 Theory of crisis and change (Adopted from Nabers [2015: 152], and modified by the author)

CORRUPTION IN THE DISCOURSE THEORY OF CRISIS AND CHANGE

The discourse theory of crisis and change (Nabers 2015) provides the structure for the empirical analysis (see Fig. 5.1):

> Any *hegemonic process* can then be traced along the lines of the political ontology: Starting with the *articulation of a particular political crisis* (of lesser or greater extent), which must in some way be connected to sedimented practices to be credible, and moving to the *competition between different political forces to hegemonize the political field*, resulting in *the acceptance of a certain interpretative framework of identification (actual hegemony)* and its eventual routinization and *political institutionalization*. This final act of institutionalization causes feedback effects on the discursive articulation of the crisis, new interpretative frames start to compete, and politics continues. Theoretically, this circle never ends. (Nabers 2015: 147)

One of the major arguments of the Dirk Nabers' theory is "that politics is about the actual process of filling the empty place of [social] identity" (Nabers 2015: 192), while imposing a certain interpretative framework for identities is an essential part of the hegemonic process. Here, it is important to explain first, what is social identity and how it is constructed and second, when does an empty space of identity occur (crisis and dislocation) in order to compete for change?

Social identity is a part of the self-perception, based on the relation to a relevant social group (Tajfel 1978; Turner and Oakes 1986; Tajfel and Turner 1986). The "group" is conceptualized as a "collection of individuals who perceive themselves to be members of the same social category, share some emotional involvement in this common definition of themselves, and achieve some degree of social consensus about the evaluation of the group and of their membership in it" (Tajfel and Turner 1986: 15). Importantly, the identifications are mostly rational and comparative, because they provide a system of orientation for *self-reference* in comparison with the *other* (Tajfel and Turner 1986: 16).

Thus, from a social psychology perspective, there are two important theoretical principles with regard to construction of social identity: First, individuals strive to achieve a positive self-concept and maintain positive social identity; and second, the evaluation of one's group is determined through favourable comparison between the positively perceived *in-group* and some relevant *out-group* (Tajfel and Turner 1986: 16).

In the discourse theory of crisis and change, the main focus is on the analysis of how the *in-* and *out-group* can be created by means of language. Here, the construction of social identities follows the logic of equivalence and difference, while articulation of signifiers in one certain way and not another is a matter of special importance:

> The logic of equivalence constitutes the fullness of a community by linking together a plurality of unfulfilled demands, while difference contradicts this logic. Different identities are grouped together in opposition to another camp to form a chain of equivalence, yet identities appear to be fixed by articulating a subject into a sequence of signifiers. (Nabers 2015: 111)

In the hegemonic struggle, any discourse tries to dominate the field of discursivity and to transform particularity into the "illusion of universality" (Nabers 2015: 115). This is done by the temporary fixation of meanings—the nodal points. The nodal point is a "discursive point around which particular signifiers get articulated into a chain of equivalence" (Nabers 2015: 115). The dominant—or hegemonic—discourse is able to provide the framework for social in- and out-group identities that are at least temporarily stable. Importantly,

> [T]he only possibility of having a true outside would be that the outside is not simply one more, neutral element but an excluded one, something that the totality expels from itself in order to constitute itself. (Laclau 2007, quoted by Nabers 2015: 112)

This means that social identities, constituted through inside and outside logic, are hierarchical, since the fact of exclusion is not neutral, but means subversion. From this perspective, relations between in-group and out-group are power relations (Nabers 2015: 114), which makes creation of social identities to the essential part of the hegemonic process.

However, the agents' identity remains incomplete, and this incompleteness guarantees the continuity of politics (Nabers 2015: 109). The antagonistic relationship between *Self* and *Other* implies "the openness of one identity to be infected by another" (Nabers 2015: 113). In other words, the antagonism opens the door for dislocation:

> *Dislocations* are crucial in the understanding of processes of social change, as they produce structural gaps that have to be filled, situations of fragmentation and indeterminacy of articulations. (Nabers 2015: 166)

In brief, in the first step of the empirical analysis my aim is to show how do the presidents create social identities according to the logic of equivalence and difference and how do they frame corruption to develop the non-corrupt *Self* through exclusion of the corrupt *Others*. In the second step, I will analyse the role of corruption in dislocation of the discourse developed by the presidents. Discourse is dislocated when it cannot integrate or explain certain "events" (Nabers 2015: 120). In this context, dislocation means crisis, leading to change "as the continuous but ultimately futile effort to gain full identity"(Nabers 2015: 193) and the beginning of new cycle.

THE CASE OF YUSHCHENKO

Discursive Context: "Fostering Democracy and Trust"

In 2001, Viktor Yushchenko moved from the Prime Minister's position under Kuchma to the leader of the opposition and promising candidate for the presidential elections in November 2004. In his opposition discourse, Yushchenko uses the *logic of equivalence and difference* to develop the inclusive *Self* by linking together a plurality of unfulfilled demands in the society and exclude regime of Kuchma as the *Other*. Yushchenko draws the line between lawless president Kuchma and himself jointly with the society as victims of the Kuchma's regime.

Only few months before elections, and symbolically, on the independence day (on 24 August 2004) Yushchenko publishes an article "Ukraine's Choice" in the *Wall Street Journal Europe* (Yushchenko 2004). This article reflects the main structure of Yushchenko's opposition discourse, consisting of three pillars: first, the country's democratic development; second, integration into the international community with western values; third, building trust into political institutions. The previous regime of Kuchma is represented as an opposite to all these positive aspirations.

> ...We thought then [1991] that our *national aspirations for freedom* had been realized and that *democracy would replace totalitarianism*. We believed our people would prosper from the combined rich natural resources and our penchant for hard work. We entrusted our elected leaders with a mandate to govern and *integrate Ukraine into the international community.*

> ... Today, an overwhelming majority of my fellow citizens –77%– believe Ukraine is heading in the wrong direction. Millions live in *poverty. Corruption pervades every social institution, from education to medicine to government.* Journalists and others who speak the truth are constantly *harassed and persecuted. Illegal searches and seizures* are common. The average *Ukrainian can rely neither on protection from law enforcement officials nor an open and fair trial in the courts.*

> ...*Today the regime of President Leonid Kuchma has reverted to complete lawlessness. Surveillance organized by state officials recently against me and my family is a feature of totalitarianism. In democracies, this would be scandalous,* but in Ukraine, the government called it common practice. (Yushchenko 2004)

The central nodal point here is devoted to the *democratic development of the Ukrainian nation*. In the article, Yushchenko refers to the Day of Independence in 1991 as a point of origin for the positive aspirations and freedom. He associates democratization with "prosperity" and "rule of law". The opposite of these is "poverty", "lawlessness", "harassment of the press"—all these in line with "corruption" as pervasive problem that is common to all social institutions.

Furthermore, Yushchenko defines another nodal point around the *integration into international community*. His narrative of democracy and rule of law is closely connected to the "European values". Thus, the chain of equivalences "prosperity" and "rule of law" is not limited to Ukraine, but includes all international community with western values. The narrative excludes Kuchma's regime as "current autocracy" with "corrupt government":

> The choice facing voters this fall is very clear. On the one hand, my vision for Ukraine proposes a *system founded on democratic European values,* which will enable each citizen *to realize their socio-economic potential* in a country *governed by the rule of law.* On the other hand, those from the ruling regime propose preserving the *current autocracy, which rules over competing financial-industrial groups. Their corrupt government bureaucrats implement unpopular policies with no respect for individual liberties and basic human rights.*
>
> There can be no doubt today Ukrainians want change – peacefully and democratically – just as they did 13 years ago. *They want an end to government corruption*, decent jobs at honest wages, and *a president whom they trust. Ukrainians share European values and yearn for democracy.* (Yushchenko 2004)

Finally, Yushchenko emphasizes *the role of trust*. Also in his book "Non-State Secrets" ("*Nederzhavni taiemnytsi*"), Yushchenko often explains his decisions as Prime Minister and later as a President from the perspective of trust building (Yushchenko 2014: 188–231). His main argument is that trust of the society in political institutions is an important economic factor, causing stability, development and sustainable collective action (Yushchenko 2014: 225). While the whole transition process from the Soviet regime to independent state was extremely non-transparent, the society lost any trust into political institutions. Therefore, Yushcheko's priority in his early political career was trust building into political institutions through transparency and communication. According to Yushchenko, widespread corruption is the reason for the low level of trust of the population of the government.[9]

To sum up, Yushchenko's opposition discourse becomes a powerful medium that creates inclusive social identity. The nodal points of democracy, European values and trust create an "illusion of universality" and unite different identities. Yushchenko's main rival in the presidential campaign—Viktor Yanukovych—is associated with Kuchma's regime and thus clearly excluded as the *Other*. "Corruption" is a strong link in the chain of equivalences, such as "authoritarian", "lawless", "poverty causing". Such powerful dichotomy of identities became central narrative of the Orange Revolution, able to accumulate support not only of the Ukrainian population but also of the Western countries for the opposition in Ukraine.

FRAMING OF CORRUPTION AS A SYSTEM

Corruption is a crucial empty signifier that Yushchenko uses in his political struggle. Already in 1994, corruption was an issue of a vital concern for the public and dominated as a topic both parliamentary and presidential elections (Birch 1998: 100). However, unlike his predecessors, Yushchenko frames corruption in a new way, not only as problem of bureaucrats and public servants, but also as an issue at the high political level. He coins the terms "system of corruption" and later on "political corruption".

In the inauguration speech on 23 January 2005 at Independence Square, the newly elected President claims:

> We will destroy the *system of corruption* in Ukraine, bring economy from shadow, taxes will be reduced, but everyone will pay them. Business will be separated from government, the [state] budget will not be the breadwinner for anyone. (Interfax Information Services, 23 January 2005)

[9] During his campaign Yushchenko said: "One of the main problems of the current Ukraine is corruption. Corruption is like erosion, corroding the state, creates a threat to the national security. Because of the high level of corruption, people do not trust the government. Almost 90% of Ukrainians consider current government corrupt and indifferent to the interests of ordinary people. Such situation has to be changed, government has to work for people, it has to be accountable to and controlled by the society." In "Posle izbraniia prezidentom Ukrainy Yushchenko podpishet ukraz o sozdanii komiteta narodnoho kontrolia s otdeleniiami v oblastiakh," UNIAN, 14 October 2004.

In this speech, Yushchenko introduces the new understanding of corruption as a system. Also in November 2005, when announcing the judiciary reform, Yushchenko indicates that during the recent years— referring to the previous Presidency of Kuchma— "the stable corrupt system was established in Ukraine" (UNIAN, 29 November 2005e). He proclaims as his central goal to bring corruption to an end.

Further content analysis of Yushchenko's speeches shows that when he talks about concrete corrupt spheres of society, he makes *corruption in high political institutions*, such as government, parliament, judiciary and law enforcement more salient than corruption among single bureaucrats and civil servants. When Yushchenko refers to the corruption cases, he mostly addresses *corruption schemes*, instead of single, occasional instances of corruption. *Corruption scheme* means that multiple actors are involved and the process of either procurement or decision-making is deliberately constructed in a way, enabling corruption. The actors in politics are connected not only by monetary, but also by social forms of corruption, such as clientelism, patronage and nepotism. Yushchenko uses the term cronyism[10]—*kumivstvo*—to describe such connections. This term is crucial, since it was used later to accuse Yushchenko of corruption himself (*Kommersant Ukraina*, 20 May 2009).

CRISIS AND CHANGE

Yushchenko was able to exclude himself from Kuchma's system of corruption as a leader of the opposition, but he did not succeed to maintain this image during his Presidency. Already at the beginning of the Presidency, Yushchenko faced accusations of corruption in his team. On 1 September 2005, Mykhailo Brodskyi, the adviser of the Prime Minister Tymoschenko from political party "Fatherland", accused Yushchenko's team—Petro Poroshenko, Head of the Security Council of Ukraine, Alexander Tretiakov, Head of the Cabinet of the President of Ukraine and Mykhailo Doroshenko, advisor to the President—of misuse of their offices for private interest and in lobbyism for oligarchs (UNIAN, 01 September 2005b). Next day, Brodskyi resigned from his position as an advisor. Few days later, on September 5, Secretary of State,

---

[10] "Yushchenko, who appears to hold a slight lead in the polls, has promised to steer Ukraine toward a more open and democratic society, ending what he calls the cronyism and corruption of Kuchma's 10 years in power" (Myers 2004).

Oleksandr Zinchenko resigned as a sign of protest against corruption in the team of the President. On September 6, already President of Russia Vladimir Putin warned Europe that Yushchenko's government is corrupt (Interfax: Monitoring, 7 September 2005). On September 7, the situation was discussed in the British newspaper *The Telegraph* in the following words:

> President Viktor Yushchenko of Ukraine was yesterday fighting to defend the credibility of the country's pro-western Orange Revolution in his worst crisis since sweeping to power last year. Simmering disagreements in his shaky coalition have exploded since his powerful chief of staff quit, accusing senior officials of corruption. (Blomfield 2005)

It is important to stress that Yushchenko personally was not accused of corruption. Besides, the accusations were supported by very little evidence, so the strongest statements were two resignations of Brodskyi and Zinchenko. The Ukrainian and international experts were united in the opinion that such a situation resulted from the internal political intrigues and conflict between the clan of Poroshenko intervening into the Tymoshenko's sphere of influence (Interfax, 14 September 2005). Yushchenko's political popularity however was irreversibly damaged.[11]

As a reaction, Yushchenko dismissed accused personalities from their political positions, although he permanently defended his team (UNIAN, 10 November 2005d). In addition, Yushchenko focused in his rhetoric on missing facts and appointed special commission for investigation of corruption in his team to save his credibility (UNIAN, 08 September 2005c). However, he was aware that independently of the evidence, his political image was massively threatened by presumptions and speculations. When insisting on political character of the accusations, Yushchenko said: "There is an anecdote: It does not really matter whether a man has a daughter or does not have a daughter. It is enough to say in public that his daughter does not behave herself well" (quoted in Myers 2005).

---

[11]According to the Razumkov Centre sociological polls, in February 2005, 46.7% of respondents indicated that they "fully support" the actions of the president, while in October 2005 this number decreased to 18.1%. Available online: http://old.razumkov.org. ua/ukr/poll.php?poll_id=67.

Nevertheless, Yushchenko followed the same strategy by accusing the Prime Minister Yulia Tymoshenko of corruption in reverse (Myers 2005) and resolving the Government. According to the experts of the leading think tank in Ukraine—Razumkov Centre—"accusations of political corruption became a tool of political struggle and public rhetoric of politicians" (Razumkov Centre 2009: 2).

In addition to losing discursive power, Yushchenko lost his structural power. On 1 January 2006 the new Constitution of Ukraine came into force.[12] According to the constitutional reform, the Parliament instead of the President became entitled to decide who was going to be part of the Government. Additionally, in the parliamentary elections on 26 March 2006, Yushchenko's bloc "Our Ukraine" became only the third force in the parliament (14%) after the political force of Viktor Yanukovych—Party of Regions—(32.1%) and Yulia Tymoshenko Bloc (22.3%). In this new constellation of power Yushchenko favoured the appointment of Viktor Yanukovych as the Prime Minister and shared executive power with his main rival.

INTRODUCING THE TERM "POLITICAL CORRUPTION"

The term of "corruption" remained useful also in the difficult situation Yushchenko found himself in 2006. Following the governmental crisis and defeat of his party in the parliamentary elections in 2006, Yushchenko coined the term of "political corruption", shifting the focus primarily to corruption in the Parliament and later in the Government. For the first time, Yushchenko articulated the term "political corruption" during his press conference in April 2007 addressing the newly elected parliament of Ukraine:

> Migration of MPs from one faction to another, in fact, abolishes elections in one or another random territory. So, if we speak about the origins the political crisis in Ukraine, it is based on the parliamentary crisis, it is based on the illegitimate processes that are becoming a norm, kind of a

---

[12]With aim to resolve presidential election crisis during the Orange Revolution in 2004 and to agree on the elections rerun, the constitutional reform was a necessary compromise. Kuchma and his presidential candidate Yanukovych demanded to change Ukraine from presidential-parliamentary republic into parliamentary-presidential one, weakening the power of president and strengthening power of the parliament.

tradition in Ukrainian Parliament. It involves not just technical migration – it involves political corruption. Democratic prospects of a nation cannot be built on political corruption... *Political corruption* has become a problem for the nation. Corruption, beginning within the walls of Parliament, namely political corruption, reaches every village council, every person, it touches your interests. (quoted in Razumkov Centre 2009: 3)

In addition, Yushchenko framed political corruption in the parliament as the source for other types of corruption in the society. Political journalist Sergei Sidorenko reflects his perceptions of this press conference as follows:

The phrase *"political corruption"* was used very often during the speech of Yushchenko. At some point he even started explaining this term to the journalists. This explanation lasted at least five minutes and apparently *it supposed to create an impression that political corruption is the reason for all troubles in Ukraine* – from the low level of prosperity to the bad investment climate of the country. (*Kommersant Ukraina*, 13 April 2007b)

One year later, political journalist Elena Geda commented on the statement of Yushchenko during the meeting dedicated to the new anti-corruption strategy:

Despite addressing corruption in all fields, his [Yushchenko's] attention was mainly on political corruption. This form of corruption in particular, Yushchenko named as a basement for corruption in all other fields: 'Only the lazy one does not tell anecdotes about the prise of the rank on the election list. Afterwards, the politician, who made it on the list, will use corrupt schemes himself and involve you into corruption'—the President gave an ambiguous look at the representatives of the law enforcement institutions. (*Kommersant Ukraina*, 16 April 2008)

Thus, Yushchenko referred primarily to political corruption in the Parliament, especially in such forms as migration between factions (*tushkuvannia*), selling of the ranks on the election lists and vote selling in the Parliament.

The broad, anti-corruption strategy that Yushchenko developed and published in the Concept for Overcoming of Corruption "On the way towards integrity" (*Kommersant Ukraina*, 3 September 2007a) reflected very well the framing of corruption as a systemic and political problem. One of the central claims of the anti-corruption strategy was to abolish parliamentary immunity. While Yushchenko didn't succeed at doing this, he favoured the regulation preventing the retail purchasing of single MPs from other factions (Riabchuk 2012: 11). This rule has foreseen that the government was created not only by a simple majority of MPs, but also by factions of parties that have enough MPs on their list to create such a majority. In addition, Yushchenko aimed at widespread replacement of staff in the law enforcement institutions and bureaucratic apparatus (*liustratsiia*) (UNIAN, 18 July 2005a). Finally, in his anti-corruption strategy Yushchenko included requirements for politicians to publish their income declarations in order to provide more transparency and control mechanisms for civil society.

Yushchenko's anti-corruption ideas found a strong resonance in the population. The answers of the respondents of the sociological polls conducted by Razumkov Centre in June 2008 and July 2009 indicate that 38% and 40.5%, respectively, considered parliamentary immunity and 43.4% and 39.9%, respectively, considered corruption in the highest levels of decision-making to be the obstacle in fighting political corruption in Ukraine.[13] 45.4% and 42%, respectively, stated that the most effective anti-corruption action would be to make it easier to prosecute politicians for corruption (e.g. to make impeachment easier by abolishing the parliamentary immunity).[14] The Parliament passed the anti-corruption legislation only in June 2009, but postponed its implementation. The package of anti-corruption laws, adopted under Yushchenko, never entered into force. New, less effective anti-corruption laws under Yanukovych replaced it.

To summarize, the use of corruption accusations in the campaigns for parliamentary elections in 2006 and 2007, as well as increasing number of journalist investigations of corruption in politics, strengthened perception of corruption as a widespread problem closely connected to the politics in Ukraine. In its study of political corruption, the experts of Razumkov Centre indicated:

> Exactly at that time (2006-2009), society learned a lot about politically corrupt behaviour of the top officials, institutes of governance, political parties and their parliamentary factions. Accusations of political corruption

[13] Available online: http://old.razumkov.org.ua/ukr/poll.php?poll_id=519.

[14] Available online: http://old.razumkov.org.ua/ukr/poll.php?poll_id=520.

became a usual method of public squabbling among politicians. This polit-
icised the very term of "political corruption" and expanded, sometimes
unreasonably, the context of its use. (Razumkov Centre 2009: 3)

Razumkov Centre sociological polls confirm that in July 2009, 82.2%
of respondents indicated that the state and 82% indicated that the entire
political sphere was corrupt.[15] While politicians became the equivalent of
"corrupt", the identity of non-corrupt agency remained contested. The
chain of equivalences around "corruption", developed in 2004 remained
the same, but the probability of non-corrupt politicians was exhausted.

THE CASE OF YANUKOVYCH

Discursive Context: "Bringing Order into Chaos"

Presidential elections in 2010 took place in the context where the term
"corruption" was increasingly politicized. While in 2004 the Orange
coalition gained broad support with the narrative of democratization,
by 2009 they disqualified themselves through mutual accusations of corruption. Yanukovych used this situation to carry the narrative of "chaos"
and "complete disorder" under the Orange coalition. To create order,
Yanukovych promised to introduce anti-corruption reforms and secure
absolute submission to law. During the pre-election speech in January
2010, Yanukovych said: "Democracy is when all laws are working, when
all are same under the law, when human rights are protected. All what
we have seen in the past five years is not the democracy. It is *chaos and
disorder* that the Orange coalition created in the country" (UNIAN, 11
January 2010).

Following this statement, Yanukovych promised to bring order and
create conditions for the absolute rule of law. The presidential candidate continued: "We certainly will introduce the reform of judiciary, *we
certainly will create an effective system to fight corruption*. Ukraine will
develop as a truly democratic state" (UNIAN, 11 January 2010).

Thus, in the election campaign, and at the beginning of his
Presidency, Yanukovych referred to corruption as an urgent problem

---

[15] The poll was held on 20–28 July 2009. 2006 respondents aged above 18 years were
polled in all regions of Ukraine. The sample theoretical error does not exceed 2.3%.
Available online: http://old.razumkov.org.ua/eng/poll.php?poll_id=516.

that he highly prioritized and aimed to resolve by bringing order into chaos, created by the Orange coalition. Further, he substantiated his main reforms, such as judiciary reform, constitutional reform and reform of public procurement sector as a necessity to counteract corruption. Ironically, all these reforms were aimed at creating *superpresidentialism* with increasingly authoritarian elements of rule (Luchterhandt 2010: 6).

FRAMING OF CORRUPTION AS A PRINCIPAL-AGENT PROBLEM

In comparison with the previous President, Yanukovych did not pay much attention to elaborate on the term "corruption". On seldom occasions, when Yanukovych assigned specific content to the term "corruption" and addressed the problem in more detail, he used the principal–agent approach to define corruption. It means that Yanukovych presented himself as a strong *principal*, willing to control corrupt *agents*, namely bureaucrats and civil servants, who strive for private enrichment: "Many civil servants turned state budget into business; their pockets are bottomless. It is inacceptable" (UNIAN, 18 March 2010).

In his first speech to the nation on 5 June 2010, Yanukovych presented the "status quo" of the sociopolitical situation as follows:

> *Ineffective state*, detached from people, *turned into bureaucratic machine that takes care only of interests of public officials.* Conflicts and dualism of executive brunch of power, weak self-governance, corrupt and dishonest courts, underdeveloped political parties – these are only few aspects of the problem. *We have lost five years to talking about political reform...I suggest deep reforms and systemic modernisation of the country.* (*Holos Ukrainy* 5 June 2010, no. 102)

This quotation[16] suggests not only the definition of the problem, but also its diagnoses: Yanukovych indirectly suggested that the reason for a critical situation lay in 5 years of the previous Presidency.

---

[16] Similarly, Yanukovych addressed corruption in the second year of his Presidency at the National Anti-Corruption Committee meeting in June 2011, as a problem that is closely attached to the bureaucratic apparatus: "We all are very well aware that *corruption in Ukraine became a medium for existence of bureaucratic apparatus* and the reason for widespread shadow economy, it bears a threat to the security of our country. Stealing from the strategic assets and resources in Ukraine, of the land and natural resources, became a permanent news in our state". See "Vsledstvii korruptsii obshestvo iezhegodno teriaiet 20 mlrd. Hrn—Yanukovich", UNIAN, 8 June 2011.

According to Yanukovych, inefficiency of the state government is one of the consequences of corruption. In his annual state of the union address to the Parliament in April 2011, Yanukovych articulated his dissatisfaction with the governmental work in the first year:

> Where is this inefficiency coming from? In 2010 we witnessed that both government and the society were not ready to accept suggested changes. The *state bureaucracy machine,* that used to survive under every government, *uses the momentum to safe its usual mechanisms of administrative resources and corrupt schemes of shadow income.* (*Uriadovyi Kurier,* 8 June 2011)

Yanukovych used a similar argument in the annual state of the union address in the Parliament one year later, in July 2012: After announcing his steps towards modernization, Yanukovych admitted that main challenge for his reforms is "persistence and resistance of corrupt bureaucracy" (*Uriadovyi Kurier,* 4 July 2012).

Suggested Remedies

Unlike Yushchenko, who did not even succeed to pass the anti-corruption legislation until the last year of his term, Yanukovych managed very early to consolidate his power. The next day after entering into office, he ordered (per decree) to establish the *National Anti-Corruption Committee (NAC).* In line with the principal–agent logic, the NAC was directly subordinated to the President and governed by the Minister of Justice. The main task of NAC became to coordinate all anti-corruption actions and to elaborate new anti-corruption laws.

As mentioned above, the parliament adopted in 2009 an *extensive package of anticorruption laws,* elaborated under Yushchenko in consultation with international agencies. However, Yanukovych postponed entering into force of these laws in 2010 and replaced them completely in 2011 with the new ones.[17] The main difference was that the new package excluded regulations of obligatory declarations of expenditures by public officials (Sushko and Prystayko 2012: 586).

---

[17] In-depth analysis of the law "On the Principles of Prevention and Countering of Corruption" Nr 3206-VI is from 15 March 2011 (Khavroniuk 2011a).

The rational choice logic of the principal–agent approach implies increasing material and moral costs to corrupt "agents" by *applying administrative and criminal sentences for corruption* as a measure of counteraction. This is reflected in Yanukovych's suggestions to introduce fines for corruption (UNIAN, 8 June 2011) and to open criminal investigations against corrupt officials (UNIAN, 2 Feburary 2011). However, legal analysis of the anti-corruption laws shows that vague definitions and normative collisions allowed selective prosecution to generate "statistical cases" instead of just investigations (Khavroniuk 2013, 2011b).

In early 2010, Yanukovych initiated substantial *reform of judiciary*. In his address to the nation in June 2010, Yanukovych said:

> I initiate the judicial reform in order to establish rule of law. The goal of this reform is to provide real independency of courts, judges and lawsuits, to protect citizens, to fight corruption in all spheres of society and at all levels of government, to return trust of the society to the judicial system. The judicial reform is based on our experience, suggestions of the Venice Commission and requirements of international organisations with regards of justice. (*Holos Ukrainy*, 5 June 2010, no. 102)

However, Freedom House report of 2011 estimated this reform as "reducing the independence and integrity of the law enforcement and judicial systems... in an aggressive, sweeping, and methodological" way (Sushko and Prystayko 2011).

Further, Yanukovych suggested, *"fighting bureaucracy"* as one of the central remedies. During the Council of Regions meeting in December 2010, he announced widespread administration reform that he was going to control personally:

> Fight against bureaucracy, reducing the level of corruption and increasing efficiency of the state governance– these are my priorities for 2011....*Bureaucracy with its conservatism, corruptibility and predatory attitude to the people became the subject to the change.* (UNIAN, 13 December 2010)

Briefly, in course of anti-corruption rhetoric and policy implementation, Yanukovych used all means to increase the control capacity of the President. He presented himself as a principal, who is willing and able to control corrupt agents. Obviously, at the beginning citizens sympathized with the image of the President, who decisively brings order. According to the sociological polls, conducted by the Razumkov Centre,[18] in April 2010 40.9% of respondents indicated to fully support Yanukovych's actions, while in February 2010 these were 28.4%, respectively. However, already one year later, in May 2011 only 9.7% indicated to fully support the President.

CRISIS AND CHANGE

Very early in Yanukovych's presidency, it became clear to the public that his rule was heading into authoritarian direction and the private enrichment of his family was a priority (Huss 2015). Journalists' investigations, especially about the privatization of Mezhyhiria—the area where Yanukovych built his luxurious private property, and exponential enrichment of his older son,[19]—were permanently questioned in the society and showed the discrepancy between the anti-corruption rhetoric and the President's action.

In case of critical questions in the public, Yanukovych re-accused his opponents of corruption. For instance, in the TV show "Talk with the country" a journalist asked when the anti-corruption law project will be finally adopted. Yanukovych responded by explaining that corrupt individuals were hindering this process. In his eyes, the journalists experienced a similar pressure as well:

> I believe, you [the journalists] experience it as well. Yes or no? Say it honestly. I'll not believe you that no one tried to bribe you to produce "instructed" content to criticize the current government, to look for weak spots in the government. And these all hinders to speak truth. (UNIAN, 25 Feburary 2011)

In fact, Yaunukovych suggested that in the press all critical voices are corrupt. At a rare press conference, in 2011, an investigative journalist Mustafa Nayyem asked Yanukovych "Why is it the country is suffering so much but everything is turning out so well for you?" Under the Presidency of Yanukovych, Nayyem was one of the few journalists who

---

[18] Available online: http://old.razumkov.org.ua/ukr/poll.php?poll_id=67.

[19] Some examples are published here: "Yanukovich's Assets," http://yanukovich.info.

managed to question Yanukovych directly about Mezhyhirya. Nayyem is well known for asking blunt questions (Yaffa 2016). In the press conference in 2011, Yanukovych responded that he was overworked and had little time to enjoy "a sweet life". He chuckled awkwardly, telling Nayyem, "You are always talking about my family. I would like to tell you that I don't envy you. We know and understand each other very well... the rest you can think yourself".[20] Given that in a similar situation during the TV talk show in 2009, Yanukovych stated to Mustafa Nayyem "If you are not my friend, you are my enemy",[21] the citation from 2011 can be interpreted as a direct threat to the journalist.

In short, Yanukovych was not able to change the dominance of the discourse of political corruption developed under Yushchenko. Quite the opposite. Through his actions, he strengthened the chain of equivalences between "corruption" and "politics" in the public perception. Razumkov Centre sociological polls[22] in October 2013 indicated that 82.3% of respondents felt that the state and 79.6% indicated that the entire political sphere was corrupt. The numbers were very similar to 2009. As a result, the identity of non-corrupt remained empty, while the chain of equivalences around the political corruption discourse kept the structure from the time of Orange Revolution: Democracy, rule of law, prosperity and integration into EU maintained the equivalence with non-corrupt, while Ukrainian politicians were excluded as corrupt *Other*.

The *event* when Yanukovych refused to sign the Association Agreement (AA) with the European Union in November 2013 triggered a political *crisis* that resulted in the Maidan revolution. Yanukovych's decision challenged the aspirations for integration into the European community that many Ukrainians had. Considering the structure of the dominating corruption discourse, where non-corruption is equivalent with democracy and European integration, the rejection of the AA destroyed the link of many Ukrainians to create the social identity of Ukraine as *non-corrupt* and democratic European country. The Maidan

[20] Video "Presskonferentsiia V. Yanukovicha," 21 December 2011. https://www.youtube.com/watch?v=1ZxCGr-kLc4.

[21] Video "Mustafa vs. Yanukovich: Mezhigorie," https://www.youtube.com/watch?v=LJyGzfxZO1I, 4:35–4:50.

[22] The poll was held on 30 September–8 October 2013. 2010 respondents aged above 18 years were polled in all regions of Ukraine. The sample theoretical error does not exceed 2.3%. Available online: http://old.razumkov.org.ua/eng/poll.php?poll_id=516.

Revolution received the name "Revolution of Dignity", which gave an opportunity to finally fill up the empty space of "non-corrupt" identity. Since the Maidan revolution was bottom-up without dominant political power in front, this event created the space for identity of protestors in line with equivalences as European, democratic and non-corrupt, constituted differentially and through recourse to an antagonistic *Other* embodied in corrupt Yanukovych's "Family".

After the Revolution, the major lines in the anti-corruption policy institutionalized the establishment of a new social identity of Ukrainian civil society as an in-group and corrupt politicians as an out-group. For instance, creation of politically independent institutions (National Anti-Corruption Bureau) for corruption control, special anti-corruption Prosecutor, co-selected by the civil society, suggests that no top-down anti-corruption can be effective when coming from the state (Huss 2016b). Importantly, the civil society enjoys much higher level of trust in the population than the political institutions.[23] This fact allows assuming the hegemony of the discourse, where politics are still associated with corruption, but the identity of non-corrupt is assigned to the non-governmental institutions. Obviously, the best position the new President—Petro Poroshenko—and politicians in the new Government can take in order to shape a positive image is the one of non-disturbing civil society in their control function over the politicians. However, the reality is different.

Concluding Remarks

The aim of this chapter was to analyse the role of corruption as an empty signifier for crisis and change in Ukraine. Accordingly, the main questions were: *What meaning do the Presidents of Ukraine assign to corruption as an empty signifier and to what extent does this temporarily fixed meaning unfold potential to create social identities?* The analysis shows

---

[23]According to the 4–9 November 2016 survey conducted by the Razumkov Centre, 65.5% of respondents trust volunteer organizations, 58.8% trust church, 51.8% trust NGOs. The Parliament (13.1%), political parties (12.5%) and courts (10.5%) enjoy the lowest levels of trust. See Andrii Bychenko "Assessment of the situation in the country by the citizens of Ukraine, their attitudes towards social institutions, electoral orientations," Razumkov Centre, 22 November 2016. http://www.razumkov.org.ua/napryamki/sot-siolohichni-doslidzhennia/otsinka-hromadianamy-sytuatsii-v-kraini-stavlennia-do-suspil-nykh-instytutiv-elektoralni-oriientatsii.

that the empty signifier of corruption fits perfectly to analyse political crisis, since "corruption" is not only the subject to the change, but also the medium used in the hegemonic struggle for "construction of new collective identities out of distinct concrete demands" (Nabers 2015: 113).

At the beginning of the Presidency, both Yushchenko and Yanukovych used the empty signifier of corruption to create what Dirk Nabers calls "binary discourse relying on a black-and-white picture of the world, based on relations of equivalence, difference, and the construction of antagonistic frontiers" (Nabers 2015: 192).

Yushchenko developed the discourse of the system of corruption and political corruption in Ukraine. This framing was useful in the position as a leader of opposition to exclude the ruling regime. However, Yushchenko became the victim of his own discourse in the position as a President. First, use of corruption accusations became the widespread medium in the political struggle. As a result, mutual accusations of corruption became the trap for all politicians, since this strategy was increasingly feeding the discourse of "corrupt politicians in Ukraine" in the society. Second, with regard to suggested remedies, Yushchenko's anti-corruption strategy contained broad, effective measures. However, most measures target high level political corruption in the Parliament, therefore they were predestined to fail, since parliamentary support of such measures means political "suicide" in the logic of the system of corruption (Huss 2016b: 346).

Yanukovych did very little attempt to assign any particular meaning to corruption. However, his anti-corruption strategy and some statements clearly indicate the principal–agent approach to conceptualization of corruption. Yanukovych framed corruption in a way that allowed himself to be presented as a "strong principal", who creates order and brings control into chaos among "corrupt agents". Population supported such actions only briefly, until it became clear that all "deep reforms" announced in the presidential campaign were used to establish super-presidentialism and to move into authoritarian direction. Additionally, journalists' investigations showed Yanukovych's blatant misuse of his political power, which all together even strengthened the domination of "political corruption" discourse in Ukraine.

Sociological polls indicated that citizens strongly associate Ukrainian politics with corruption. The Euromaidan did not challenge the dominant discourse of political corruption; however, the Revolution generated new identities of active non-governmental groups in the society as opposite to the corrupt state. It is doubtful, whether the current discourse of "corruption in politics" and "anti-corruption in the civil society" is a stable one. Meanwhile, it is possible to recognize three challenges, feasibly leading to the dislocation. First, lately we notice action by politicians trying to discredit civil society, e.g., accusations against MP Serhii Leshchenko (Mylovanova and Yurmanovych 2016), investigations against AntAC (Reanimation Package of Reforms civil platform 2016), law on assets declarations for NGOs (Makarenko 2017). Facts of corruption in the civil society organizations might destroy the "illusion of universality" and undermine their identity as the opposite to corrupt politicians. The second challenge is coming from the active role of oligarchs, who are intensively founding NGOs and becoming increasingly active in the civil society (Leshchenko 2015). This tendency might undermine the homogeneity of the civil society and weaken the dichotomy of the society's opposition to the political. Third, since western countries fund many civil society organizations and the discourse of non-corrupt is currently closely connected to integration into the democratic West, the big challenge might be in the shift of the image of the West. Political situation in the USA and increasingly active populist anti-EU parties in Europe can bring the dislocation of this discourse in the future.

To overcome the system of corruption in Ukraine, the new generations of politicians need to consider changing the traditional "story" and the traditional narratives about corruption in order to change the future of the country. Perhaps excluding the topic of corruption and anti-corruption from the next election campaign might be a first step. Instead, the focus shall be on the question, what is the opposite to corruption beyond anti-corruption? Instead of attempts to win a rigged game in an uneven playing field (output side), the focus shall be on the question how to create a new game (input side)? How to channelize collective action towards sustainable institutional design that will replace the functions of corruption in the country? These questions shift the perspective from destruction ("fight" against corruption, de-oligarchisation, punishment and control) to construction (institutional design, generation and communication of interests, raising bottom-up social movements and political parties, creating open-access order). They can open new discussions, generate new ideas and disrupt the hopeless discourse of political corruption in Ukraine.

REFERENCES

Birch, S. 1998. "Electoral Systems, Campaign Strategies, and Vote Choice in the Ukrainian Parliamentary and Presidential Elections of 1994." *Political Studies* 46 (1): 96–114.

Blomfield, A. 2005. "Ukraine's Orange Revolution Loses Its Lustre," September 6. http://www.telegraph.co.uk/news/worldnews/europe/ukraine/1497849/Ukraines-Orange-Revolution-loses-its-lustre.html. Accessed January 27, 2018.

Dahlberg, S., and S. Holmberg. 2014. "Democracy and Bureaucracy: How Their Quality Matters for Popular Satisfaction." *West European Politics* 37 (3): 515–37.

Darden, K. 2008. "The Integrity of Corrupt States: Graft as an Informal State Institution." *Politics & Society* 36 (1): 35–59.

Debiel, T., and B. Pech. 2010. "Mit Korruptionsbekämpfung Zum Take off Bei Den MDGs? Zu Möglichkeiten Und Grenzen Einer Entwicklungspolitischen Strategie." In *"Simplizistische Lösungen Verbeiten Sich" - Zur Internationalen Zusammenarbeit Im 21. Jahrhundert*, edited by Eckhard Deutschner and Hartmut Ihne. Baden-Baden: Nomos.

Entman, R. M. 1993. "Framing: Toward Clarification of a Fractured Paradigm." *Journal of Communication* 43 (4): 51–58.

Franziskus, U. Ruh, and M. Sievernich. 2014. *Korruption und Sünde: eine Einladung zur Aufrichtigkeit.* Herder-Spektrum 6684. Freiburg im Breisgau: Herder.

Gephart, M. 2009. "Contextualizing Conceptions of Corruption: Challenges for the International Anti-corruption Campaign." Working Paper 115, GIGA Working Papers, German Institute of Global and Area Studies, Hamburg. http://www.ssrn.com/abstract=1534589. Accessed January 27, 2018.

Gupta, S., H. Davoodi, and R. Alonso-Terme. 2002. "Does Corruption Affect Income Inequality and Poverty?" *Economics of Governance* 3 (1): 23–45.

Hale, H. E. 2015. *Patronal Politics: Eurasian Regime Dynamics in Comparative Perspective.* Problems of International Politics. New York: Cambridge University Press.

Halling, S., and S. Stewart. 2016. "Die 'Deoligarchisierung' in Der Ukra.ne," Stiftung Wissenschaft und Politik. http://www.swp-berlin.org/fileadmin/contents/products/aktuell/2016A69_hll_stw.pdf. Accessed January 27, 2018.

Heidenheimer, A. J. 2002. "Perspectives on the Perception of Corruption." In *Political Corruption: Concepts & Contexts*, 3rd ed., edited by A. J. Heidenheimer and M. Johnston. New Brunswick, NJ: Transaction Publishers.

Huss, O. 2015. "Family Business Ukraine: Centralisation of Political Corruption under the Presidency of V. Yanukovych." Presented at ECPR General Conference, Montreal.

Huss, O. 2016a. "Anti-corruption Reform in Ukraine: Prospects and Challenges." In *Engaging Crimea and Beyond: Perspectives on Conflict, Cooperation and Civil Society Development*, edited by D. Carment and M. Nikolko. Global Dialogues 11. Duisburg: Käte Hamburger Kolleg/ Centre for Global Cooperation Research (KHK/ GCR21).

Huss, O. 2016b. "The Perpetual Cycle of Political Corruption in Ukraine and Post-revolutionary Attempts to Break Through It." In *Revolution and War in Contemporary Ukraine: The Challenge of Change*, edited by O. Bertelsen. Soviet and Post-Soviet Politics and Society. Stuttgart: Ibidem.

Interfax. 2005. "Zapadnaia pressa schitaet glavnymi prichinami krizisa na Ukraine peredel sobstvennosti I peregrupirovku sil pered parlamentskimi vyborami," September 14.

Interfax Information Services. 2005. "Yushchenko nazyvaiet sebia prezidentom vsei Ukrainy i obeshaet narodu izmenit' zhizn'," January 23.

Interfax: Monitoring. 2005. "Putin iskliuchaet svoio vydvizhenie na tretii srok," September 7.

Kaufmann, D. 2006. "Human Rights, Governance, and Development." World Bank Institute Development Outreach Special Report, October. http://siteresources.worldbank.org/EXTSITETOOLS/Resources/KaufmannDevtOutreach.pdf. Accessed January 27, 2018.

Khavroniuk, M. 2011a. *Naukovo-praktychnyi komentar do zakonu Ukrainy "Pro zasady zapobihannia koruptsii."* Kyiv: Atika.

Khavroniuk, M. 2011b. "Pravyl'no Vyznachaite Slova..." ZN.ua. *DT.ua*, July 8. https://dt.ua/LAW/pravilno_viznachayte_slova__.html. Accessed January 27, 2018.

Khavroniuk, M. 2013. Za koruptsiiu peresliduvatymut' usikh: vid uchyteliv i medsestr do cpivrobitnykiv zhekiv Centre of Policy and Legal Reform. http://pravo.org.ua/ua/news/4754. Accessed January 27, 2018.

Klitgaard, R. 1988. *Controlling Corruption.* Berkeley, CA: University of California Press.

Klitgaard, R. 1998. "International Cooperation Against Corruption." *Finance and Development* 35 (1). Reprinted in *New Perspectives on Combating Corruption*, A Joint Publication of Transparency International and the Economic Development Institute of the World Bank, 1998.

Klitgaard, R. 2009. *Controlling Corruption.* Berkeley: University of California Press.

Koechlin, L. 2013. *Corruption as an Empty Signifier: Politics and Political Order in Africa.* Leiden and Boston: Brill.

Kommersant Ukraina. 2007a. "Kak prezident nameren pobedit' korruptsiiu," September 3.

Kommersant Ukraina. 2007b. "Viktor Yushchenko podal izbiratelnyi golos," April 13.

Kommersant Ukraina. 2008. "Viktor Yushchenko skhlesnulsia s korruptsiei," April 16.

Kommersant Ukraina. 2009. "Prezident pomenial Viktora Balogu na Veru Uliachenko," May 20.

Laclau, E. 2007. *Emancipation(s)*. London: Verso.

Langseth, P. 2002. "Global Dynamics of Corruption, The Role of the United Nations Helping Member States Build Integrity to Curb Corruption." Vienna: United Nations ODCCP, Centre for International Crime Prevention. https://www.unodc.org/pdf/crime/gpacpublications/cicp3.pdf. Accessed January 27, 2018.

Leshchenko, S. 2015. "Oligarkhi Ustali Ot Novoi Vlasti. Tainaia Vstrecha v 'Khaiiate'," August 4. http://blogs.pravda.com.ua/authors/leschenko/55c1023769875/. Accessed January 27, 2018.

Luchterhandt, O. 2010. "Der Kampf um das Regierungssystem der Ukraine – eine unendliche Geschichte." *Forschungsstelle Osteuropa an der Universität Bremen, Ukraine-Analysen* 80 (October): 2–6.

Makarenko, O. 2017. "Supporting Transparency or Fighting It? New Law on Assets Declarations for NGOs Raises Scandal in Ukraine." *Euromaidan Press*, March 28. http://euromaidanpress.com/2017/03/28/new-law-on-e-declarations-for-anti-corruption-ngos-seen-as-return-to-authoritarianism-in-ukraine/. Accessed January 27, 2018.

Melnykovska, I. 2015. "Big Business and Politics in Ukraine: The Evolution of State-Business Relations." *Employment and Economy in Central and Eastern Europe 1*. http://www.emecon.eu/fileadmin/articles/1_2015/1%202015%20MelnykovskaN.pdf. Accessed January 27, 2018.

Miller, W. L., Å. B. Grødeland, and T. Y. Koshechkina. 2001. *A Culture of Corruption? Coping with Government in Post-communist Europe*. Budapest: Central European University Press.

Myers, S. L. 2004. "Farce and Drama Mix as Election Day Nears in Fierce Ukraine Race." *The New York Times*, October 11. https://www.nytimes.com/2004/10/11/news/farce-and-drama-mix-as-election-day-nears-in-fierce-ukraine-race.html. Accessed January 27, 2018.

Myers, S. L. 2005. "Deal for Ukraine Company Renews Charges of Abuse." *The New York Times*, September 15. https://www.nytimes.com/2005/09/15/world/europe/deal-for-ukraine-company-renews-charges-of-abuse.html. Accessed January 27, 2018.

Mylovanova, Z., and V. Yurmanovych. 2016. "Legal Analysis of the Apartment Scandal: Leshchenko, Lyashko or Khomutynnyk—Whose Abuse Is Worse?"

VoxUkraine, September 14. https://voxukraine.org/2016/09/14/leshchen-ko-en/. Accessed January 27, 2018.

Nabers, D. 2015. *A Poststructuralist Discourse Theory of Global Politics.* Houndsmills and New York: Palgrave Macmillan.

Pleines, H. 2009. "The Political Role of the Oligarchs." In *Ukraine on Its Way to Europe. Interim Results of the Orange Revolution*, edited by J. Besters-Dilger. Frankfurt/Main: Peter Lang.

Razumkov Centre. 2009. "Political Corruption in Ukraine: Actors, Manifestations, Problems of Countering," 7 (111). National Security and Defence. Kyiv: Ukrainian Centre for Economic and Political Studies named after Olexander Razumkov.

Reanimation Package of Reforms Civil Platform. 2016. "Open Appeal to the President of Ukraine Petro Poroshenko to Put an End to the Pressure on the NGO 'Anticorruption Action Center' Exerted by the Prosecutor General's Office of Ukraine." *Reanimation Package of Reforms*, March 29. http://rpr. org.ua/en/news/open-appeal-to-the-president-of-ukraine-petro-poroshen-ko-to-put-an-end-to-the-pressure-on-the-ngo-anticorruption-action-center-exerted-by-the-prosecutor-general-s-office-of-ukraine/. Accessed January 27, 2018.

Riabchuk, M. 2012. *Gleichschaltung: Authoritaian Consolidation in Ukraine 2010–2012.* Kyiv: K.I.S.

Rose-Ackerman, S. 1978. *Corruption: A Study in Political Economy.* New York: Academic Press.

Rothstein, B. 2005. "Social Traps and the Problem of Trust." *Theories of Institutional Design.* Cambridge, UK and New York: Cambridge University Press.

Rothstein, B. 2011. *The Quality of Government: Corruption, Social Trust, and Inequality in International Perspective.* Chicago and London: University of Chicago Press.

Rothstein, B. 2014. "What Is the Opposite of Corruption?" *Third World Quarterly* 35 (5): 737–52.

Rothstein, B., and M. Tannenberg. 2015. *Making Development Work: The Quality of Government Approach.* Stockholm: Swedish Government Expert Group for Aid Studies. http://eba.se/wp-content/uploads/2015/12/Making_development_work_07.pdf. Accessed January 27, 2018.

Rothstein, B., and A. Varraich. 2014. "Corruption and the Opposite to Corruption a Map of the Conceptual Landscape." http://anticorrp.eu/wp-content/uploads/2014/10/D1.1-State-of-the-art-report-on-theories-and-harmonised-concepts-of-corruption.pdf. Accessed January 27, 2018.

Rothstein, B., and A. Varraich. 2017. *Making Sense of Corruption.* Cambridge, UK and New York, NY: Cambridge University Press.

Sushko, O., and O. Prystayko. 2011. "Freedom House Report, Nations in Transit 2011, Ukraine." Nations in Transit. Freedom House. https://freedomhouse.org/report/nations-transit/2011/ukraine.

Sushko, O., and O. Prystayko. 2012. "Freedom House Report, Nations in Transit 2012, Ukraine." Nations in Transit. Freedom House. https://freedomhouse.org/report/nations-transit/2012/ukraine. Accessed January 27, 2018.

Tajfel, H., ed. 1978. *Differentiation Between Social Groups: Studies in the Social Psychology of Intergroup Relations.* European Monographs in Social Psychology 14. London and New York: Published in Cooperation with European Association of Experimental Social Psychology by Academic Press.

Tajfel, H., and J. C. Turner. 1986. "The Social Identity Theory of Intergroup Behaviour." In *Psychology of Intergroup Relations*, edited by S. Worchel and W. G. Austin. Chicago, IL: Nelson-Hall.

Turner, J. C., and P. J. Oakes. 1986. "The Significance of the Social Identity Concept for Social Psychology with Reference to Individualism, Interactionism and Social Influence." *British Journal of Social Psychology* 25 (3): 237–52.

United Nations Convention Against Corruption. 2003. United Nations Office on Drugs and Crime. http://www.unodc.org/documents/treaties/UNCAC/Publications/Convention/08-50026_E.pdf. Accessed January 27, 2018.

UNIAN. 2004. "Posle izbraniia prezidentom Ukrainy Yushchenko podpishet ukraz o sozdanii komiteta narodnoho kontrolia s otdeleniiami v oblastiakh," October 14.

UNIAN. 2005a. "Yushchenko podcherkivaet neobkhodimost' polnoi zameny starykh kadrov v rukovodstve MVD," July 18.

UNIAN. 2005b. "Brodskii zaiavliaet o koruptsii v okruzhenii Yushchenko," September 1.

UNIAN. 2005c. "Yushchenko zaiavliaet, chto obvinenie v koruptsii koe-koho iz eho okruzhenia, bylo sdelano dlia razrushenia osnovy komandy," September 8.

UNIAN. 2005d. "Yushchenko podcherkivaet, chto vse obvineniia eho okruzhenia v koruptsii nosily iskliuchitelno politicheskii kharakter," November 10.

UNIAN. 2005e. "Sleduiushim etapom posle sudebnoi reform stanet reorganizaciia SBU, prokuratury, drugikh silovykh struktur," November 29.

UNIAN. 2011. "Yanukovich schitaet, chto korruptsionery pytaiutsia vliiat' na zhurnalistov," February 25.

Varraich, A. 2014. "Corruption: An Umbrella Concept." *QoG Working Paper Series* (5): 5. https://qog.pol.gu.se/digitalAssets/1551/1551604_2014_05_varraich.pdf. Accessed January 27, 2018.

Way, L. 2005. "Kuchma's Failed Authoritarianism." *Journal of Democracy* 16 (2): 131–45.

Wickberg, S. 2016. "Scandales et corruption dans le discours médiatique français : la partie émergée de l'iceberg?" *Éthique publique* 18 (2). http://journals.openedition.org/ethiquepublique/2745. Accessed January 28, 2018.

Yaffa, J. 2016. "Reforming Ukraine After the Revolutions." *The New Yorker*, May 9. http://www.newyorker.com/magazine/2016/09/05/reforming-ukraine-after-maidan. Accessed January 27, 2018.

Yushchenko, V. 2004. "Ukraine's Choice." *Wall Street Journal*, August 24. http://www.wsj.com/articles/SB109329771672198865. Accessed January 27, 2018.

Yushchenko, V. 2014. *Nederzhavni Taiemnytsi Notatky Na Berehakh Pamiati*, edited by O. Zinchenko. Kharkiv: Folio.

CHAPTER 6

Gender Role Scenarios of Women's Participation in Euromaidan Protests in Ukraine

Tamara Martsenyuk and Iryna Troian

INTRODUCTION

As gender remains not only the key division in society but also one of the main systems of inequality (Connell 2002), it is important to highlight the fact that gender equality and women's question in particular became the key issues in the processes of democratization. Contemporary egalitarian state demands equal participation and representation of all its citizens' interests (both men's and women's) in all powers of the state (legislative, executive, and judiciary). In post-Soviet Ukraine, gender (in) equality issues have been critically debated by both Ukrainian (Kis 2007, 2012; Martsenyuk 2012, 2014; Plakhotnik 2008; Tolstokorova 2012; Zherebkina 1999; Zhurzhenko 2004, 2011) and international scholars (Hankivsky 2012; Kebalo 2007; Phillips 2014). Particular attention was

T. Martsenyuk (✉)
Department of Sociology,
National University of Kyiv-Mohyla Academy, Kyiv, Ukraine

I. Troian
Independent Researcher, Kyiv, Ukraine

© The Author(s) 2018
E. Resende et al. (eds.), *Crisis and Change in Post-Cold War Global Politics*, https://doi.org/10.1007/978-3-319-78589-9_6

129

paid to the development of women's (feminist) movement in Ukraine (Hrycak 2006; Kebalo 2007; Plakhotnik 2008; Zychowicz 2011).

On the one hand, the independent Ukrainian state declared that democratic principles and legislation enhancement create foundations for establishing gender equality (Hankivsky 2012). On the other hand, development of national state required reinvention of myths and traditions and had resulted in "patriarchal renaissance" (Rubchak 2011; Zhurzhenko 2004, 2011). This caused resurrection of "traditional national values" and reconstruction of "traditional" gender roles for men and women that enhance gender polarization and prescribe expressive roles for women and instrumental—for men (Kis 2007; Zhurzhenko 2004, 2011).

With getting the independence in 1991, the processes of nation and state building had started in Ukraine. The complex transition of Ukraine from command-administrative to free-market economy and from totalitarian communist regime to a democratic one presupposed not only deregulation, privatization, trade, and market liberalization, but also strengthening the common identity of the nation to transform people into the active political subjects (Kuzio and Wilson 1994: 18–19). Therefore, project of nation and state building required mobilization of the cultural resources to create the authentic path of "new-born" (after collapse of Soviet bloc) Ukrainian state.

Current Ukrainian gender order was reflected in the modes of men's and women's participation in Euromaidan protests that took place from November 2013 to February 2014 (Khromeychuk 2015; Martsenyuk 2014; Onuch and Martsenyuk 2014; Popova 2014). Except for people's aspirations for the further European integration and democratization, these series of protests were accompanied by the emotionally exalted expectations connected with emergence of a new Ukrainian nation as a community united by a sense of collective unity and common values. Despite the presence of both men and women, gender aspects of their participation were in general seen in the gendered division of labor and functions performed by women and men during the protests (Martsenyuk 2014; Onuch and Martsenyuk 2014; Phillips 2014; Popova 2014). The modes of women engagement in the protests varied significantly during different stages of the protests—from peaceful demonstrations to violent clashes (Khromeychuk 2015; Martsenyuk 2014; Onuch and Martsenyuk 2014). Militarization of the protest and spread of nationalistic discourse has greatly contributed to the glorification of male heroes as "true revolutionaries" and fighters for freedom, while women's contribution to the protests was neglected or stood invisible and their role was treated as auxiliary (Popova 2014).

At the same time, despite limitations of gender role stereotypes allocated to women (expected performance of reproductive labor), female protesters were engaged in diversity of activities that made possible for them to criticize sexism (Martsenyuk 2014; Onuch and Martsenyuk 2014; Phillips 2014). Moreover, Euromaidan protest provided women with the space and the ability to accept and affirm egalitarian gender roles, expressing themselves as leaders and active citizens. Empathy and solidarity among citizens contributed to their ability to mobilize as well as to challenge stereotypes, which is favorable for transformation of society toward greater participation and inclusion. Taking into account the existing controversy in the perception of women's role into the protests, it is reasonable to argue that there were different gender role scenarios of women's participation in the protests according to the functions they performed and the way in which they represented themselves. Apart from understanding of the crisis as undesirable and unpredictable, the events demanding response to manage them, the enabling potential of the crisis for desirable interventions of social agents should be stressed. In particular, it is necessary to underline the empowering potential of the series of the Euromaidan protests for increasing women's visibility in the public space due to discursive changes that help to articulate and question the power relation within existing gender order.

Therefore, this chapter aims to define the major gender role scenarios of women's participation in Euromaidan protests. The empirical basis for this chapter was the sociological survey data from research jointly conducted by two major sociological research institutions in Ukraine—the Kyiv International Institute of Sociology (KIIS) and the Ilko Kucheriv Democratic Initiatives Foundation (DIF) in three phases—during 7–8th of December 2013,[1] on December 20, 2013,[2]

---

[1] The first phase of research was conducted on December 7–8, 2013, "Maidan: who is standing, why and for what?" via face-to-face interview with 1037 respondents. The theoretical margin of error does not exceed 3.2% for indicators close to 50%, 2.8% for indicators close to 25%, 1.9% for indicators close to 10%, 1.4% for indicators close to 5% (The design effect is close to 1).

[2] The second phase of the research was conducted on December 20, 2013, "Maidan-camp" via face-to-face interview with 515 respondents.

and on February 3, 2014,[3] that helped to understand the changes of socio-demographic profile of the protesters during different stages of the protests. The sample included representation and weighing of different segments within Maidan protest space and ensured random selection of respondents from each segment to provide data saturation.

The qualitative methodology was used to define major gender role scenarios of women's participation in the protests through the analysis of 32 selected online texts—articles devoted to the topic of women's participation in Euromaidan protests that had been published in the Ukrainian or foreign online media from November 2013 up to November 2014. Relying on the method of qualitative content analysis, the media articles on women's participation in the protest activity were analyzed. Social constructivist approach toward gender roles identification was used. Nation/state building process in post-Soviet Ukraine was analyzed from a feminist perspective based on international and local authors.

EUROMAIDAN PROTESTS 2013–2014 AND WOMEN'S PARTICIPATION

The recent events in central Kyiv and other Ukrainian cities became famous as a so-called Euro Revolution, better known as "Euromaidan." Protests of Ukrainian citizens against their government commenced in November 2013, when President Yanukovych announced a decision to turn Ukraine away from the European Union, and continued for about three months (even after the Yanukovych regime had fallen). Protests or social movements in their conventional definition presuppose existence of not only clearly defined opponents, informal social network of peoples united by the collective identity (Della Porta and Diani 2006: 23–24), but also a series of campaigns designed to promote their ideas or satisfy demands (Tilly 2004: 8).

Women were actively participating in all form of activities in the protest space. Besides cooking, cleaning, and entertaining, women were fighting on barricades, making negotiations and participating in peacekeeping, providing medical support, maintaining information support,

---

[3] The third phase of the research was conducted on February 3, 2014 ($n = 502$), "Maidan-Sich" via face-to-face interview with 502 respondents.

Table 6.1 Women's and men's participation in Euromaidan protests in Kyiv, Ukraine

Survey period	December 2013 (%)	January 2014 (%)	February 2014 (%)
% of women	43	15	12
% of men	57	85	88
Total	100	100	100

participating in legislative work and logistics, and providing education for protesters and huge organizational support. There are results of surveys to provide figures of female participation in Euromaidan. First of all, according to the Ukrainian Protest Participant Survey (Onuch and Martsenyuk 2014: 88), on *the Maidan Nezalezhnosti* between November 26, 2013, and January 10, 2014, men did in fact represent a slim majority of overall protesters at 59%, and women represented 41%. Onuch and Martsenyuk add that "men were also more likely, from the very beginning, to protest more frequently and later at night. But we can still confidently say that until January 10, 2014, women made up almost half of the protest participants" (Onuch and Martsenyuk 2014: 88).

These findings of gendered trends in the average participation of women in the Euromaidan protests could be compared with surveys results conducted by the KIIS and the DIF. KIIS and DIF conducted surveys on large organized protest days (December 7–8, 2013, and December 20, 2014), as well as surveyed people residing on the Maidan (February 3, 2014) (see Table 6.1).

In the beginning of the peaceful protests and mass demonstrations, women composed almost half of the protesters (43%), but later stages lead to its transformation into semi-military area of permanent residence of the protesters—women composed among them only 12%. The increased danger of violent repressions resulted in many women's exclusion from protest zone. On the one hand, it was a display of "caring about women." On the other hand, one can argue that women were not perceived as "responsible" enough to make decisions and choices about their safety on their own or not strong enough to take care of themselves.

Empirical Study of Gender Roles in Euromaidan: Methodology

As far as Euromaidan was a heterogeneous space of diverse protests activities (Martsenyuk 2014; Phillips 2014), it is important to analyze women's gendered roles in it using qualitative methods. *Qualitative content analysis* presupposes attentive reading of texts and their interpretation accompanied by selection and aggregation of the most significant fragments of the text that correspond to developed theoretical model. This procedure helps to identify the dominant topics, patterns, links, as well as exclusions (what had been "silenced" in the text); it is based on flexibility of analytical categories that have to provide data saturation (Ivanov 2013: 71).

The *purposive (relevance) sampling* was used for the research to understand a phenomenon, rather than to enable generalizations from study samples. Relevance sampling aims to selecting all textual units that contributes to answering given research questions and definition of the gender role scenarios of women's participation in Euromaidan. Thus, the articles for analysis were selected according to such criteria as *informativeness* and *relevance* (Krippendorff 2003: 118–9).

Firstly, sampling of relevant electronic written texts—articles and publications in online journals, newspapers, and blogs—was based on the *key-words search* in the Google according to request "Women+(Euro)maidan" both in English and in Ukrainian. Another criterion for sampling was the *period when publications had been made*—from November 2013 up to November 2014. Excluding textual units that did not possess relevant information, 32 online articles were selected from the national and international media (Table 6.2).

Such number of selected texts is considered to be sufficient for the pilot research as point of data saturation was reached, when other texts

Table 6.2 Sample of articles for qualitative content analysis: Women in Euromaidan protests

	National media	International media
Key-word(s) of Google search	Жінки (*Zhinky*) (Євро)майдан (*Yevromaydan*)	Women (Euro)maidan
Number of article	23	9
Total	32	

did not reveal new information and contained repeats. *Units of analysis* were those semantic phrases or fragments of the text that contain description of women's activities during Euromaidan protests and heroines' own reflections on their experience (quotations and statements).

EMPIRICAL STUDY OF GENDER ROLES IN EUROMAIDAN: CONCEPTUALIZATION

Social constructivism interprets dichotomy between sexes and gender roles as culturally and socially constructed, where gender relationships are socially organized relations of power and inequality that operate both on the institutional and individual levels. From Peter Berger and Thomas Luckmann's perspective, subjects not only learn and reproduce gender roles and relationships, but also create them through permanent social construction (Berger and Luckmann 1966: 36–39). The differences between sexes are endowed with social meaning—stereotypes embedded in all institutions of the society.

Connell (2002: 55–56) interprets gender as a system of stratification operating on different levels in the form of gender order (the way relationship between men and women is organized and regulated within particular societies), gender regimes (at the level of institutions and organizations), and gender relationship (interpersonal communication and interaction, everyday practices). Performativity of gender is culturally predetermined as it varies in different cultures and in different times and reflects a gender order of a particular society. To understand how gender order is created and reconstructed, it is important to analyze the macro-context of social interaction—state policy, economic relationship, collective imaginations, traditions, images of men and women into the culture.

Different variants of gender roles performance in particular situations or contexts are called gender role scenarios, and they contain patterns of behavior and expression that are expected for men and women and predetermined by biological sex. It should be recognized, however, that women in a movement, politics, in the public arena, and in the disruptive fields of activism face the burdens of gender expectations and transcend these expectations. Gender role scenarios refer to the ways in which women participated in the protests and represented themselves according to the contributions that they made and functions they performed. Taking into account the existing approaches toward definition of the level of equity of men and women in particular activity, the patriarchal and egalitarian scenarios can be distinguished.

Patriarchal scenario is based on gender polarization (portraying men's and women's "nature" and roles as completely opposite), maintains traditional "women's" roles, and underlines their essentialist features representing them as those who serve the needs of other and perform expressive functions through revealing empathy and moral support to the other members of society. In contrast, egalitarian scenario presupposes equity of opportunities and rights for men and women, making them independently choose the roles they wanted to perform. As a result, women can perform more emancipative roles that helped them express leadership, own civil position and represented them as experts or professionals. Gendered roles of women depend not only on individual factors (such as their abilities and willingness, skills, and knowledge) but also from structural ones (state politics on gender equality issues) that form gender order of the particular society. That is why macro-picture of gender roles in the Ukrainian society should be discussed.

GENDER AND NATION/STATE BUILDING OF UKRAINIAN SOCIETY

Nation-state might be analyzed as a masculine institution, where masculinity is embodied in the policy of nationalism. From this perspective, the culture existing in a nation-state greatly contributes to the spread, support, and reconstruction of such masculine cultural norms as dignity, patriotism, courage, and sense of duty, making them universal and defining conventional ways of their expression both for men and women. In this case, women who are involved in the processes of state building as citizens, national representatives, activists, or leaders play the role that reflects masculine definition of femininity and the "proper" place of women in nation in the national discourse and collective action (Yuval-Davis 1997).

According to Brubaker (1996: 61–62), the development of national ideology in post-Soviet space was predetermined by national politics in USSR. It had implicitly propagated ethnic version of nationalism (not the state or cultural one) through differentiation of the citizenship and ethnicity and simultaneous suppression of any manifestations of nationalism or national consciousness. As Zhurzhenko has argued, approaching the nation as a symbolical community deserves creation of common imagination about the past and the present of the nation that include reinterpretation of the traditional myths. Such a shift toward nation-state building caused emergence of "neo-traditionalism," an element of the cultural decolonization that could be interpreted as a reaction of the independent Ukrainian state to a former repressive Soviet policy and the attempt of the Ukrainians to distance themselves from the totalitarian past (Zhurzhenko 2004: 23–24). The new ideological discourse of "neo-traditionalism" had significantly affected the gender order of independent Ukraine, as it prescribed the "expressive" roles for women and "instrumental" roles for men as the most beneficial for harmonious functioning of society. Hence, this discourse serving for nation-state building purposes had a profound effect of new political and legal order.

At the same time, as a result of Ukrainian integration into international community and "transition" toward liberal democracy with a market economy, the gender order in Ukraine became a fragmented combination of numerous heterogeneous discourses (Tolstokorova 2012: 48–49). Thereby, mass-communication messages as data surveys in Ukraine revealed the presence of such "discourse–mixture":

1. A discourse about emancipation of family from the state invasion;
2. A global feminism or gender equality discourse (Zhurzhenko 2004: 39–40);
3. A nationalistic discourse about women's "natural" destination with deep nostalgia for the "traditional family values" (Tolstokorova 2012: 49).

Yuval-Davis (1997) defines the following ways of women's engagement into national processes: Women are biological agents of ethnic communities' reproduction; they also appear to be agents of boundaries' reconstruction between ethnic and national groups as well as agents of cultural transmission in the processes of socialization (participants of ideological reconstruction of community). Representing ethnic and national differences, women become central elements and symbols in ideological discourses, but also they are also participants of national, economic, political, or military struggle. As Beard (2014: 12) points out, there is a process of silencing women through making them invisible in the public space, even if they are physically present there. This process presupposes allowing women to speak out only in certain capacities—as "victims and as martyrs" or "legitimately rise up to defend their homes, their children, their husbands or the interests of other women."

Analysis of historical publications by Kis drew the conclusion that "women's history appeared to be an element in the history of Ukrainian nation building" (Kis 2012: 158). According to her, a mythical image *Berehynya*[4] had become a starting point for construction of the "authentic Ukrainian femininity" and an embodiment of cultural and national identity that resists criticism or deconstruction. Since authenticity of the nation is personified and embodied in the image of women, the project of national identity's development included invention of "ideal female-citizen: mother, pure and dedicated Ukrainian women" (Hankivsky 2012: 31). Providing Ukrainian women with traditional features—orientation toward family and motherhood dedication were combined with underlining their strength and independence, autonomy and freedom, respect and recognition in the family and society. Such combination of features became a foundation for the myth of matriarchy, and it represents a special way of Ukrainian women's emancipation that, on the one hand, removes the need for Western-style feminism and, on the other hand, emphasizes the progressive nature of the nation compared to its neighbors. The constructed image of Ukrainian women represents them as essentially taking care of welfare and interests of the family, their children, or of the next generation: "Altruism and ability to sacrifice (as opposed to men's selfishness) is considered as the main motive of women's social and political activity that derives from their primary role, i.e. mother" (Zhurzhenko 2004: 36).

Unarticulated dependence of the Ukrainian feminism on the nationalistic discourse and subordination of women's question to the issue of national liberation struggle, according to Zhurzhenko (2011: 182),

---

[4]Berehynya is a character from the ancient Ukrainian mythology of pagan times that symbolizes a strong and independent woman as a guardian of household and as a spirit-protector. According to the Ukrainian researcher Oksana Kis, the concept that refers to the role model of "traditional and authentic" Ukrainian femininity was constructed in mass consciousness in late Soviet Union period and reinforced during the national revival in 1980s; it stresses eternal "matriarchal" past and underlines exceptionally high social status of women and gender equality inherent to the Ukrainian culture.

are inherent features of women's activism in independent Ukraine. This argument is built on the fact that most women's NGOs are traditional, social, and business-oriented, when NGOs with essential feminist orientation, which raise the question of female self-consciousness, identity, and subjectivity, occupy a marginal position. This situation allowed Zherebkina (1999: 41–42) to argue that "in Ukrainian women's movement the unconscious substitution of women's individuality and freedom values with more abstract goals of nation-state building took place." At the same time, Plakhotnik (2008: 195–6) suggested that "local specificity" of women's activity in post-Soviet countries is characterized with attempts to distance themselves from feminism and carried out "under any other name" without articulation of the issue of women's rights, but gradually undermining the existing gender order.

According to Bohachevsky-Chomiak, the formation of national states (nationalism) and women's emancipation (feminism) are a single process of political and social modernization. A pragmatic feminism characterizes a situation of women in the stateless nations on the periphery of Europe, and it is expressed in the subordination of women's interests to the ideas of nation building, when women use emancipatory democratic potential of the national liberation movement to achieve equal rights and self-affirmation space for participation in the public life. Actually, women's collective agency in national movement had always played a secondary role (Kebalo 2007: 39). As long as the struggle for power of persons deprived of power would continue instead of forcing the changes of power relations in society, the so-called national liberation leads to more oppression of women and other disadvantaged groups in the new social order.

Prejudices about nationalism and feminism in Ukrainian society had originated from the Soviet "iron curtain" and isolation period, when construction of the opposite to the Western model of development civilizational system was accompanied by the Soviet Union's ambition to become a great power. Soviet ideology had achieved a success in "stigmatization of the nationalist movement and in de-legitimization of Western feminism" (Kebalo 2007: 58) and fixed in the public opinion negative connotations to both of these terms. As it might be seen, feminism was considered a threat and was stigmatized as "an imported Western product," because official ideology stated that women question has been already solved.

Empirical Study of Gender Roles in Euromaidan: Results

According to previously defined gender roles' characteristics, sub-categories of qualitative content analysis were identified and their explanation was provided. The following *sub-categories* could be named as patriarchal women's roles in Euromaidan participation:

1. Motherhood (reproductive—caring, serving, and helping labor, providing emotional and moral support),
2. Beauty (importance of Ukrainian visible femininity for inspiration of heroes), and
3. Victimhood (suffering of weak women, over-protective strategy from men's perspective).

Patriarchal gender role scenarios stressed essentialist features of women and portrayed their role as a supporting one. At the same time, the following *sub-categories* could be named as egalitarian women's roles:

1. Fighting with adversary (together with men building and protecting barricades, providing medical service, etc.),
2. Peacekeeping (communicating and negotiating with adversary to prevent escalation of violence), and
3. Providing information and logistic services.

Egalitarian roles are those ones that provide agency, visibility (as for men) in public discourses, glorification, and with more probability (compare to patriarchal) recognition in memory politics.

Patriarchal Gender Role Scenarios During Euromaidan Protests

Despite the equal presence of women at the protests, symbolical representation of their participation was criticized (Khromeychuk 2015; Martsenyuk 2014; Onuch and Martsenyuk 2014; Phillips 2014). Such critique highlighted inferior perception of women's contribution to the protests and reduction of their roles to such "traditional" functions as inspiration, peace building, or assistance for men as "true" revolutionaries. Partly it was caused by the fact that during the protests the nationalistic rhetoric became dominant and contributed to the reconstruction of patriarchal structures and ideology. For example, analogies of Euromaidan and *Cossack Sich*[5] led to glorification of male warriors, strengthening of the myths about the Ukrainian *Cossacks* (a masculine community where women's role was marginalized or symbolical) that caused reconstruction of an *androcentric* vision of the Ukrainian nation.

Another reason was radicalization and further militarization of the protests that had reinforced *sexist rhetoric* (Popova 2014) and gender segregation in the division of labor among protesters as well as strengthened men's privileges as warriors in the context of revolution. Such glorification of the men as fighters for freedom led to women's exclusion from participation in the hostilities as well as restricted their presence on the frontline. Such discriminatory practice of exclusion was justified with men's intention to protect "women and children" as well as elderly people who together created a "weaker" and "inferior" category of not sufficiently mature, strong, or healthy people that are in need of help and defense by the men warriors. This over-protective strategy considerably narrowed the opportunities for women to take their own decisions about acceptable risks, which illustrates the policy of exclusion and demonstrates the ways patriarchal order restricts civil rights of female citizens.

Patriarchal gender role scenarios could be explained using three major female images: *Mother, Ukrainian beauty*, and *Victim* (see Table 6.3). Traditional "women's" roles in Euromaidan protests describe women's participation in Euromaidan as mothers (caregivers and helpers).

Gender labeling of women as "other" at the protest space corresponded to the expected women's functions that were reduced to mainly reproductive work—to take care of other, to cook meal, to clean the protests space, to provide emotional help. As it is mentioned in one of the articles: "Women had to be there at least to support emotionally the men. No one said that they had to be at the forefront, but they were necessary to fulfill the most important mission—to be Berehynias, mother and woman as an independent rear" (see Table 6.3). The logic of voluntary engagement in the protests by searching for the place where one can be most useful allowed both women and men to perform a great

---

[5] Cossack Sich—a fortified territory on the islands of Dnipro River (near contemporary Zaporizhzhya region of Ukraine), where in the sixteenth to eighteenth centuries the unregistered Ukrainian army composed of men warriors (the Cossacks) was located.

Table 6.3 Patriarchal gender role scenarios of women's participation in Euromaidan protests

Scenario	Descriptive features	Examples (quotations from articles)
Mother	Women were mostly mentioned in the context of kitchen, cleaning and serving the needs of others (mainly performing reproductive labor as an exclusive realm of their competence). Such women see their function in taking care about others, providing psychological, emotional, and moral support	"Women, when you see garbage: clean it up! The revolutionaries will be grateful" "God, we were neither for Europe nor for Russia, we just felt it necessary to protect the children who stayed at Maidan" "Our strong and brave men needed attention, assistance and just talk! With women, men are more brave and courageous. So on Maidan we should be together" "The women shouted to the security forces "there is no alien children," "authorities, do not kill our children" "Women had to be there at least to support emotionally the men. No one said that they had to be at the forefront, but they were necessary to fulfill the most important mission – to be Berehynias, mother and woman as an independent rear"
Ukrainian beauty	Underlining the physical attractiveness and appearance of women that is strategically used by them for keeping up men's good spirits at barricades and entertaining them	"We want to cheer them up, and we want to support them. They smile, and they say thank you for the tea, and sometimes ask for our telephone numbers." And we say, "No, boys, only after you bring us victory" "Men must show documents and women have to smile" to enter the Ukrainian House" "Ukrainian beauty is on the Revolution's side!"
Victim	Women are represented as weaker category expressing need in male's defense and exhibiting admiration of their strength and courage	"A woman has the right to be weaker, and the calling of women here is to help the guys, and this situation revealed them as real men" "We have to be proud of our defenders - men. There is no place for cowards near us"

variety of duties (building barricades, information support "Euromaidan SOS," medical or provision supply, and so on). But segregation on the gender basis appeared only in the moments when violence or clashes had started, and this signifies the masculine nature of war.

Martsenyuk (2014) argues that such division of labor reflected the gender order in Ukraine, where such labor is considered the domain of women's competence and responsibility, but does not have prestige, is unpaid and invisible. The announcement found in the kitchen: "Dear women, if you see garbage – clean it up, [the male] revolutionary will be pleased" is a clear example of a patriarchal attitude toward gender roles. Moreover, female activists on Euromaidan heavily criticized it (as well as the other examples of sexism). At the same time, women internalized traditional gendered role of mother and strategically used it to communicate with the "enemy": The women shouted to the security forces, "There are no alien children"; "Authorities, do not kill our children."

The second gender role scenario of women's participation in the protests is portrayed as "beautiful women" of Maidan who were also involved in a number of activities. The Ukrainian women were called "The Muses of Revolution," in which beauty (that it is important in the patriarchal perception of femininity) is an important factor to be underlined. Women were making space beautiful (painted barricades into bright colors), and they were performing ballet on barricades. Some pictures from the military protests' space demonstrate "visible femininity" where women came with pink or other bright cloth, in wreaths, and with flowers, to bring love, communication, and understanding to the protest space. "Smile" was a traditional feminine feature of the Ukrainian women. It was also requested in the protest space: "Men must show documents and women have to smile" to enter the "Ukrainian House."

Finally, the third gender role scenario of women's participation in the protests is connected with victimhood. Ukrainian women are portrayed as victims of a cruel regime or relationships with Russia. What is more, the Ukrainian nation is portrayed via a *victimized* female image as a *suffering nation* (with slogans like "Russia, hands of Ukraine" or "Leave me alone, big country"). Also, some posters show a crying (or even bleeding) woman who suffers for the destiny of their nation.

At the same time, it is necessary to understand that the domination of masculine ideologies and patriarchal discourse, such as nationalism, could not be total because its internal contradictions enabled the existence of other alternative and competing discourses (Hirschmann 2006: 203).

Despite being less visible, alternative discourses alter the dominant order, reinforce new norms transforming power relations, and provide space for different symbolical minorities' subjectivity expression. As Phillips pointed out, "Euromaidan has created a space for citizens' discussion of new strategies for their rights articulation" (Phillips 2014: 414–5).

On November 21, 2014, in his speech commemorating the first anniversary of the Euromaidan protests, President Petro Poroshenko thanked not only the men, but also the women who died during the protests, as well as both male and female volunteers for their roles in the events. This discourse of *inclusivity* and *recognition* of women who participated in the protests encourages a broader analysis of women's involvement in Euromaidan. Three sub-categories for egalitarian scenarios of women's participation in Euromaidan protests mentioned earlier will be discussed.

EGALITARIAN GENDER ROLE SCENARIOS DURING EUROMAIDAN PROTESTS

As a heterogeneous space containing not only patriarchal gender roles, but also the egalitarian ones, Euromaidan was represented in various forums (Martsenyuk 2014; Phillips 2014). These authors stressed heterogeneity of the Euromaidan protest space with regard to women's gender role scenarios of participation in the protests. When patriarchal and traditional gender roles were reconstructed in protestors' division of labor, women had an opportunity to criticize sexism and create alternative initiatives.

Although such critique is fair and definitely should be voiced to highlight the problems with women's misrecognition, discrimination, or humiliation in the nationalistic or military discourse, it should be considered that such perspective eliminates the manifestation of female agency during the protests. Therefore, selective stressing of discrimination against women represents the latter as "monolithic" victimized objects "without historical and political agency" (Mann 2012: 365) who experienced submission and were oppressed by the reinforced and partly legitimized patriarchal order during the protests. As a result, such approach might also have destructive consequences because it represents women's activism as completely subordinated by the masculine cultural norms leaving no space for resistance and changes.

Despite the heterogeneous civilian composition, during the second half of December, Euromaidan was "centered around the militarized symbolism of the national liberation movement" (Khromeychuk 2015). Female volunteers at Euromaidan were helping protesters by risking their lives. The best known example is a 21-year-old volunteer Olesya Zhukovska, who, after having been struck in her neck by a metal bullet, tweeted: "I am dying." Olesya survived and became known in Ukraine and abroad because of her dangerous situation.

Because of mainly patriarchal views regarding the role of women in society as mothers and beautiful subjects, and a lack of women's access toward decision-making in the top politics of the public sphere, it is difficult for the Ukrainian women to fulfill alternative gender roles. Despite societal and stereotypical challenges, women were engaged in alternative to "traditional" forms of participation at Euromaidan.

Egalitarian gender role scenarios could be explained using three major female images: *Female warrior, Peacekeeper*, and *Information and Logistics Provider* (see Table 6.4).

We call the first egalitarian gender role scenario "Female warrior." Women were building barricades together with men and constantly carrying scarce resources (used tires and firewood) on their own. One of the outstanding examples of women's inclusiveness in the Euromaidan protests was the creation of both military and non-military women's "sotni"[6]—"the hundreds" or squadrons as a reminiscent from the Cossacks' times, traditionally masculine Ukrainian military structures. There were formal squadrons (the 39th Women's Squadron of Euromaidan Self-Defense), female platoon [*Zhinocha Chota*] squadrons (the 16th Squadron of "Maidan Self-Defence"), and informal or non-registered squadrons (the 1st Women's Squadrons,[7] the

---

[6]Sotni (literary translated as "hundreds")—a military unit such as squadron within the Cossack army composed of one or several hundreds of soldiers. During the Euromaidan protests in 2013–2014, the protesters adopted this name for self-organization and protection units.

[7]The 1st Women's Squadron was a non-military initiative of women's solidarity that occurred on Euromaidan as an opposition to the other male-dominated squadrons (sotni) and was the first unit composed of women who provided humanitarian aid and moral support for the Ukrainian warriors.

Table 6.4 Egalitarian gender role scenarios of women's participation in Euromaidan protests

Scenario	Descriptive features	Examples (quotations from articles)
Female Warrior	Creation of both military and non-military women's "*sotni*" ("the hundreds"), building barricades together with men, and constantly carrying scarce resources (used tires and firewood) on their own	"Apart from cooking and serving food, they help the wounded protesters in hospitals, keep night watch at barricades, and give medical aid to the injured"
		"Their professions and ages vary, but one thing remains certain: they are the faces of not only fighters, but leaders"
		"I helped get fire wood when it was −15 C, and built snow barricades … Women were making Molotov cocktails. Hundreds of men and women were bringing bags filled with medication and food for the protesters"
Peacekeeper	Women as initiators of peaceful actions and flesh-mobs in order to prevent clashes and escalation of violence. They perform function of mediators between conflicting forces	"Servicemen will be presented cards and gate or of every military building would be door decorated with the rose as a symbol of peace, our gratitude, love and kindness"
		"Now we with other women of Maidan had organized maternal movement. We walk close to the border with police, we ask them to come to the Ukrainian people's side. It's a peaceful action"
Information and logistics provider	Coordination and participation in hotlines, providing logistics, informational, legal, and educational support	"We wanted to make women's voice at Maidan more noticeable, so it would really be heard, that women are involved not only at the kitchen, but also in Automaidan and in hospital rounds. The community Euromaidan SOS is mostly managed and coordinated by women too"
		"We published our newspaper for Maidan with our own money. We organized the screenings of documentaries about peaceful resistance"
		"At Maidan University, an informal education center in the square, the women's hundred invited lecturers to speak about feminist theory"

Women's Squadron of Zaporizhzhya,[8] the Sisterhood Squadron in Dnipropetrovsk,[9] the Olga Kobylianska Female Squadron,[10] and others).

At the same time, female activists' self-organization during the Euromaidan protests into traditionally masculine Ukrainian military structures—*Sotni*—raised the question whether women's presence and participation in the masculine institutions could transform them according to the feminine interests and needs and whether women were capable of achieving the same recognition of their achievements as men. Women's practices of self-organization into sotnias and their reflections on their roles help to evaluate the emancipative prospects of Euromaidan. Phenomena such as creation of women's defense structures might also signify a manifestation of collective women's agency and their response to patriarchal exclusion policy as well as to the traditional gender division of labor.

Olga Kobylianska Female Squadron was not officially registered as part of Maidan self-defense to stay outside of its highly patriarchal structure and to reveal publically the contributions of women to the Euromaidan. Such initiative might be seen as a form of protest against reconstruction of gender inequality and attempt to confront habitual gender politics at Euromaidan through rejection of traditional feminine roles. Olga Kobylianska Female Squadron emerged during the Euromaidan events in late January 2014, as an initiative of feminists and activist women who were outraged with the sexist aspects of Euromaidan. The initiative aimed to provide visibility to all kinds of participation on the part of women at Euromaidan. It suggested that women "made the revolution" alongside with men. The group has a Facebook page with almost 3376 followers as of June 2015.

Other women's sotnias had appropriated new masculine norms and partly enjoyed masculine privileges. Kovalenko, who formed the 39th

[8]Women's Squadron of Zaporizhzhya—the regional unit of women's self-organization during the Euromaidan protests in Zaporizhzhya city that stood for peace and organized protests against police's violence (later was registered as women's civil organization).

[9]Sisterhood Squadron (in Dnipropetrovsk)—the unit of female protestors that was spontaneously created by women-activists after January 29, 2014, in Dnipropetrovsk city when participants of peaceful demonstration were beaten.

[10]Olga Kobylianska Female Squadron—the squadron that united women-protestors was named after the Ukrainian modernist writer and feminist (1863–1942) in order to distinguish this unit from other Euromaidan's Squadrons composed by men.

official all-female sotnia, argued that "[We] were all equally involved in that war. It did not matter to me that I was a girl" (Khromeychuk 2015). Following her argumentation, willing women could not simply join existing male-units, because it could damage discipline inside them. Female-unit was called to make women's desires correspond to their capabilities through intensive training in martial arts, first aid, etc. She recalls meeting recognition from other male *sotnyks*[11] that considered her their "sister in arms" due to her adoption of some of the manners traditionally associated with men and usage of some of traditional masculine form of self-presentation. The creation of all-female unit was an attempt to formalize women's presence on Euromaidan, achieve their recognition, and overcome obstacles.

The Women's Squadron of Zaporizhzhya and the Sisterhood Squadron in Dnipropetrovsk are examples of units that exercised nonviolent methods of resistance. Through such tactics, they tried to draw public attention to the peaceful nature of Euromaidan protests and made obvious the unjustified violence of the state against peaceful, unarmed people. Women were initiators of peaceful actions and flesh-mobs—such as nonviolent communication with police—in order to prevent clashes and escalation of violence. They performed the function of mediators between conflicting forces. As far as often this communication was under risk of violence, it was decided to place it into the egalitarian gender role scenario. Actually, medical support of Maidan including initiatives such as "Safety transportation" or "Initiative E+," "Hospitals guard" [*Varta v likarni*] could also be perceived as nonviolent peacekeeping initiatives where women played an important role.

Finally, the third scenario combines information and logistics provision of the protest space. There were many other grassroot Euromaidan projects and initiatives, where women were leaders and participants: "Euromaidan SOS" or "Euromaidan SOS Europe" and other hotlines, "Open Maidan University," "Student center," "Civic sector of Maidan," "Єлюди—maidaners" (life stories about people from Maidan), and others. Informational, legal, and educational support also played an important role during protests.

---

[11] Sotnyk: a position of the person who headed the military and administrative-territorial unit called "sotnia" in sixteenth to eighteenth centuries that was elected by the Cossacks-warriors (the structural units of people during the Euromaidan protests were also headed by elected Sotnyks).

Egalitarian scenarios of women's participation in Euromaidan protests support the critical view toward bipolar conceptions of gender power and men's dominance over women. As we could observe from some women's initiatives, women may actively participate in the process of modifying their gender roles. At Euromaidan, women were actively participating in all forms of activities in the protest space. Proposed gender role scenarios could overlap; some women's initiatives could combine features of both of them—patriarchal and egalitarian.

According to Nabers' theory of crisis and change in global politics (Nabers 2015), any transformation of the social boundaries connected to the questions of inclusion and exclusion, power and subordination is engendered by crisis. As crisis might be seen as a source of opportunities, the analysis of the meanings' production and transmission through discourse helps to articulate the social changes. In particular, it clarifies how during the Euromaidan protests meaningful acts of women (creation of units of female protesters, communication of their meanings, and distinctive features) contributed to the shift in discourse and made visible collective attempts of social agents to redefine the role of women amid protests and, therefore, to frame the uncertain moments to claim the need for change of gender order to a more egalitarian one.

Concluding Remarks

Gender roles can be defined as socially expected behavior predefined by values and norms regarding masculinity and femininity. They are internalized by individuals in the processes of differentiated socialization. According to biological deterministic approaches, relationship between men and women is gender polarized and different, as far as based on biological foundation. On the contrary, social constructivist approaches interpret dichotomy in gender roles as culturally and socially constructed, where gender relationships are based on power and inequality that operate both on the institutional and individual levels. The differences between women and men also depend on gender stereotypes embedded in all institutions of the society.

Gender role scenarios are different versions of female and male role performance in particular situations or contexts. Traditional gender roles are based on biologically determined explanations of gender differences and presuppose gendered division of labor—productive labor is expected for men and reproductive—for women. A patriarchal scenario reflects gender polarization (men's and women's roles as opposite) and maintains traditional "women's" roles (serving the needs of the others, revealing empathy and moral support to the other members of society). A patriarchal scenario does not expect agency from women who are dependent on men. An egalitarian scenario presupposes equity of opportunities and rights for men and women, allowing them to independently choose the roles they want to perform. In an egalitarian scenario, women perform more emancipative roles, such as leaders and experts.

Gender roles scenarios could be explained by the macro-picture of gender roles regulation. Results of international reports (e.g. Women in National Parliaments and Global Gender Gap Report) demonstrate the fact that women in Ukraine do not hold egalitarian roles (such as equal participation in decision-making). Ukraine has a rather well-developed legal framework concerning gender issues. However, the declared principles still require the development of the institutional mechanisms. On the micro-level of analysis, it is pointed out that there are gender stereotypes about "lack of women's interest or capability" to succeed in male-dominated politics that could contribute to the reconstruction of "traditional" gender roles and beliefs that women could not perform independently in public area.

In the theoretical literature on gender and nation from Yuval-Davis, women are seen as biological agents of ethnic communities' reproduction, agents of cultural transmission in the processes of socialization. There are diverse opinions on possibilities of gendered scenario performance for women in the process of nation or state building. Scholars such as Zhurzhenko mention the problem of "women's question" subordination to the issue of national liberation struggle while other researchers, such as Bohachevsky-Chomiak, stress that women could use emancipatory democratic potential of the national liberation movement to achieve equal rights.

At the beginning of the peaceful protests, women composed almost half of the protesters (KIIS survey results). However, by February 2014, women were excluded from the protest zone and constituted only a marginal minority among the protesters. The militarization of the protest space reinforced sexist rhetoric and gender segregation in the division of labor among protesters as well as strengthened men's privileges as warriors.

According to our qualitative content analysis of 32 online articles, patriarchal gender role scenarios were explicated via three major female images: Mother, Ukrainian Beauty, and Victim. Women internalized traditional gendered roles and performed them during Euromaidan. Women were mainly among those who provided so-called reproductive labor for Maidan: cleaning, cooking or brining food, caring about clothes, etc. Women were also represented as a "weaker" category (compared to men) expressing need for male's defense and exhibiting admiration for their strength and courage.

At the same time, women had an opportunity to criticize sexism and create alternative initiatives. Egalitarian gender role scenarios were explicated via three major female images: Female Warrior, Peacekeeper, and Information and Logistics Provider. Women were participating in all forms of activities in the protest space. Besides cooking, cleaning, and entertaining, women were fighting on barricades, making negotiations and participating in peacekeeping, providing medical support, maintaining information support, participating in legislative work and logistics, and providing education for protesters and sizable organizational support. During Euromaidan protests, gender roles were reaffirmed (expressing patriarchal gendered scenarios) as well as contested (providing egalitarian scenarios).

References

Beard, M. 2014. "The Public Voice of Women." *London Review of Books* 6 (36): 11–14.

Berger, P. L., and T. Luckmann. 1966. *The Social Construction of Reality. A Treatise on Sociology of Knowledge*. Harmondsworth: Penguin Books.

Brubaker, R. 1996. *Nationalism Reframed: Nationhood and the National Question in the New Europe*. Cambridge: Cambridge University Press.

Connell, R. W. 2002. *Gender*. Cambridge: Polity Press.

Della Porta, D., and M. Diani. 2006. *Social Movements: An Introduction*, 2nd ed. Malden: Blackwell Publishing.

Hankivsky, O. 2012. "Legacies, Opportunities, and Milestones in Post-Soviet Ukraine." In *Gender, Politics, and Society in Ukraine*, edited by O. Hankivsky and A. Salnykova. Toronto: University of Toronto Press.

Hirschmann, N. J. 2006. "Response to Friedman and Brison." *Hypatia* 4 (21): 201–11.

Hrycak, A. 2006. "Foundation Feminism and the Articulation of Hybrid Feminisms in Post-socialist Ukraine." *East European Politics and Societies* 20 (1): 69–100.

Ivanov, O. V. 2013. "Klasychnyy kontent-analiz ta analiz tekstu: terminolohichni ta metodolohichni vidminnosti." In *Visnyk Kharkivs'koho natsional'noho universytetu imeni V. N. Karazina. Sotsiolohichni doslidzhennya suchasnoho suspil'stva: metodolohiya, teoriya, metody* 30 (1045).

Kebalo, M. K. 2007. "Exploring Continuities and Reconciling Ruptures: Nationalism, Feminism, and the Ukrainian Women's Movement." *Aspasia* 1 (1): 36–60.

Khromeychuk, O. 2015. "Gender and Nationalism on the Maidan." In *Ukraine's Euromaidan. Analysis of a Civil Revolution*, edited by D. R. Marples, F. V. Mills, and Ibidem Verlag. New York: Columbia University Press.

Kis, O. 2007. "'Beauty Will Save the World': Feminine Strategies in Ukrainian Politics and the Case of Yulia Tymoshenko." *Spacesofidentity.Net* 7(2). http://pi.library.yorku.ca/ojs/index.php/soi/article/view/7970/7101. Accessed February 12, 2017.

Kis, O. 2012. "(Re)Constructing Ukrainian Women's History: Actors, Authors, and Narratives." In *Gender, Politics, and Society in Ukraine*, edited by O. Hankivsky and A. Salnykova. Toronto: University of Toronto Press.

Krippendorff, K. 2003. *Content Analysis: An Introduction to Its Methodology*. London: Sage.

Kuzio, T., and A. Wilson. 1994. *Ukraine: Perestroika to Independence*. London and New York: St. Martin's Press.

Mann, S. A. 2012. *Doing Feminist Theory. From Modernity to Postmodernity*. Oxford: Oxford University Press.

Martsenyuk, T. 2012. "Ukraine's Other Half: International Women's Day Brings Disappointment and Hope for the Sex Largely Excluded from Power in Kyiv." *The Stanford Post-Soviet Post*. http://postsovietpost.stanford.edu/discussion/ukraines-other-half. Accessed February 12, 2017.

Martsenyuk, T. 2014. "Gender and Revolution in Ukraine: Women's Participation in Euromaidan Protests of 2013–2014." *Perspectives on Europe: War, Sovereignty and Social Change in Ukraine* 44 (2): 15–23.

Nabers, D. 2015. *A Poststructuralist Discourse Theory of Global Politics*. New York: Palgrave Macmillan.

Onuch, O., and T. Martsenyuk. 2014. "Mothers and Daughters of the Maidan: Gender, Repertoires of Violence, and the Division of Labour in Ukrainian Protests." *Social, Health, and Communication Studies Journal* 1 (1): 105–26.

Phillips, S. D. 2014. "The Women's Squad in Ukraine's Protests: Feminism, Nationalism, and Militarism on the Maidan." *American Ethnologist* 41 (3): 414–26.

Plakhotnik, O. 2008. "Postsovetskiy feminizm: ukrainskiy variant." *Gendernyye issledovaniya* 17 (1): 183–98.

Popova, D. 2014. "Seksyzm na Maydani." *Spil'ne: zhurnal sotsial'noyi krytyky*. http://commons.com.ua/seksizm-na-majdani/. Accessed February 12, 2017.

Rubchak, M., ed. 2011. *Mapping Difference: The Many Faces of Women in Contemporary Ukraine*. New York and Oxford: Berghahn Books.

Tilly, C. 2004. *Social Movements*. Boulder: Paradigm Publishers.

Tolstokorova, A. 2012. "Mosaic Model of Gender Democracy in Ukraine." In *Gender, Politics, and Society in Ukraine*, edited by O. Hankivsky and A. Salnykova. Toronto: University of Toronto Press.

Yuval-Davis, N. 1997. *Gender and Nation*. London: Sage.

Zherebkina, I. 1999. "Kto boitsya feminizma v byvshem SSSR?" In *Femina Postsovetica. Ukrainskaya zhenshchina v perekhodnyy period: ot sotsial'nykh dvizheniy k politike*, edited by I. Zherebkina. Khar'kov: KHTSGI. https://www.researchgate.net/profile/Irina_Zherebkina.

Zhurzhenko, T. 2004. "Strong Women, Weak State: Family Politics and Nation Building in Post-Soviet Ukraine." In *Post-Soviet Women Encountering Transition: Nation Building, Economic Survival, and Civic Activism*, edited by K. Kuehnast and C. Nechemias. Washington, DC: Woodrow Wilson Center Press.

Zhurzhenko, T. 2011. "Feminist (De)Constructions of Nationalism in the Post-Soviet Space." In *Mapping Difference: The Many Faces of Women in Contemporary Ukraine*, edited by Marian J. Rubchak. New York and Oxford: Berghahn Books.

Zychowicz, J. 2011. "Two Bad Words: FEMEN & Feminism in Independent Ukraine." *Anthropology of East Europe Review* 29 (2): 215–27.

CHAPTER 7

Memory, War, and Mnemonical In/Security: A Comparison of Lithuania and Ukraine

Dovilė Budrytė

INTRODUCTION

Drawing on the concept of "mnemonical security" (Mälksoo 2015), this chapter will analyze the interaction of discourses associated with World War II and its aftermath and the formation of related cultural, social, and political practices in Ukraine in comparison with Lithuania. The focus will be on what can be considered a hegemonic war memory in the two countries—discourses about the anti-Soviet partisans and their memorialization. It is argued that these memories are intersecting with constructed national traumas that have become known as genocides—Stalinist repressions and deportations in Lithuania, and Holodomor in Ukraine.

"Mnemonical security" is used to describe securitization and consolidation of certain memory discourses that are associated with the processes of "defending" memory and can lead to security dilemmas. In the context of Ukraine, several relevant powerful discourses with related practices could be identified, including a discourse with a focus on the "Great Patriotic War" (World War II) supported by various actors

D. Budrytė (✉)
Political Science, Georgia Gwinnett College, Lawrenceville, USA

© The Author(s) 2018
E. Resende et al. (eds.), *Crisis and Change in Post-Cold War
Global Politics*, https://doi.org/10.1007/978-3-319-78589-9_7

in Russia, and a discourse with a focus on the crimes committed by totalitarian regimes, among others. The contentious discourse about the anti-Soviet partisans intersects with these other discourses, especially the discourse about the "Great Patriotic War," strengthening the borders between "us" and "them" and perpetuating conditions to "defend memory." Thus, by tracing the evolution of discourses about the anti-Soviet partisans and related historical developments, it may be possible to understand the processes of memory politics—especially as they relate to ontological security—and construction of collective identities. Comparisons with similar discourses and their interaction in Lithuania will be made.

In both cases (Lithuania and Ukraine), there was a "crisis of history" that intersected with the disintegration of the Soviet Union in 1991. This was the time when new discourses challenging the legitimacy of the story about the "Great Patriotic war" were created. In both cases, powerful new discourses about anti-Soviet partisans became alternative discourses to the old discourse about the "Great Patriotic war," and eventually these discourses about the anti-Soviet partisans became state-supported discourses, which, coupled with discourses about national genocides, rose to a hegemonic status. These discourses can be described as "fighting and suffering" narratives. In Lithuania, legal acts acknowledging the legitimacy of anti-Soviet resistance were passed in 1999, and in Ukraine, the anti-Soviet resistance fighters—the Organization of Ukrainian Nationalists, or the OUN, and the Ukrainian Insurgent Army, or the UPA—have increasingly received state recognition since the Orange Revolution, most recently in 2015, with the decommunization laws.

In both cases, the institutionalized memory of partisans and national genocides has been constantly challenged and disputed, not only by domestic, but also by international actors, and it has played an important role in the relations between these countries and Russia. My hope is that a comparison of these cases will help to sketch the impulses to "defend memory" (mnemonical in/security) as well as capture the intersections between crisis and memory, as outlined in the post-structuralist and constructivist literature on crisis and change. Pioneered by Jutta Weldes (1999), this literature tends to view crises as "socially constructed openings for change" (Widmaier et al. 2007: 747).

As suggested by Dirk Nabers, crises can be conceptualized as "a qualitative feature of the social" without falling into the trap of endless "crisis management" in international relations (Nabers 2015: 2). Such conceptualization of crises makes ontological security of society relevant to a better understanding of social change. Nabers views crisis as "a permanent attribute of the social, not some momentary condition that surfaces from time to time" (Nabers 2015: 2). To him, crisis of the social is linked to the "transformation of the social," and therefore, it becomes important to ask "what the social must look like for crisis to become possible" (Nabers 2015: 3).

Nabers suggests a clear structure for empirical investigations of relations between crisis and change. He argues that the articulation of a particular political crisis must "in some way be connected to sedimented practices to be credible" (Nabers 2015: 146–147). After the crisis is articulated, there is "a competition between different political forces to hegemonize the political field, resulting in the acceptance of a certain interpretative framework of identification (actual hegemony) and its eventual routinization and political institutionalization. This final act of institutionalization causes feedback effects on the discursive articulation of the crisis, new interpretative frames start to compete, and politics continues" (Nabers 2015: 147). Following this framework, crisis is an "engine" of discourses, and politics is constantly linked to identity struggles.

The analysis below is inspired by Nabers' framework, tracing the articulation of the crisis of history that occurred with the disintegration of the Soviet Union, and the struggles for hegemonic war memory that continued. Prior to starting empirical analysis, the following section will explore the concept of "defending memory" and relate it to the framework of crisis and change. Having briefly reviewed relevant works on war memory in Ukraine and Lithuania, the other sections will focus on empirical analysis, tracing "the competition between different political forces to hegemonize the political field" (Nabers 2015: 147), the emergence of hegemonic memory about the anti-Soviet partisans, its routinization, political institutionalization, and continued contestation. In addition to surveying attempts to create hegemonic mnemonic discourses in national politics, I will also trace the developments related to public debates about monuments and memorialization of anti-Soviet partisans.

Methodologically, this chapter engages a comparative method, comparing "defending memory" discourses related to anti-Soviet partisans used in Lithuania and Ukraine. Although the status of two states is different (with Lithuania being the member of the European Union and NATO), they have been engaged in memory wars related to World War II and its aftermath with Russia. In both cases, it is possible to discern powerful discourses that present the armed anti-Soviet resistance in a very positive light, as essential to sovereignty, and often tend to leave out less heroic aspects of these fights, such as the involvement of some of the fighters in the Holocaust. These discourses that "defend memory" have intersected with others, sometimes feeding into domestic and international memory wars. Furthermore, there have been attempts in both cases to democratize history by debunking myths about heroic timeless anti-Soviet struggle and acknowledging the crimes of the past.

Mnemonical In/Security, Crisis, and Change

In her article "'Memory Must be Defended': Beyond the Politics of Mnemonical Security," Maria Mälksoo has described "the securitization of memory," a phenomenon that is common in Eastern and Central Europe and beyond. In many contexts, especially Ukrainian–Russian and Baltic–Russian relations, historical remembrance is a security issue. These actors (the states) are creating biographical narratives, and these processes of narrative creation are inseparable from historical remembrance. Biographical narratives provide these communities with "a sense of being in the world by situating them in an experienced space and an envisioned space, ordered from a particular place and delineated through horizons of experience and of possibility, respectively." (Berenskoetter 2014: 282). Thus, biographical narratives are sources of security and guides in interactions with other states. They are likely to be simplified stories where some memories are left out, and others highlighted. No matter how carefully constructed, the narratives will include tensions and contradictions that political agents will try to hide, but these tensions and contradictions can be revealed by others, thus triggering contestation of story lines (Berenskoetter 2014: 280).

Such phenomena can lead to new security dilemmas and negatively affect the sense of security of the involved parties. "Our" narrative, "our" past is viewed as being completely misunderstood and distorted by the "Others," whose own vision of the past is seen as a danger to "our" existence. Thus, it becomes critical to defend "our" memory, which is essential to the survival of "our" state. As explained by Maria Mälksoo, similar dynamic can be detected in the interactions between Russia and its former satellites in Eastern Europe in relation to their interpretations of World War II. Constant attempts to "defend memory" become inseparable from insecurity and ongoing animosity (Mälksoo 2012: 178–179).

Conceptualized in this way, mnemonical in/security becomes essential to the study of crises in international relations. The study of mnemonical in/security is inseparable from the study of the construction of biographical narratives of the states. As argued by Felix Berenskoetter, it is important to understand who "has the authority to create a hegemonic master narrative and how/under what conditions alternative narratives emerge, capable of challenging and replacing, or significantly altering, the master narrative" (Berenskoetter 2014: 280). The construction of state narratives is "an active and elaborate process" with multiple agents, both domestic and international, involved, and the narrative becomes hegemonic when "a critical mass of social actors accepts it and buys into it as a social fact" (Subotić 2016: 615).

WAR MEMORY IN UKRAINE AND LITHUANIA: INTERNATIONAL AND DOMESTIC DISCOURSES

Many authors have pointed out the importance of World War II and the postwar era discourses in the developments surrounding the current crisis in Ukraine and acrimonious memory wars between Kyiv and Moscow that have accompanied it. For example, Tatiana Zhurzhenko argued that "the reinterpretation of the Second World War and its role in Ukrainian history is directly linked to the 'postcolonial' search for national identity and the problem of geopolitical choice between Russia and the West" (Zhurzhenko 2015a: 171). In another article, she traced the beginning of the current memory wars to 2005, when the 60th anniversary of the end of World War II became a "loyalty test" conducted by Moscow of its former satellites. Since then, according to Zhurzhenko, a new sort of memory politics have emerged, in which hard (military) power is intersecting with the use of discourses related to World War II (Zhurzhenko 2015b).

As recently noted by Andreas Umland (2017), the discourses defending the OUN and the UPA in Ukraine have played and will continue to play a negative role in Ukraine's relations with the West. Russia often uses these discourses to "prove" that "fascism" is alive in Ukraine. Although the two organizations fought the Soviet domination in Ukraine, their collaboration with the Nazi occupying forces and participation in the Holocaust are often obscured. Umland is especially critical of discourses produced by the Ukrainian government's memory institute (The Ukrainian Institute for National Remembrance, or UINP), which, in his words, "has coupled its current decommunization campaign with a comprehensive nationalization and partial 'Banderization' drive in public remembrance and official discourse" (Umland 2017). The UINP cooperates with an NGO called Center for Research into the Liberation Movement, or TsDVR, which, according to Umland, "presents the wartime Ukrainian ultra-nationalist movement as the pinnacle of Ukrainian patriotism and love of freedom" (Umland 2017).

Similarly, the participation in the Holocaust of some of the anti-Soviet Lithuanian partisans is an extremely painful topic, and it has been part of Lithuanian–Russian relations and local Lithuanian domestic memory wars. The publication of Rūta Vanagaitė's book *Mūsiškiai (Ours)* (2016) was one of them. In this book, the author has openly acknowledged that her own relative, a former widely respected anti-Soviet resistance fighter, has also participated in the Holocaust. Her book brought the issue of the participation in the Holocaust home through its title. *Mūsiškiai* is the Lithuanian first person plural possessive pronoun, "ours," which in this case signifies "our people." In writing a popular book about Lithuanian Holocaust perpetrators, calling them "our own kind," Vanagaitė revealed the experience of the Holocaust in the national memory of ethnic Lithuanians (Davoliūtė 2016). Moreover, by noting that one of her own relatives participated in the murder of Jews, Vanagaitė told a moving personal story. The book was wildly popular: 2500 copies were sold in several days in the country of three million people, and it was number-one bestseller for several weeks in a row (Makhotina 2016). Yet this book did cause an eruption of a scandal, with many public figures denouncing her for factual errors and even "betrayal."

Most recently, in October 2017, statements made by Rūta Vanagaitė became the focus of another memory war. Vanagaitė made several inflammatory statements about Adolfas Ramanauskas-Vanagas (no relation), a prominent leader of the Lithuanian anti-Soviet partisans. Specifically, she suggested that he may have cooperated with the Soviet secret police and may have even participated in the Holocaust. These statements were immediately discredited by historians who have researched the anti-Soviet resistance, and Vanagaitė was widely criticized. Alma Littera, Vanagaitė's publisher, announced that it was ending its relationship with her and recalling her books from stores. Vanagaitė apologized publically for her remarks, but this did not change the public attitude toward her.

Even a glimpse at such memory wars raise further questions, such as: How did this contentious memory about anti-Soviet partisans become state-supported war memory? What has happened to other war memories? How is memory about anti-Soviet partisans institutionalized and routinized, and what are the sources of resistance?

FROM A MEMORY CRISIS TO "DEFENDING MEMORY": THE EMERGENCE OF "FIGHTING AND SUFFERING" MEMORY DISCOURSES IN LITHUANIA AND UKRAINE

Lithuania

The Soviet and German occupations during World War II, the anti-Soviet resistance and its repression through mass deportations after World War II have become pivotal traumatic events with a long-lasting impact on political identities in Lithuania. The losses resulting from these traumatic events were substantial. According to the Genocide and Resistance Research Center of Lithuania (a state institution), during the Holocaust, 240,000 people (200,000 Jews) were killed. In 1944–1953, during the second Soviet occupation (the first one was in 1940–1941), 186,000 were arrested or imprisoned, and 118,000 were deported. An estimated number of 20,500 anti-Soviet partisans and their families were killed during an intense war of anti-Soviet resistance. Many of those who were deported after World War II were either active anti-Soviet resistance fighters themselves or related to someone who was an active resistance fighter (Genocide and Resistance Research Center of Lithuania, n.d.-a).

It is estimated that during 1944–1953, there were at least 50,000 active anti-Soviet resistance fighters (partisans) in Lithuania. If one includes those who provided them with various kinds of assistance (messengers and reserve fighters), this number increases to 100,000. Following the mass deportations of 1949 and the successful collectivization of agriculture, the partisan movement lost many of its supporters. This movement ended in the early 1950s (Genocide and Resistance Research Center of Lithuania, n.d.-a).

Soviet authorities in Lithuania vilified resistance fighters as "bandits" and "enemies of the state" (Girnius 1990: I). Some of them had cooperated with the Germans before joining the anti-Soviet resistance, and such cases were highlighted in the public sphere to discredit the whole anti-Soviet partisan movement. In the late 1980s, however, the tide has reversed, and the anti-Soviet resistance fighters became heroes. The national revival movement in Soviet Lithuania even used the same name as the anti-Soviet armed resistance in 1949, "Sajūdis."

After the restoration of independence in 1991, there was a clear focus on the losses experienced during the Soviet occupations. The German occupation, including the Holocaust, received less attention. Initially, the focus of remembrances and commemoration was on repression and mass deportations under Stalin that started to be called genocide. The term was borrowed from the Lithuanian diaspora, which had used it to gain political currency during the Cold War.

Deportations and repressions by the Soviet Union became the backbone of the "fighting and suffering" memory discourse created in Lithuania shortly before it regained its independence from the Soviet Union in 1991. According to the Web site of the Genocide and Resistance Research Center of Lithuania, approximately 156,000 individuals were imprisoned in the USSR during the period of 1941–1958, and 131,600 were deported to approximately 2500 places in the former USSR during 1940–1953 (Genocide and Resistance Research Center of Lithuania, n.d.-b).

The lifting of censorship during Gorbachev's *glasnost* in the late 1980s resulted in the surge of popular interest in historical issues, including deportations and repressions that took place in 1941 and after World War II, anti-Soviet resistance and its suppression. The memoirs of deportees, many of whom were anti-Soviet resistance fighters and their supporters, played a critical role in unveiling the crimes of the Stalinist regime and articulating the widespread suffering that took place in Lithuania. In addition, there were many commemorative events in various parts of Lithuania focusing on various types of suffering experienced during the Soviet times.

The initial process of coming to terms with the past in the late 1980s was dominated by various non-state actors that fought together with Sajūdis, such as the Freedom League of Lithuania and the Union of Political Prisoners and Deportees of Lithuania. These non-state groups publicized Soviet crimes through mass rallies, public events, and publications, and used the term "genocide" to refer to deportations and repression under Stalin. This was a way to condemn the Soviet regime.

"Genocide" later became part of a name used by a state-supported memory institution, the Genocide and Resistance Research Center of Lithuania, and its subsidiary, the Museum of Genocide Victims.[1]

Around the same time, in the late 1990s, the Lithuanian state started to institutionalize the memory of anti-Soviet resistance fighters. In 1997, a new memory day entered Lithuania's national calendar: the Day of the (anti-Soviet) Partisans (the fourth Sunday in May). In 1999, the Lithuanian parliament voted to make a declaration to defend the sovereignty of Lithuania that was signed by anti-Soviet resistance fighters in 1949 a "legal document," thus emphasizing the importance of the anti-Soviet resistance for post-Soviet Lithuanian identity. In 2009, the Lithuanian parliament announced 2009 as the year of Lithuania's freedom fighters, and revisited the 1949 declaration as "essential to the Lithuanian statehood."

In the twenty-first century, the partisan war and its official memorialization are fully accepted by government institutions and political parties. For example, in the exhibition introducing the Lithuanian statehood opened in 2016 in the Presidential palace, there is a section on the history of anti-Soviet partisans. This history is presented as an "integral history of the Lithuanian statehood" (Petrauskienė 2017: 39).

Starting in the late 1980s, the "fighting and suffering" narrative elicited strong counter-narratives, both in Lithuania and abroad. Even during the initial stages of democratization, in the mid- and late 1980s, some historians and journalists started to write about the attacks of anti-Soviet resistance fighters against the civilians and other sensitive issues, such as betrayal and the collaboration of some of the anti-Soviet resistance fighters with Nazi Germany during World War II. Other works were written later, including a recent essay "Ką pagerbė Lietuva— partizanų vadą Generolą Vėtrą ar žydų žudiką" [Who Did Lithuania Honor: The Partisan Commander General Vėtra or a Jew Killer?] by Rimvydas Valatka, a journalist (Valatka 2015).

In 2015, the monument to this partisan commander placed on the wall of the Lithuanian Academy of Sciences has become the site of public controversy. The partisan commander Generolas Vėtra, a famous anti-Soviet fighter, who worked in the Lithuanian Academy of Sciences

---

[1]In September 2017, a consensus was reached to rename this Museum to get rid of the term "genocide." The new proposed name for the museum is "The Museum of Occupations and Freedom Fights."

in 1945–1946, has also collaborated with the Nazis by signing a decree ordering the moving of the Jews to ghettos. In the recent past, as the memory of anti-Soviet partisans was institutionalized by the Lithuanian state, this fact of his biography was obscured, and he even was awarded state honors posthumously. Despite the public outcry, the monument is still in place, but the debates surrounding it demonstrated challenges to the hegemonic "fighting and suffering" narrative.

However, despite these challenges, the "fighting and suffering" narrative is still popular. It appears that the recent tensions in relations to Russia, with Russia's growing assertiveness, have even increased its appeal. Stories about heroism of anti-Soviet resistance fighters appear to increase in popularity as insecurity has increased after the Russian occupation of the Crimea in 2014. During the same year, "The Invisible Front," a film about anti-Soviet partisans created by Jonas Ohman, a Swedish documentary maker residing in Lithuania, and Vincas Sruoginis, a Lithuanian American, drew crowds and was especially popular among young Lithuanians. Similarly, a short film about the "forest brothers" (anti-Soviet partisans) in the Baltic states created by NATO in 2017 and distributed via social media became wildly popular in Lithuania.[2] This film established a connection between the irregular warfare strategies used by the anti-Soviet partisans and the current preparations for irregular warfare by special forces in the Baltic states. It received an angry reaction from Russia's Ministry of Foreign Affairs, whose spokeswoman referred to the Baltic anti-Soviet partisans as "unfinished fascists." Thousands of Internet users from Lithuania, Latvia, Estonia, and Ukraine immediately started "defending history" by opposing the remarks of the spokeswoman. This incident demonstrates the lasting popularity of the heroic narrative about the anti-Soviet resistance.

Ukraine

As in Lithuania, the topic of anti-Soviet partisans in Ukraine remains controversial and capable of eliciting very powerful public emotions. Rethinking and reconceptualizing the Soviet past in general, and anti-Soviet resistance as well as Holodomor, became the most visible problems of Ukraine's memory politics after the disintegration of the

---

[2] This video "Forest Brothers—Fight for the Baltics" is available at: https://www.youtube.com/watch?v=h5rQFp7FF9c.

Soviet Union. Holodomor, the Soviet and German occupations during World War II, the anti-Soviet resistance and its repression through mass deportations after World War II have also become pivotal traumatic events with a long-lasting impact on political identities in Ukraine. Undoubtedly, human losses associated with these historical developments were substantial. It is estimated (although there is still some debate about the exact numbers) that Ukraine lost approximately 4 million during the Holodomor, 6.5–7.4 million during World War II, and 400,000 during the postwar famine and Stalin's campaign against the anti-Soviet partisans in Western Ukraine. In addition to these losses, there were deportations to Central Asia and Far East (Liber 2016: 5).

Similarly to Lithuania, the questions about the anti-Soviet partisans some of whom were also involved in the Holocaust became an intractable "memory problem" and even a source of domestic and international tensions. A lot has been written about the "OUN-UPA problem" in Ukraine. The OUN was a nationalist underground organization founded in 1929 in Vienna whose goal was to establish an independent Ukrainian state during the interwar period. The UPA was a resistance movement associated with the establishment of a Ukrainian nation-state which was active in Western Ukraine. It fought against both Nazi and Soviet forces. Historians have noted the collaboration of the OUN-UPA with Nazi Germany and its involvement in crimes against civilians; including Jews and Poles (e.g., see Marples 2010). The OUN-UPA fought against the Soviet Union after World War II, and this is one of the reasons for the development of the OUN-UPA "cult" in Ukraine (especially Western Ukraine). The involvement of this organization in the killing of the Jews often is obscured or minimized by those who lionize these organizations.

As argued by David R. Marples, the topic of anti-Soviet partisans "continues to divide Ukraine," as Western regions of Ukraine tend to embrace the "cult" of Stepan Bandera, while east and south oppose it (Marples 2010: 26). Qualitative research conducted in Galicia (Western Ukraine) reveals further divisions in the families, where at least one grandparent came from Eastern Ukraine or Russia (Wylegała 2017: 783). However, after the 2014 Euromaidan event, there is a clear tendency of rehabilitate historical figures associated with the OUN-UPA, including Stepan Bandera. Negative attitudes toward these heroes have even subsided over time (Shevel 2016: 259), which is a change from the late 1980s and early 1990s, when, in the wake of the disintegration of the Soviet Union, the OUN-UPA fighters were still described in mass media as "bourgeois nationalists" and "the worst enemies" of the Ukrainian nation (Marples 2010: 27). Thus, similarly to the Lithuanian case, it appears that the changes in security environment after 2014 have coincided with the increase in support for the anti-Soviet fighters.

If deportations and repressions conducted during the time of Stalin have been regarded as genocide by many Lithuanians—and thus have constituted a collective historical trauma—the famine of 1932–1933, or Holodomor, has served this function in Ukraine. First and foremost, this event, which entailed the deaths of several million people and enormous suffering, must be acknowledged as a historical trauma of enormous proportions. At the same time, as shown by many studies conducted by scholars who study memory politics, every historical trauma requires cultural memory work to become part of collective consciousness. This memory work can involve attempts to "defend memory." As explained by Georgyi Kasianov, "periodically, the strong emotional charge of the problem even brings out a measure of social hysteria, and in that context scholarly appeals for a sober and rational examination of the question may be regarded (and often are regarded by a segment of the public) as a challenge to public opinion or as a show of disrespect for the memory of victims" (Kasianov 2008: 201–2).

As demonstrated by Per Rudling, preoccupation with Holodomor as Ukrainian genocide is relatively recent, and it dates back to the 1970s. In 1983, a campaign to commemorate the 50th anniversary of Holodomor was organized, and since then this traumatic event became an "identity marker" for the Ukrainian diaspora (Rudling 2011a: 751). As several other chapters in this volume suggest (see Buhari-Gulmez's and Nikolko's chapters in this volume), traumatic events are capable of mobilizing diasporas and playing an important role in identity politics.

The Ukrainian diaspora in the West (especially in Canada) was responsible for the development of the "fighting and suffering regime," in which the OUN and the UPA were portrayed as brave heroes who died for an independent Ukrainian state, and Holodomor was constructed into a major Ukrainian national trauma. The construction of this memory discourse included creation of narratives focusing on monumental "national" traumas and building of monuments to commemorate Holodomor and resistance fighters (e.g., a monument to Roman Shukhevych in Edmonton, Canada, and a monument to the Ukrainian war veterans also in Edmonton) (Rudling 2011a).

Rudling documented the influence of the Ukrainian diaspora on the formation of memory discourses in independent Ukraine. Even though the

Ukrainian diaspora did not exert significant influence on politics in Ukraine after the disintegration of the USSR, it made an impact on the formation of memory politics, especially related to the construction of monumental national traumas. The influence of the Ukrainian diaspora was especially pronounced after 2004, the Orange Revolution, which strengthened the construction of new national myths (Rudling 2011b: 24). In the case of Lithuania, its Western diaspora was very influential in both politics and the formation of memory discourses. The use of the term "genocide" to describe the Stalinist deportations and repressions was also started by the Lithuanian diaspora, and later this term was adopted by politicians and historians in Lithuania after it regained its independence in 1991.

In Ukraine, *glasnost* has also unleashed a wave of popular interest in similar topics, including the crimes of the Soviet regime, Holodomor, and the anti-Soviet resistance. As in Lithuania, many former Communists became nationalists and, as explained by Kasianov, "with no less zeal than their recent opponents (nationalists), set about publically condemning the 'crimes of the totalitarian regime', thereby neutralizing possible accusations against themselves" (Kasianov 2008: 1999). During *glasnost*, mass consciousness (related to the former Communist crimes) changed as more and more people became aware of the Stalinist crimes. The discourse of Holodomor as a crime of the Stalin regime became part of public discussions, and it was an important instrument in Narodnyi Ruch's program to delegitimize the Soviet regime (Zhurzhenko 2011: 601). Similarly to Lithuania, the term "genocide" was already used in debates related to the Soviet crimes (in the case of Ukraine, Holodomor), but in the words of Tatiana Zhurzhenko, "without special emphasis." Chernobyl nuclear disaster and Holodomor were among the collective traumas that were used in opposition to the Soviet rule.

However, it would probably be erroneous to assert that the period of *glasnost* led to the emergence of a coherent hegemonic memory discourse in Ukraine. As argued by Andryi Portnov (2013: 235), most dramatic changes related to memory politics during early post-Soviet years took place in East Galicia and Western Ukraine, the areas which were annexed by the USSR in 1939 (later than other territories). This region is where the statues of Lenin were replaced by monuments to the leaders of the Ukrainian nationalist movements, including Stepan Bandera and Roman Shukhevych. Meanwhile, there were no systematic attempts in Eastern and Southern Ukrainian cities to drastically change memory landscape.

Interestingly, even when memorials to Ukrainian nationalist leaders were built in Western Ukraine, they coexisted with monuments erected to the Soviet soldiers who, according to Portnov, were "neither dismantled not vandalized" (Portnov 2013: 237). Instead, sculptures of the Virgin Mary, a Catholic symbol, mourning the deaths of the soldiers, were added in these sites. Such pluralism in the sites of memory attests to the "contingent and multivectored nature" of memory politics in Ukraine during the transition period (Portnov 2013: 238; see also Portnov 2008). During the same time, the sites associated with the commemoration of World War II ("the Great Patriotic war"), such as the IX fort in Kaunas or a monument to the fallen Soviet soldiers in Gargždai remained intact in Lithuania as well, but these sites became marginal in national memory landscape which was consumed with commemoration of Stalinist deportations (the "Soviet genocide") and war of anti-Soviet resistance.

A COMPARISON OF MEMORY DISCOURSES

It appears that in 2017, there are some important similarities between leading memory discourses in Lithuania and Ukraine. In both cases, we can detect discourses associated with "defending memory" of the anti-Soviet resistance fighters and discourses of victimization related to "national genocides." In both cases, political developments described as "revolutions" (Sąjūdis in Lithuania, the Orange Revolution and Euromaidan in Ukraine) have coincided with major discursive changes regarding memory politics. However, it appears that there are differences in the timing and conditions that surrounded the emergence of these memory discourses. In the case of Lithuania, the contours of the "fighting and suffering" memory discourse focused on the narratives about the anti-Soviet fighters and mass deportations and repressions emerged during *perestroika*, as the Soviet Union was disintegrating.

It is fair to suggest that similar themes, genocide and anti-Soviet resistance, became prominent in Ukraine only after the Orange Revolution and Euromaidan. During the protests associated with Euromaidan, banners with the images of Stepan Bandera, the leader of the anti-Soviet resistance, were flown, and songs associated with the anti-Soviet resistance were sung.

Prior to President Yushchenko's memory politics focusing on Holodomor, there were some rather ineffective attempts to address the controversial memories of UPA. President Kuchma, who was elected in 1994, tried to do his best to avoid the topic of the UPA in all of his speeches during May 9 (which marks the end of the Great Patriotic War) celebrations. It is noteworthy that during his administration a commission to study the OUN and UPA was created in 1997. Its final conclusions were published in 2005, already during the times of the Orange Revolution, and they supported official recognition of the UPA fighters "as veterans of the Second World War" (Portnov 2013: 239). The findings of this commission did not result in proclaiming the former UPA fighters as "veterans of the Second World War," thus demonstrating how complicated this problem has been in Ukrainian memory politics. This is in contrast to the developments in Lithuania, where the beginning of the process of rehabilitation of the former resistance fighters started with the reestablishment of the Lithuanian statehood in 1991, and, as noted earlier in this paper, in 1999 the Lithuanian state attempted to link itself to the anti-Soviet resistance movement by officially honoring a partisan declaration from 1949.

In Lithuania (as in Ukraine), attempts to rehabilitate anti-Soviet resistance fighters coincided with domestic and international tensions. In the early 1990s, when the process was taking place, the Lithuanian bureaucracy was still in its infancy and was not able (or perhaps even willing) to conduct careful investigations of all former resistance fighters, deportees, and their supporters, all of whom were considered to be victims of the Soviet regime. In addition, there was a strong urge from many members of society to "defend" a newly constructed memory about the evils of the Soviet regime and show respect to the victims. Thus, by spring 1991 the Law on the Reconstitution of Legal Rights of the People Repressed for the Resistance to Occupation Regimes (2 May 1990) rehabilitated over 50,000 people[3] (Geleževičius 2003: 10), some of whom have participated in the Holocaust (Geleževičius 2003: 14). There was strong criticism of these rehabilitations by international actors, including the ones based in the USA and Israel. In response, in 1991, the Lithuanian government rejected 500 requests for rehabilitation as a proof that it was not pursuing "indiscriminate rehabilitation" by

---

[3] This information is from the Web site of the Genocide and Resistance Research Center of Lithuania. "The Armed Anti-Soviet Resistance in Lithuania in 1944–1953," Genocide and Resistance Research Center of Lithuania (2017), http://genocid.lt/centras/en/2390/a/ and see "Tremties ir kalinimo vietos," http://genocid.lt/centras/lt/1491/a/.

rehabilitating those who participated in genocide and killing of unarmed civilians (Pettai and Pettai 2015: 178).

This resistance to "indiscriminate rehabilitation" of the anti-Soviet resistance fighters may have been linked to the rise of the so-called double genocide theory. According to this "theory," there were two major genocides in Lithuania, the Soviet one (consisting of deportations and repressions) and the Holocaust. Both were extremely tragic events, and, according to some defenders of memory, they should be even viewed as equal. Yet some proponents of this "theory" took the argument even further than merely asserting that there were two equally tragic developments in Lithuania. They argued that some Lithuanian Jews supported the occupying Soviet forces, and those Lithuanians who were participating in the Holocaust, were retaliating for the losses experienced during the first Soviet occupation. In other words, some Jews were participating in the "Soviet genocide" against the Lithuanians. Needless to say, this "theory" is flawed on many different levels. However, it did reflect a relatively popular way of thinking in the mid- and late 1990s.

In the case of Ukraine, attempts to rehabilitate the OUN-UPA can be traced back to the period of *glasnost* when such discussions started to take place. In April 1991, the Ukrainian parliament adopted the law "On the rehabilitation of victims of political repressions in Ukraine." However, this law did not include the UPA as a group to be rehabilitated, and Article 2 of the law prohibited those who were sentenced for "betraying the motherland" and similar crimes, thus making the former members of the UPA ineligible for rehabilitation (Shevel 2011: 148). The OUN and UPA members were explicitly mentioned in 1993 in the law of "On the status of war veterans and guarantees of their social protection." This law mentioned those UPA fighters "who took part in the armed struggle against the German occupiers in 1941–1944, and who did not commit crimes against peace and humanity, and who were rehabilitated under the 1991 law on victims of political repression" (Shevel 2011: 149–150). As explained by Oxana Shevel, the 1993 law did not solve the issue of OUN-UPA fighters because fighting against the Soviet state "was by itself sufficient to disqualify the person from veteran status, even if that person did not commit war crimes" (Shevel 2011: 150). In 2000–2009, there were many legislative initiatives aimed at giving formal status to the OUN-UPA, including social protection, but they were not successful.

Yet there were other initiatives to lionize the OUN-UPA during the same time. In June 2007, President Yushchenko officially celebrated the 100th year anniversary of UPA commander Roman Shukhevych, and shortly after it named Shukhevych a posthumous Hero of Ukraine. Yushchenko also started commemorating Yaroslav Stetsko, who was the leader of the Ukrainian government proclaimed in 1941. In 2010, Yushchenko made Stepan Bandera a posthumous Hero of Ukraine, and called on local governments to name schools, streets, and squares after the leaders of the OUN-UPA. Arguably, as this memory discourse of fighting and suffering was gaining strength (with Holodomor being part of suffering), the memory of the Holocaust was obfuscated (Himka 2012: 219). Similarly to the developments in Lithuania, there were negative international reactions to the discourses focusing on fighting and suffering. For example, in 2008, Yad Vashem expressed concerns about the commemoration of Roman Shukhevych and demanded that his hero status was revoked. In response to Yushchenko's decision to make Stepan Bandera "the hero of Ukraine," there were protests from the chief rabbi of Ukraine and the Polish government. Timothy Snyder described this development as "ma[king] a hero of a long-dead Ukrainian fascist" (Snyder 2010).

Yet these protests did not seem to have a profound effect on historical consciousness of some Ukrainians who have continued to lionize the OUN and UPA. As explained by Snyder, Stepan Bandera remains "for some Ukrainians a symbol of the struggle for independence during the twentieth century" (Snyder 2010). This is despite Bandera's support for one-party fascist dictatorship without national minorities, and the fact that his supporters were engaged in killing of Jews and Poles. As in the case of Lithuania, structural political changes appear to be related to increased support for nationalist myths. The attempts to create nationalist mythology separate from the Soviet past, drawing on the OUN and UPA, intensified after the Orange Revolution and during and after the Euromaidan. After the 2014 uprising, the Ukrainian government has definitely taken decisive steps to demonstrate a movement away from the Russian influence.

The four decommunization laws adopted in May 2015 are a case in point. Prepared in cooperation with the Ukrainian Institute of National Memory (created under President Yushchenko), these laws have once again attempted to rehabilitate the wartime Ukrainian nationalist leaders, including Stepan Bandera. Similarly to the Lithuanian case, the laws include a condemnation of the communist and nationalist socialist regimes and prohibition of propaganda of their symbols and the replacement of the Soviet term "The Great Patriotic War" with the Second World War. May 8th was established as a day to remember the end of World War II. "The recognition of fighters for the Ukrainian independence in the twentieth century" has been probably one of the most controversial laws, as it gave this status to the OUN and the UPA and forbade "public display of disrespectful attitudes" toward the well-known independence fighters and "public denial of the legitimacy of the struggle for Ukraine's independence in the twentieth century" (Shevel 2016: 261). Thus, these laws embody attempts to "defend history."

As in the case of Lithuania, the complicated geopolitical situation and increasingly assertive Russian foreign policy (especially after the occupation of Crimea in 2014) seem to be correlated with increased support for nationalist mythology about anti-Soviet resistance and suffering. For example, in 2010, 60% of people nationwide in Ukraine viewed Holodomor as genocide against the Ukrainian people (Shevel 2016: 259). By September 2015, this percentage increased to 81%, and according to Oxana Shevel, "it was a majority view in every region of Ukraine," though admittedly there were some regional differences (Shevel 2016: 259). Given this set of circumstances, is it possible to identify any significant changes in the memory landscape, challenges to the hegemonic portrayal of the anti-Soviet resistance fighters? Could the recent 2016 attempts to commemorate the 75th anniversary of Babi Yar in Ukraine and the public march to commemorate the victims of the Holocaust in Molėtai in Lithuania be a start of different memory politics?

In 2016, commemorations of one of the worst tragedies that marked the beginning of the "final solution" in September 1941 in Kyiv included many commemorative activities and many international actors, both governmental and non-governmental. The attention that this anniversary has attracted from the government of Ukraine and even the public was different from the usual victimization (seeing themselves as victims, first from the Soviets, and then from the Nazis; this view is common in Lithuania as well). Prior to the commemoration activities, in December 2015 President Poroshenko addressed the Israeli Knesset, asking for forgiveness:

> We must remember the negative events in history, when collaborators helped the Nazis seek the Final Solution. Following its establishment, Ukraine asked for forgiveness, and I am doing it now at the Israeli Knesset in front of the children and grandchildren of victims of the Holocaust, who experienced that horror first hand. I am doing this in front of all the citizens of Israel. (quoted in Tabarovsky 2016)

In Lithuania, public willingness to learn about the Holocaust and participation in commemorative activities have also increased recently, partially as a result of the activities of non-state actors. In 2016, there was a march in Molėtai to honor the memory of Jews of this small town murdered during the Holocaust.[4] Inspired by Marius Ivaškevičius, a famous playwright and attended by thousands, this march triggered soul-searching and discussions about the roles that ordinary Lithuanians played during the Holocaust. An official apology to the Israeli Knesset was issued by President Brazauskas as early as 1995; however, this gesture did not receive a lot of domestic support at that time.

It remains to be seen whether these attempts to commemorate the Holocaust and admission of guilt can challenge the hegemonic accounts of heroic anti-Soviet partisan resistance, consistent with what Burakovskiy (2011) has described as the perception of history as a "battle for liberation." This is not to deny or obscure the important attempts to democratize the Ukrainian and Lithuanian histories and adopt more critical views of the past. Examples include academic work, including a suggestion by a commission of historians to democratize historical memory from 2007 until 2009, when twelve historians from various regions of Ukraine led by Natalia Yakovenko discussed the results of their review of the textbooks and proposed the content for a future history textbook. Yakovenko and colleagues proposed a different approach to history: Viewing it not through a national prism, but through the prism of individuals and groups who lived in the territory of today's Ukraine. Instead of conceptualizing the Ukrainian nation as a live being which needs to be "defended," the proposal was to "treat the social life of all communities on Ukrainian territories… as an inseparable part of the Ukrainian history" (quoted in Shevel 2011: 158). Similar attempts to deconstruct the myth about an "organic" Lithuanian nation have been made by historians and political scientists in Lithuania as well, reconceptualizing and rewriting the Lithuanian history from multicultural perspectives. Admittedly, it is much more difficult to politicize such stories and reduce them to myths about heroism and suffering which occurs when states feel ontologically insecure and try to create biographical narratives that inspire loyalty.

---

[4] There was a death march in Molėtai in 1941, when the entire Jewish community was killed by the Nazis and their local collaborators.

Concluding Remarks

This essay has attempted to compare various trajectories of "defending history" discourses related to anti-Soviet partisans and national traumas described as genocides in Lithuania and Ukraine. In both cases of Lithuania and Ukraine, there was a "crisis of history" which coincided with the disintegration of the USSR when the account about the "Great Patriotic war" popularized by the Soviet government lost its legitimacy. In both cases, discourses about anti-Soviet partisans and national sufferings became hegemonic, state-supported narratives. These discourses became essential for identities of Lithuania and Ukraine, and they became an important part of interactions with Russia.

The analysis presented in this essay suggests that political developments described as "revolutions" (Sąjūdis in Lithuania, the Orange Revolution and Euromaidan in Ukraine) have coincided with major discursive changes regarding memory politics. It is during those times that narratives extolling the virtues of anti-Soviet partisans and dwelling on losses associated with national tragedies, described as genocides, have attracted more supporters willing to "defend history." However, this interpretation of such political developments does not suggest that the multidimensional nature of memory can be erased. As demonstrated by a brief analysis of politics of monuments in Ukraine and Lithuania, different monuments to different heroes can coexist in the same landscape, even during the most polarized political times. In addition, hegemonic memory narratives have produced strong counter-narratives opposing heroic portrayal of anti-Soviet partisans, thus perpetuating contestation and, as explained by post-structuralist perspectives on crisis and change, continuing politics.

This comparative analysis of the two cases enriches post-structuralist and constructivist accounts on crises and change by demonstrating how crises yield opportunities for memories to be challenged and defended. During Sąjūdis in Lithuania and Euromaidan in Ukraine, when major discursive changes related to memory politics took place, and new hegemonic historical accounts were created, another development followed—the determination to defend these newly created historical accounts. In both cases, these impulses to defend memory were inseparable from the feelings of security. Understanding this securitization of memory is essential for relations between "us" and "them"—not only domestically, but also internationally.

Acknowledgement Research for this contribution was supported by a SEED grant awarded by Georgia Gwinnett College in 2016–2017. I would like to thank Charlie Marburger and Mandy Crane, my research assistants, for their help with this article. Previous versions of this contribution were presented at the European International Studies Association's Annual Conference (EISA) in Barcelona in September 2017 and the Association for the Study of Nationalities Annual Conference at Columbia University in May 2017. I would like to thank the discussants and the participants of these conferences for their comments and suggestions.

REFERENCES

Berenskoetter, F. 2014. "Parameters of a National Biography." *European Journal of International Relations* 20 (1): 262–88.

Burakovskiy, A. 2011. "Holocaust Remembrance in Ukraine: Memorialization of the Jewish Tragedy at Babi Yar." *Nationalities Papers* 39 (3): 371–89.

Davoliūtė, V. 2016. "Two-Speed Memory and Ownership of the Past." Transitions Online, September 1. http://www.tol.org/client/article/26264-two-speed-memory-and-ownership-of-the-past.html. Accessed January 28, 2018.

Geleževičius, R. 2003. *Holokausto teisingumas ir restitucija Lietuvoje atkūrus nepriklausomybę, 1990–2003.* Vilnius: Lietuvos teisės universitetas.

Genocide and Resistance Research Center of Lithuania. n.d.-a. "The Armed Anti-Soviet Resistance in Lithuania in 1944–1953." http://genocid.lt/centras/en/2390/a/. Accessed January 28, 2018.

Genocide and Resistance Research Center of Lithuania. n.d.-b. "Tremties ir kalinimo vietos." http://genocid.lt/centras/lt/1491/a/. Accessed January 28, 2018.

Girnius, K. K. 1990. *Partizanų kovos Lietuvoje.* Vilnius: Mokslo leidykla.

Himka, J. 2012. "Interventions: Challenging the Myths of Twentieth-Century Ukrainian History." In *The Convolutions of Historical Politics*, edited by M. Lipman and A. I. Miller. Budapest: Central European University Press.

Kasianov, G. 2008. "Revisiting the Great Famine of 1932–33: Politics of Memory and Public Consciousness (Ukraine after 1991)." In *Past in the Making: Historical Revisionism in Central Europe After 1989*, edited by M. Kopeček. Budapest: Central European University Press.

Liber, G. O. 2016. *Total Wars and the Making of Modern Ukraine, 1914–1954.* Toronto: University of Toronto Press.

Makhotina, J. 2016. "We, They and Ours: On the Holocaust Debate in Lithuania." Cultures of History Forum, September 27. http://www.cultures-of-history.uni-jena.de/debates/lithuania/we-they-and-ours-on-the-holocaust-debate-in-lithuania/. Accessed January 28, 2018.

Mälksoo, M. 2012. "Nesting Orientalisms at War: World War II and the 'Memory War' in Eastern Europe." In *Orientalism and War*, edited by T. Barkawi and K. Stanski. New York: Columbia University Press.

Mälksoo, M. 2015. "'Memory Must Be Defended': Beyond the Politics of Mnemonical Security." *Security Dialogue* 46 (3): 221–37.

Marples, D. R. 2010. "Anti-Soviet Partisans and Ukrainian Memory." *East European Politics and Societies* 24 (1): 26–43.

Nabers, D. 2015. *A Poststructuralist Discourse Theory of Global Politics.* Houndmills, Basingstoke, and New York: Palgrave Macmillan.

Petrauskienė, A. 2017. *Partizaninio karo vietos: Įamžinimas ir įpaveldinimas nepriklausomoje Lietuvoje.* Unpublished PhD dissertation, Vilnius University, Vilnius.

Pettai, E., and V. Pettai. 2015. *Transitional and Retrospective Justice in the Baltic States.* Cambridge: Cambridge University Press.

Portnov, A. 2008. "Pluralität der Erinnerung. Denkmäler und Geschichtspolitik in der Ukraine." *Osteuropa* 58 (6): 197–210.

Portnov, A. 2013. "Memory Wars in Post-Soviet Ukraine (1991–2010)." In *Memory and Theory in Eastern Europe*, edited by U. Blacker, A. Etkind, and J. Fedor. Houndmills, Basingstoke: Palgrave Macmillan.

Rudling, P. A. 2011a. "Multiculturalism, Memory and Ritualization: Ukrainian Nationalist Monuments in Edmonton, Alberta." *Nationalities Papers* 39 (5): 733–68.

Rudling, P. A. 2011b. "The OUN, the UPA and the Holocaust: A Study in the Manufacturing of Historical Myths." *The Carl Beck Papers in Russian and Eastern European Studies*, no. 2107. The Center for Russian and East European Studies, University of Pittsburgh.

Shevel, O. 2011. "The Politics of Memory in a Divided Society: A Comparison of Post-Franco Spain and Post-Soviet Ukraine." *Slavic Review* 70 (1): 137–64.

Shevel, O. 2016. "The Battle for Historical Memory in Postrevolutionary Ukraine." *Current History* 115 (783): 258–63.

Snyder, T. 2010. "A Fascist Hero in Democratic Kiev." *The New York Review of Books*, February 24. http://www.nybooks.com/daily/2010/02/24/a-fascist-hero-in-democratic-kiev/. Accessed January 28, 2018.

Subotić, J. 2016. "Narrative, Ontological Security and Foreign Policy Change." *Foreign Policy Analysis* 12 (1): 610–27.

Tabarovsky, I. 2016. "Babi Yar at 75: Filling in the Blanks in Ukrainian History," September 27. Woodrow Wilson Center, Kennan Institute. https://www.

wilsoncenter.org/article/babi-yar-75-filling-the-blanks-ukrainian-history. Accessed January 28, 2018.

Umland, A. 2017. "The Ukrainian Government's Memory Institute Against the West." *New Eastern Europe*, March 7. http://neweasterneurope.eu/articles-and-commentary/2284-the-ukrainian-government-s-memory-institute-against-the-west. Accessed January 28, 2018.

Valatka, R. 2015. "Ką pagerbė Lietuva—partizanų vadą Generolą Vėtrą ar žydų žudiką?" (Whom Did Lithuania Honor: The Leader of Partisans General Vėtra or a Jew killer?). *Delfi*, July 26. http://www.delfi.lt/news/ringas/lit/r-valatka-ka-pagerbe-lietuva-partizanu-vada-generola-vetra-ar-zydu-zudika.d?id=68576988. Accessed January 28, 2018.

Vanagaitė, R. 2016. *Mūsiškiai*. Vilnius: Alma Littera.

Weldes, J. 1999. *Constructing National Interests: The United States and the Cuban Missile Crisis*. Minneapolis: University of Minnesota Press.

Widmaier, W. W., M. Blyth, and L. Seabrooke. 2007. "Exogenous Shocks or Endogenous Constructions? The Meanings of Wars and Crises." *International Studies Quarterly* 51 (4): 747–59.

Wylegała, A. 2017. "Managing the Difficult Past: Ukrainian Collective Memory and Public Debates on History." *Nationalities Papers* 45 (5): 780–97.

Zhurzhenko, T. 2011. "'Capital of Despair': Holodomor Memory and Political Conflicts in Kharkiv After the Orange Revolution." *East European Politics and Societies* 25 (3): 597–639.

Zhurzhenko, T. 2015a. "Shared Memory Culture? Nationalizing the 'Great Patriotic War' in the Ukrainian–Russian Borderlands." In *Memory and Change in Europe: Eastern Perspectives*, edited by M. Pakier and J. Wawrzyniak. New York and Oxford: Berghahn Books.

Zhurzhenko, T. 2015b. "Russia's Never-Ending War Against 'Fascism': Memory Politics in the Russian–Ukrainian Conflict." *Eurozine*, May 8. http://www.eurozine.com/russias-never-ending-war-against-fascism/. Accessed January 28, 2018.

PART III

International/Regional Dimensions of the Crisis in Ukraine

Framing of Crimean Annexation and Eastern Ukraine Conflict in Newspapers of Kazakhstan and Kyrgyzstan in 2014

Katja Lehtisaari, Aziz Burkhanov, Elira Turdubaeva and Jukka Pietiläinen

INTRODUCTION

Central Asia faces similar challenges of democratization after a long era of authoritarian rule, as do many other developing countries. Civic unrest is a problem for many developing countries that face challenges caused by ethnic conflicts or political disagreement. The media can play a central role in either spreading these conflicts or promoting peaceful

K. Lehtisaari (✉) · J. Pietiläinen
Aleksanteri Institute, University of Helsinki, Helsinki, Finland

A. Burkhanov
Graduate School of Public Policy, Nazarbayev University,
Astana, Kazakhstan

E. Turdubaeva
Department of Journalism and Mass Communications,
American University of Central Asia, Bishkek, Kyrgyzstan

© The Author(s) 2018   181
E. Resende et al. (eds.), *Crisis and Change in Post-Cold War Global Politics*, https://doi.org/10.1007/978-3-319-78589-9_8

solutions (on cases related to Kyrgyzstan, see, for example, Freedman 2009 and Kulikova 2008). The article focuses on media's role in Kazakhstan and Kyrgyzstan public discussion around Crimea in spring 2014. Thus, the article adds to the existing research literature creating new insights for understanding the role of media in process of social transformation in post-Communist conditions.

Inspired by Nabers' (2015) approach to framing global politics in the "crisis and change" paradigm, we look at the crisis around Crimea in 2014 as a possible catalyst of social changes in these Central Asian societies. Nabers' approach is based on the four interrelated and mutually constitutive elements: sedimented practices and dislocation on the one hand, as well as antagonism and the institutionalization within a so-called imaginary on the other. We also build up on Nabers' conceptualization of critical discourse analysis as an interrelation between the discourse and linguistics. As Nabers asserts, "language no longer remains a neutral linguistic system but acquires the status of a scheme of socially regulated values of good and bad, strong and weak. The signifier 'worker' acquires no meaning as long as it is not linked to another signifier, for example, 'wage,' 'woman,' 'children,' 'German' or 'British.' It is only via the relationship between different signifiers that mutual integration, and the establishment of a chain of equivalences, becomes possible" (Nabers 2015: 135).

While the overall historical context of the Central Asia media has been elaborated in a number of studies (Freedman 2012; Juraev 2002; Junisbai 2011; Junisbai et al. 2015; Kulikova and Perlmutter 2007; Kulikova and Ibraeva 2002), a number of academics have pointed out the lack of academic research of the post-Soviet media systems—even though the number of studies on individual ex-Soviet countries and regions is growing (Freedman and Shafer 2014). However, they have drawn the conclusion that, after a relatively short period of vibrant media development, the process of building independent institutions of the Fourth Estate came to a halt.

This chapter examines how the process where Russia annexed Crimea in 2014 was reported in the Kazakh and Kyrgyz press and if the security perceptions offered in the media outlets depended on the different language or ownership background of the outlet. In both Kazakhstan and Kyrgyzstan, in addition to Kazakh- and Kyrgyz-language media, outlets operating in Russian language such as TV, radio stations and newspapers are widely available and are among nationally important news media. The main questions addressed are how the newspapers wrote on the Crimea events of 2014 and how they described the reasons behind Russian intervention, and gave comparisons with other similar situations and prognosis. The main hypothesis is that the situation is framed in more pro-Russian way in the editions of Russian-language media outlets compared to publications printed in Kyrgyz and Kazakh languages and that the coverage in state-owned publications is more inclined towards official statements of the state officials and thus presenting hegemonic processes.

Our sample includes newspapers published in February–April 2014, which gives us an opportunity to look at how the development of Crimea-related events was covered while they were ongoing, as well as reactions and reflections in both Kazakhstan and Kyrgyzstan soon after the annexation. For this chapter, we combine elements of framing analysis and discourse analysis. The discourse analysis helps to track patterns and main storylines in the reporting, as well as differences in reporting of different outlets. We also look at the difference between locally published Kazakh/Kyrgyz-language and Russian-language newspapers, and Kazakh/Kyrgyz editions of Russian-language newspapers.

The research material was gathered by choosing all articles (news items, analysis, etc.) in a selection of newspapers in the given time frame of 1 February–30 April 2014 including word Crimea in any form. We utilized also a list of keywords (democracy, democratization, freedom, revolution, civil society, conflict, demonstration, Crimea, Russia, West, Kyrgyzstan and Ukraine) to see if some topics are of greater interest. In the analysis, also the main framing function (as described by Entman 1993: 52) was identified. According to Entman, framing is "selecting some aspects of a perceived reality and mak[ing] them more salient in a communicating text, in such a way as to promote a particular problem definition, causal interpretation, moral evaluation, and/or treatment recommendation" (Entman 1993: 52). Frames are constructed through the strategic use or omission of certain words and phrases. Entman suggested that frames in news can be examined and identified by "the presence or absence of certain keywords, stock phrases, stereotyped images, sources of information and sentences that provide thematically reinforcing clusters of facts or judgments" (Entman 1993: 52). Thus, in our analysis, we aim to discuss what are the main topics, or problems raised in the context of Crimean annexation, what causes the media stories give for these problems, if there are moral judgements, and if the media stories offer and justify treatments of the problem or predict their likely effects.

KAZAKH AND KYRGYZ MEDIA

Since Kazakhstan gained independence, the number of media outlets operating in the country has grown dramatically. In the late 1980s, the total number of registered media outlets only included ten republic-level printed media and twenty-one TV and radio channels. In July 2016, the total number of registered media outlets at all levels was 2763, including 1156 newspapers and 1269 magazines (Ministry of Information and Communications 2017). The Agency for Public Service and Anti-Corruption, interestingly, provides rather different statistics in 2016: according to them, there are 1364 newspapers and 522 magazines, out of which 24 and 33%, respectively, are state-owned. Thus, the state in Kazakhstan remains a significant player in the media market. The language in which the media outlets operate remains a very important factor for defining political orientation of a particular outlet in both Kazakhstan and Kyrgyzstan. In Kazakhstan in May 2013, 344 media outlets operated in only Kazakh, 758 in only Russian, 727 in both Kazakh and Russian, and 282 in Kazakh, Russian and other languages, which suggests presence of two major linguistic realms in the media industry.

As part of a larger Central Asian sociocultural and sociopolitical entity, the Kyrgyzstani press system adapted many traits of the Soviet model imposed during seventy years of Communist ideology (Freedman 2011: 2). In the post-Soviet period, significant changes in ownership occurred and part of the media outlets became privately owned. Nowadays public, state-run, private as well as international media coexist in Kyrgyzstan.[1] State sovereignty led not just to the development of independent from the state media outlets but also to the new language policy in the media sphere. Kyrgyzstan as a multi-ethnic country with large Russian and Uzbek minorities adopted a bilingual system of Kyrgyz and Russian. As Russian was the dominating language during the Soviet era, the positions of Kyrgyz language were enhanced through a special law that required transmitting at least 50% of all TV

---

[1]According to the Ministry of Justice (2013), the three newspapers with the largest circulations rates appear in Bishkek: the dailies *Vecherniy Bishkek* (150,000), *Super Info* (120,000) and the weekly *Delo No.* (16,000). Many other newspapers have more limited circulation.

and radio programming in Kyrgyz (Kyrgyz Public Television and Radio Corporation law).[2] Taking into consideration that 85% of the population (5.1 million citizens) of Kyrgyzstan in 2016 were Internet users (National Sustainable Development Strategy for the Kyrgyz Republic for the period 2013–2017), we may conclude that news websites or their information reproduced through social networks gains appeal among a wide readership. Since 2010, there have been fewer legal cases against the press and fewer attacks against journalists than in previous years. However, the government occasionally pressures outlets for coverage of certain issues while most media outlets that are anxious to avoid trouble with the government and political forces order their journalists to frame coverage in certain ways.

THE CRIMEAN CRISIS

The Crimean crisis erupted in the aftermath of a violent regime change in Ukraine in late February 2014 in context of which President Yanukovych left Kyiv on February 22. Shortly after these events, armed soldiers without any identification badges or insignia started to appear on the streets of several cities in Crimea. They quickly established control over key administrative buildings in the Crimean capital, Simferopol, and blocked the Ukrainian military bases stationed in the peninsula. The soldiers refused to talk to journalists and remained silent, while continuing to secure access to major governmental buildings, police and military stations and were quickly labelled "Polite Men." The Crimean assembly gathered and, allegedly under pressure from the military, voted in favour of holding a referendum on joining Russian Federation. The referendum was held on March 16, 2014 in Crimea and was largely criticized internationally as illegal. The Russian official discourse, however, implied that the military deployment was done in order to protect the Russian-speaking population of Crimea, many of whom were Russian citizens (mainly in Sevastopol). On March 18, 2014, Russian President Putin signed the bill on inclusion of Crimea to the Russian Federation.

---

[2] It aimed mostly at the regulation of television and radio broadcasting, having left out the Internet-based media. However, the majority of news agencies and websites take the bilingual approach by default and publish materials both in Kyrgyz and in Russian languages.

There were numerous criticisms of the way the plebiscite was organized and most countries refused to consider it legal. In our research, we look at how the discourses were built in Kazakhstan and Kyrgyzstan, countries with a remarkable Russian media supply. In what follows, we describe our approach to analysis of the media coverage of the Crimean events in both Kazakh and Kyrgyz media outlets.

COVERAGE OF CRIMEAN EVENTS IN KAZAKHSTAN AND KYRGYZSTAN

The media outlets play two major societal roles. First, media have the "agenda-setting" capacity in their respective societies by informing their audiences and shaping their perceptions of certain issues by framing/interpreting news in a positive or negative fashion. As a generator of discourses, media, as also Nabers (2015) puts it, frames global politics in the "crisis and change" paradigm. Second, the media also largely reflect the broader societal stances towards certain issues, by following their audiences' preferences (at least how they perceive them).

The research on foreign news has indicated that trade between countries is the principal predictor of news coverage about foreign countries in most of the countries and that geographic distance and population of a country play a significant role in the developing countries while in developed countries GDP is an exclusive predictor of news coverage (Wu 2003: 19–20). Pietiläinen (2006: 226) stated that both the foreign news and the foreign trade of individual countries depend on geographic, political and cultural proximity, historical connections and many other factors and in many cases these factors result in a similar distribution of both trade and news. Not only the news flows in quantitative terms but also their content is largely dependent on cultural and political ties between countries, which may also change when political changes happen. Therefore, the study of Crimean crisis in Central Asian media is extremely interesting: just few decades ago all the countries were part of the same empire, and now Russian and Ukrainian versions of the conflict are very different. Therefore, it is interesting to see how the case is framed in Kazakhstan and Kyrgyzstan.

KAZAKHSTAN AND KYRGYZSTAN MEDIA UNDER RESEARCH

We chose four Kazakhstan's nationwide print newspapers with the largest circulation size for purpose of this project: *Egemen Qazaqstan* [Independent Kazakhstan] and *Zhas Alash* [Young Alash] which are published in Kazakh language, and *Kazakhstanskaya Pravda* [Truth of Kazakhstan] and *Vremia* [Time], which represent the Russian-language segment. *Kazakhstanskaya Pravda* and *Egemen Qazaqstan* are government-owned nationwide newspapers that usually express the regime's officially sanctioned views on political and social issues in Kazakhstan. They were both created in the early 1920s and build up on a legacy of the official papers of the Communist Party of Soviet Kazakhstan. In the post-independence period, both of these papers remained being government newspapers, albeit having adjusted their practices in order to appear as genuine newspapers and not ideological messengers. These newspapers also possess largest circulation figures in Kazakhstan—circulation of *Kazakhstanskaya Pravda* in 2017 is estimated at approximately 100,000 copies, while *Egemen Qazaqstan* has more than 200,000 copies. *Vremia* and *Zhas Alash* represent an opposite segment—both of these papers are privately owned, and, as such, possess a greater degree of freedoms when it comes to voice societal concerns *vis-à-vis* certain issues. *Zhas Alash* leans towards the stances of the Kazakh-speaking intelligentsia, including those with rather nationalist views; and its circulation size is estimated at 50,000 copies. *Vremia* is under the patronage of the state-owned corporation, Kazakhmys, but managed to preserve its quasi-independent editorial policies and its circulation is approximately 180,000 copies.

The material regarding Kyrgyzstan follows the same pattern: We analysed privately owned *Alibi* and state-backed *Kyrgyz Tuusu* printed in Kyrgyz language; and privately owned *Vecherniy Bishkek* and state-controlled *Slovo Kyrgyzstana* published in Russian language. *Alibi* is a privately owned Kyrgyz-language newspaper, which is published once a week. It has a circulation of 10,000 copies, and the main audience is Kyrgyz-speaking audience living in regions. *Kyrgyz Tuusu* is a state-owned Kyrgyz-language newspaper, and it is published twice a week. It has 15,000 copies of circulation, and it is mainly read by Kyrgyz-speaking audiences. *Slovo Kyrgyzstana* is state-owned Russian-language newspaper and comes out twice a week. It has Russian-speaking audience living in capital city and regions. The circulation is 15,000. *Vecherniy Bishkek* is published twice a week and is privately owned. The circulation is 150,000. The readers consist of local Russian-speakers living in the capital city and rural areas.

News Coverage in Kazakhstan and Kyrgyzstan

In our analysis, it came clear that the coverage of state-owned or state-sponsored media differed from that of the independent publication. Also, the language question had influence.

Domestic Developments in Ukraine

Substantial focus of the coverage of the Crimean crisis was in Kazakh press dedicated to the analysis of the domestic crisis in Ukraine and Yanukovych's overthrow after several weeks of protests and violent riots in the late February 2014. In general, the state-sponsored papers embraced the narrative that was part of the Kazakhstan's regime discourse about primacy of the economic reforms before political liberalization. Kazakhstan's officials, starting from the President Nazarbayev, at many occasions have mentioned the "Economy first, then politics" principle, largely trying to replicate the Southeast Asian paternalistic transitional models, inspired by Singapore, Malaysia and Taiwan. The regime's discourse tried to portray cases of Kyrgyzstan, Ukraine and Georgia and regime changes there as failures, specifically due to the violation of this principle and overpolitization of societies. For example, in an article called "Ukraine: The Impact of Crisis," the state-backed *Egemen Qazaqstan* narrates about the Yanukovych overthrow and connects the regime collapse with the overpolitization of the country. The journalists shared their impressions from a recent trip to Ukraine:

> The Ukrainian society has become too politically aggressive and has turned into an arena for the struggle of political parties for power. In such situations, no one will ever pay attention to the economy. During our recent trip to Ukraine, we were amazed by the richness of the natural resources of the country, which was highly developed in the Soviet era. But we've also seen bad roads, poor houses and dark streets. The fact that Ukraine's GDP per capita is only $7,000, while the country has so much wealth and sits in

the middle of Europe, tells us something. But they have a lot of political parties pulling people to their sides, using newspapers and TV channels. That is why all people talked about was the party they wanted to see in power. (*Egemen Qazaqstan*, 26 February 2014)

The state-backed papers repeatedly mentioned Ukraine's economic troubles in the aftermath of the Yanukovych overthrow and Crimea annexation. Russian-language state-backed paper *Kazakhstanskaya Pravda* also highlighted Ukraine's economic troubles. In an article called "Ukraine-2014: Chronicle of Events," the paper narrates about economic consequences of the Yanukovych overthrow and suggests that the country might declare default. Interestingly, the paper also mentions that tourism in Crimea (still controlled by Ukraine at the moment of printing) was also to be affected by the economic slowdown. (*Kazakhstanskaya Pravda*, 1 March 2014)

Zhas Alash, being a privately run newspaper associated with the Kazakh intelligentsia and nationalist circles, takes a more critical and anti-Yanukovych position in the discourse, but also draws similarities to Kazakhstan. For instance, in an article called "It is Possible to Seize Power from the Hands of one Person," published right after Yanukovych was ousted, the newspaper says:

> Yanukovich said he does not want to leave power. He said on the TV: "I am legally elected president. I will not resign. This decision [of the Supreme Rada] is illegal." Yanukovich clearly reminds us the former Kyrgyz President Kurmanbek BaKyiv. He also did not want to leave the power, yet he fled to Belarus. What has Yanukovich left behind? Yanukovich wants Ukraine to be divided into two. The situation in Ukraine is a lesson for our government. (*Zhas Alash*, 25 February 2014)

CRIMEA ANNEXATION

The Crimea annexation by Russian troops put Kazakhstan into a very challenging position. Kazakhstan does preserve close relations with Russia, yet at the same time, a clear violation of the international law made Kazakhstan feel vulnerable against potential attacks from Russia, given the demographics of Northern Kazakhstan. The state-backed papers reflected the regime's position on these developments, remaining prudent and only publishing short notices regarding the Ministry of

Foreign Affairs statements. For instance, *Egemen Qazaqstan*, in an article called "Putin has signed documents recognizing independence of Crimea" (*Egemen Qazaqstan*, 18 March 2014), narrates in a very neutral tone that Crimea has been incorporated into Russian Federation after the formal recognition of its independence, the submission of a petition to join the Russian Federation, followed by the formal approval by the Russia's State Duma.

Similarly, state-owned *Kazakhstanskaya Pravda*'s was careful and neutral. The paper initially reported about the intervention to Crimea by quoting Ukrainian officials, such as Minister of Interior Avakov. He stated that "the Government of Crimea reported that its building has been occupied, the Ministry of Interior deploys troops and police forces" (*Kazakhstanskaya Pravda*, 27 February 2014). The paper went on to add "Ministry of Interior of Ukraine accused Russia in the armed intervention to Crimea" (*Kazakhstansiaka Pravda*, 28 February 2014). The paper finally looked at Ukraine in mid-March when it printed a statement by the MFA of Kazakhstan regarding the situation in Crimea. The statement itself caused many criticisms, as it included three paragraphs, two of which seemed to contradict each other:

> Kazakhstan confirms its commitment to the fundamental principles of the international law and UN Charter [...] Kazakhstan considered the referendum in Crimea as a free expression of the will of the population of this autonomous republic and understands the decision of the Russian Federation in the existing conditions. (*Kazakhstanskaya Pravda*, 19 March 2014)

This statement of the Ministry of Foreign Affairs was criticized domestically: *Zhas Alash* printed an article called "It Would Have Been Better to Remain Silent rather than Making a Statement in Support of Russia":

> While the international community condemns Russia's involvement in the Crimea, the Ministry of Foreign Affairs of Kazakhstan said "it considers the decision of the Russian Federation with understanding..." The official statement of the Ministry of Foreign Affairs on the issue of Crimea, which has caused a crisis between Russia and the West, was confusing. One of the experts said that through this statement, Kazakhstan was supporting Russia, and one of the experts said it's a sign that the Aqorda was shocked by Russia's involvement. (*Zhas Alash*, 20 March 2014)

Only later, when the situation started to explode in the eastern parts of Ukraine, the state-backed Kazakh paper *Egemen Qazaqstan* took a more critical position towards the Donetsk and Luhansk referendums, while admitting the controversy of the issue. The article tried to present both sets of views, pro-separatist and pro-Kyiv, while somewhat inclining to support the latter (*Egemen Qazaqstan*, 13 May 2014).

The private newspapers were much less limited in expressing their position vis-à-vis the Crimea situation. The *Zhas Alash*, private Kazakh-language newspaper, was the most vocal in the discourse regarding Crimea annexation. In their discourse, the paper criticized both the Russian occupationist policy and how Kazakhstan's government handled the situation. For instance, in an article called "Kazakhstan did not assess Russian occupationist policy," the paper expressed criticism of the Kazakhstan's diplomatic approach and said that "while criticizing Russia's aggressive policy, Western states are considering applying anti-Moscow measures, and Kazakhstan's President Nursultan Nazarbayev has left for Moscow to discuss the situation in Ukraine" (*Zhas Alash*, 6 March 2014). The newspaper further mentioned that Kazakhstan should have taken a more proactive stance on this and express solidarity with Ukraine. Russian involvement in staging the referendum in Crimea was also mentioned by the paper: in an article called "Russia's involvement in Crimea is now obvious," the paper argues:

> The result of the referendum that took place within three weeks after the capture of the Crimean parliament building by armed men without distinctive marks is not surprising. Since the fall of Yanukovich, Russia has deployed 14,000 troops in Crimea. The United States has said it will not recognize the referendum conducted under "the pressure of the Russian army." The Crimean Tatars, who have long opposed Russia's accession, have announced a boycott to the referendum. (*Zhas Alash*, 18 March 2014)

In Kyrgyzstan, a private newspaper *Alibi* gave a platform for both pro-Russian and pro-Ukrainian voices. The information sources for *Alibi* were both local pro-Russian and pro-Western political experts and government statements of both Russia and Ukraine. *Alibi* did not refer to Kyrgyz government's official position on Crimean issue neither stating Ministry of Foreign Affairs nor the Kyrgyz government.

State newspapers in Kyrgyzstan took pro-Russian position on annexation of Crimea, while also being rather silent on the issue. Kyrgyz-language state-owned newspaper *Kyrgyz Tuusu* published only one article on Crimean issue. *Kyrgyz Tuusu* in an article called "Protesting people, growing army" (*Kyrgyz Tuusu*, 18 March 2014, no. 19) narrated in a pro-Russian position by stating Mihailov, a Russian politician:

> Look at recent history. Crimea was before part of Russia. The reason why it was given to Ukraine is the political blindness of the first secretary of Communist Party at that time Nikita Hrushtshov and after before the collapse of Soviet Union of Boris Yeltsin......There is a situation in Kyiv and regions of Ukraine which is turning into an anarchy. Current Kyiv government has just remembered the legacy of Soviet Union which was given to it after the collapse of USSR and started suing Russia by blaming it. (*Kyrgyz Tuusu*, 18 March 2014, no. 19)

The author of the article mentioned the geopolitical confrontations of big powers over the Crimean issue:

> Because there are interests of big powers and geopolitical confrontations behind the issue of returning Crimea to Russia which is making this issue popular. It seems that the confrontations of Russia, EU and US will not end soon. (*Kyrgyz Tuusu*, 18 March 2014, no. 19)

Another state-owned, but Russian-language newspaper *Slovo Kyrgyzstana* also wrote about the results of the referendum in Crimea. In the article "Crimea will become a part of Russia" from 18 March 2014, *Slovo Kyrgyzstana* refers to Mikhail Malishev, the head of referendum commission in Crimea:

> About 96.77% of residents voted on Sunday at a referendum for the entry of autonomy into the Russian Federation.......Referendum asked two questions, "Are you for the reunification of the Crimea with Russia as a subject of the Russian Federation?" and "Are you for the restoration of the Constitution of the Republic of Crimea in 1992 and for the status of the Crimea as part of Ukraine?." In turn, most of the observers from 20 countries of the world who came to Crimea noted the absence of any irregularities in the voting. (*Slovo Kyrgyzstana*, 18 March 2014)

Slovo Kyrgyzstana published a news article "Republic Crimea is a federal subject of Russia" in 21 March 2014 where the author writes that

Crimea was reunited to Russia and raises concerns why West doesn't accept it. In the article, Russian viewpoint is not problematized. The same author Irina Koshova published another news article "No way back" in the next issue of *Slovo Kyrgyzstana* from 25 March 2014 where she uses the narrative "self-proclaimed Republic of Crimea" and narrates that "The State Duma of the Russian Federation ratified the Treaty on the accession of the Crimea and Sevastopol to the Russian Federation. Earlier, representatives of the self-proclaimed Republic of Crimea and President Vladimir Putin signed an agreement on this." (*Slovo Kyrgyzstana*, 25 March 2014). The author also noted that Kyrgyzstan supported Russian Federation on annexation of Crimea and recognized the legitimacy of the referendum in Crimea:

> It is worth noting that Russia's actions to annex Crimea were sharply criticized by the West. Also Ukraine, all EU countries, including usually standing alone Great Britain (total of 28 states), Canada, Japan, South Korea, Iceland and Turkey do not consider the referendum to be legitimate. But still there are states that supported the Russian Federation: Kazakhstan, Abkhazia, Belarus, the Ministry of Foreign Affairs of Kyrgyzstan in its statement expressed its opinion that the results of the referendum in the Crimea represent the will of the absolute majority of the population of the Crimea. A few more states do not say anything about the signed agreement yet, but consider the Crimean referendum legitimate: Venezuela, North Korea (DPRK), Syria. (*Slovo Kyrgyzstana*, 25 March 2014)

GEOPOLITICAL GAME OF WORLD POWERS

Alibi, a privately run Kyrgyz-language newspaper, took a rather neutral position in the coverage of Crimean crisis—largely like *Zhas Alas* in Kazakhstan. In its pages, the newspaper criticized both the Russian occupationist policy and Western countries' regime handling the situation. For instance, in an article called "Crimea: The Conflict of the Century" the paper expressed criticism of Russia and said:

> First of all the peninsula Crimea which N. Hryushev gave to Ukraine in 1954 and which is the gate to the Black sea is very important for Russia and for all world powers who are interested in this region. That is why Russia is holding its "Black Sea navy" here by paying 97 million USD annually. In spite of this as this territory is a part of Ukrainian territory, it is evaluated by world community as an invasion to Ukrainian territory....

The fact that President Vladimir Putin got the approval of Federal Council to send its military weapons to the peninsula of Ukraine Crimea is scaring the world community. (*Alibi*, 4 March 2014, no. 15)

In the same article, the paper also criticized the Western countries and stated that "Western countries are trying to include Ukraine to EU and supporting nationalists like Stepan Bandera's generation in Ukraine" (*Alibi*, 4 March 2014, no. 15). Russian-language private newspaper *Vecherniy Bishkek* in an article "Peninsula Crimea" from 18 March 2014 also narrated about the geopolitical game in the region:

The step of the American side can only be explained by an irresistible desire to maximally politicize an already difficult situation, in order to satisfy its geopolitical interests, to continue to increase internationally around Ukraine. (*Vecherniy Bishkek*, 18 March 2014)

Building up on similar narrative, a number of articles in Kazakh media, too, were dedicated to further implications and consequences of the Ukrainian crisis for Kazakhstan. As Kazakhstan was about to sign a Eurasian Economic Union (EEU) Treaty at the end of May of 2014, many voiced their concerns of enhancing any cooperation with Russia further after the Crimea crisis. *Zhas Alash*, for instance, narrated about anti-Eurasian movement, which brought together several prominent opposition leaders, nationalists and pro-Western activists. In an article called "Let's Stop the Kremlin!" the newspaper in its editorial article emotionally called to manifest against the signing of the EEU, which was scheduled for the late May 2014. The newspaper argued:

The decision of the Russian President Vladimir Putin to send the Russian troops to the independent, sovereign, Ukrainian territory undermined the international community and the world. Having violated the 1994 Budapest Treaty, UN documents and all human moral principles, and using "protection of Russia and Russian citizens" as an excuse for using force against Kyiv, the Putin's regime is turning into a fascist nature and is ready to commit crimes against humanity! Can we be allies with such a state? The international community can block and sanction any aggression of a fascist regime. The Russian leadership is overwhelmed by the great Russian chauvinism and imperial ambitions. If Russia attacks Ukraine today, there is no guarantee that tomorrow the Russians will not incorporate the northern regions of Kazakhstan! (*Zhas Alash*, 4 March 2014)

Interestingly, the paper interviewed Sergei Duvanov, a prominent Kazakhstani journalist and formerly an opposition activist. *Zhas Alash* rarely invites ethnic Russian opinion-makers to be interviewed on its pages; this perhaps represents that pro-Western and Kazakh nationalist groups' interests overlapped when being juxtaposed against the Russian annexation of Crimea. In his interview to *Zhas Alash* Duvanov said:

> I recently visited four Ukrainian cities: Kyiv, Odessa, Nikolaev and Kharkov. My goal was not to meet with famous politicians or public figures, but rather to talk to ordinary people. I talked to people at the train stations, shops, buses, cafes, hotels, all the places I went through. I concluded that there is no fascism in Ukraine, and this is just Putin's propaganda. True, there are some nationalists, including radicals. But show me a country that doesn't have this kind of people. These people have no influence on the policies of the present government. (*Zhas Alash*, 27 March 2014)

Another article about anti-Eurasian movement in *Zhas Alash*—called "If We Were Talking about Saving Our State"—narrates further about challenges that await Kazakhstan in the EEU. The paper narrated about surveys that were conducted in Ukraine before conflict, in which even in Crimea and Eastern Ukraine, more than 80% expressed their loyalty to Russia rather than Ukraine. The paper says:

> Are there any such surveys in the northern Kazakhstan? No, of course. And if there were, it would not be impossible to imagine that more than half of Petropavlovsk, Pavlodar and Kostanai residents would choose Russia over Kazakhstan. We should avoid danger. We need to be careful about the situation. What do people living on the border with Russia think about? Do they consider Kazakhstan as their homeland? What do we need to do in order to make them not pro-Russian, but our fellow countrymen, pro-Kazakhstan? (*Zhas Alash*, 27 March 2014)

The excerpt above reflects a sense of insecurity felt in identity terms, in rather direct way. The anti-Eurasian forum gathered in Almaty on April 12, 2014. *Zhas Alash* published the resolution issued by the Forum. By some accounts, this was a substantial mobilization of people around anti-Eurasianist agenda; yet, the critics said it failed to attract a mass support and only managed to get a few hundred people on board. The paper expressed viewpoint that all agreements and documents should be openly published and that "It is impossible to join any alliance with Russia when the Russian army invaded Ukraine and annexed the Crimea with an illegal referendum" (15 April 2014).

HISTORICAL REFERENCES

Part of the media coverage used historical references and combined them with current topics. Kyrgyz *Alibi* published the last words of S. Miloshevitch on the position of Russians and Yugoslavia, in a statement on information war between Russia and the West (*Alibi*, 4 March 2014, no. 15). At the same issue of the newspaper, another article was published on Crimean issue "Nationalists came to the power in Ukraine." In this interview with a local political expert Toktogul Kakchekeev on annexation of Crimea, the expert took a pro-Russian position.

In a short note "Is Putin an enemy of Ukraine?" from 25 March 2014, no. 21, *Alibi* writes about ex-prime minister of Ukraine Yulia Timoshenko's reaction to annexation of Crimea:

> After the annexation of Crimea Ukrainians are hating Russia. Ex-prime minister of Ukraine Yulia Timoshenko who was recently let free from jail declared on Ukrainian TV Channels that "the number one enemy of Ukraine is Putin." Besides this she also declared that "as Putin could not take over the Crimea with political pressures, he was ought to take it with military power. However eventually Ukraine will return Crimea to its own territory. (*Alibi*, 25 March 2014, no. 21)

Russian involvement in staging the referendum in Crimea was also mentioned by the paper: in an interview with Tursunbek Akun, public Ombudsman who was an observer from Kyrgyzstan during the referendum in Crimea titled "Even if we blame Putin, he did not lie," from 1 April 2014, the paper refers to Tursunbek Akun's following statement:

> 70% of population of Crimea are Russians that is why mostly they showed up during referendum. And Ukrainians in Crimea showed up very few. And Tatars who are 14% of the population did not show up at all. And their votes were falsified, because the information that 97% of population showed up at referendum is not true at all. Tatars not only did not show up, but also did not assign an observer at elections. As all members of the commission were Russians, they did what they want. All these are violations of law. Russians brought to Crimea about 30 000 army and the

border was protected by Chechens. One more thing to mention is that, they already hang the Russian flag before the referendum. At night on 26 February to 27 February, unknown people seized the Crimean Rada (Parliament) building and the next day they brought Rada members and made them to vote to hold a referendum on greater autonomy of Crimea on 25 May 2014.

The Ombudsman continues by expressing his pro-Russian view and criticizing Barack Obama and supporting Putin:

> Even if we blame Putin, he did not lie at all. He is doing it openly and talking about it openly. And Barack Obama is bombing Syria, providing weapons to its opposition, destroyed Iraq and Libya and lying that he did not do it all. In general Putin's position is right. He is building an alternative to US who is trying to build its dominance in the world. (*Alibi*, 1 April 2014, no. 23)

In the Russian-language state-owned newspaper *Slovo Kyrgyzstana*, only four articles were dedicated to annexation of Crimea over the period between 1 February and 30 April 2014. One of the stories was an interview with local political expert and director of Political Research Foundation in Kyrgyzstan. The story, "Anxiety and pain are common," was based on material in Vesti.kg from 5 March 2014. The interviewee talked in the interview how Kyrgyzstanis, "who survived the two revolutions, understand the Euro-Maidan passions." This quote shows proximity to the events in the post-Soviet region. The expert also mentioned the information war between Russia and the West and expressed his anxiety that parallel to Ukrainian protests the local Kyrgyz opposition will also try to shake the situation in Kyrgyzstan. The expert took pro-Russian position by stating that

> What was happening in Ukraine did not leave indifferent any of the residents in the post-Soviet space. Kyrgyzstan cannot be related to this conflict. However, in the event of a situation out of control, we must find ourselves on the Russian side, considering our relations with the Russian Federation, including within the framework of the CSTO. In any case, we should pray for Ukraine and hope that the parties will be able to find a sound force and come to a consensus on this issue. (*Slovo Kyrgyzstana*, 5 March 2014)

Annexation of Crimea was seen in some articles as a threat of Russia's territorial emancipation to Central Asia.

In an article "Will we lose our land together with our people?" from 22 April 2014, the author of a story in *Alibi* writes about "separate and govern" policy of Russia towards Ukraine. The author named his subtitle "Russia took over the Crimea, who is next..." (*Alibi*, 22 April 2014, no. 21). The author asked questions like "Will Ukrainian crisis repeat in Kyrgyzstan in the future?" and "What is the intention of Russia?" and tried to answer them by stating the following:

> Putin said that one of the two world camps during "cold war" NATO is still existing and the Warsaw Pact disappeared. That is why Russia will try not to lose its world influence. It can be observed from Russia's foreign policy that it is trying to form USSR which was destroyed in 1991 in another form. For this purpose, Russia brought its military first to Crimea, Abkhaziya and south Osetiya and conquered these territories. There are assertions that the next will be Central Asia. It is clear even if it is not declared openly that Kazakhstan moved its capital from Almata to Astana because it doubted of Russia. (*Alibi*, 22 April 2014, no. 21)

The article raises the issue of migration from Central Asia particularly from Kyrgyzstan to Russia and sees it as a threat to Central Asia that Russia will initiate similar referendum like in Crimea in Central Asia, too:

> Many migrants from Kyrgyzstan are getting Russian citizenship. By increasing the number of citizens by giving them Russian citizenship the Russian government will try to make a referendum like in Crimea to annex Central Asia in the future. (*Alibi*, 22 April 2014, no. 21)

Russian-language private newspaper *Vecherniy Bishkek* also narrated on the possible influence of "Crimean campaign" of Russia on integration projects in CIS (*Vecherniy Bishkek*, March 2014). The main topic of the interview with local political experts and independent journalists "No one wants war" from March tells about the consequences of the Maidan on the regional security for Russia, Ukraine and Central Asia and raises the issue of the probability of the development of the same scenario in Central Asia. The news article in *Vecherniy Bishkek* from 19 March 2014 "Putin's Appeal" writes about the Russian President Vladimir Putin's address at the St George's Hall of the Grand Kremlin

Palace to the Federal Assembly of the Russian Federation, residents of Russia, the Crimea and Sevastopol in connection with the request of the Republic of Crimea and Sevastopol to join the Russian Federation. The author referred to Putin's appeal: "According to Putin, Crimea has been in the heart and mind of people of Russia and remains part of Russia." (*Vecherniy Bishkek*, 19 March 2014).

CONCLUDING REMARKS

Analysis of the Kazakhstan's and Kyrgyzstan's media discourse in different languages reveals that their perspective towards Russia is rather complicated. In Kazakhstan, the official discourse in both state-sponsored Russian and Kazakh newspapers in general is in accordance with the country's policy towards preserving closer political and economic engagement as well as strong cultural ties with Russia, seen as a traditional foreign policy ally and strategic partner. However, when the Crimean crisis escalated, later Russian foreign policy initiatives, including calls for further political integration within the EEU, "Russian World" and tensions with Ukraine over Crimea provoked more resistance and criticism (even if initially limited) across Kazakhstan's media, especially private Kazakh-language outlets. Russian-language newspapers had a more nuanced view towards Russia (and Soviet experiences are oftentimes projected to modern Russia); while some tend to recall the widespread famine in the 1930s, mass repression and deportations, as well as the policy of forced Russification, others praise Soviet industrial modernization and express nostalgic feelings towards the social security and stability.

The main discourses in Kyrgyz press differed according to the ownership and language of the print outlets. Russian language, both state-owned and private newspapers' coverage of annexation of Crimea was pro-Russian and not balanced by providing a platform mainly for pro-Russian voices over the issue of annexation of Crimea. The voices of pro-Ukrainian political experts and neutral political experts were not heard on the pages of these newspapers. They took pro-Russian position and narrated about annexation of Crimea as justified and supported Russia's actions in Ukraine and Crimea. They also referred to government of Kyrgyzstan in relation to recognition of referendum in Crimea legitimate which Kyrgyz language, both state-owned and private newspapers did not. Russian-language press discourses contributed to the construction of a narrative of crisis that made the annexation of Crimea possible. The analysis of both content and discourse analysis of the stories of Russian-language press shows that there was a more pro-Russian coverage in Russian-speaking press, and that they contributed in some extent to the political consequences of these discourses and narratives for the legitimation of the annexation.

Findings include that the amount of coverage was rather small in official, state-published or sponsored newspapers while in privately owned newspapers, the amount and spectrum of coverage is wider. It seems also that in Kazakhstan, the Kazakh-language papers are less controlled by the officials and therefore more varied in their views than Russian-language papers. In some private newspapers, the similarities of Northern Kazakhstan and Crimea were discussed while the state media reported only the official version that the annexation is against international law but that the people of Crimea also have right to organize a referendum. In Kyrgyzstan, the coverage had broadly the same pattern, Kyrgyz-language privately owned newspapers being the most varied and critical in their views.

In Kazakhstan, projection to Eurasian union discussion was visible. This track was also visible in Kyrgyzstan, particularly in *Vecherniy Bishkek*. Its stories were about possible influence of "Crimean campaign" of Russia on integration projects in CIS, CSTO and EEU. There were also projections on the information war between Russia and the West, and speculations if some nearby location would be taken over by Russia.

REFERENCES

Entman, R. M. 1993. "Framing: Toward Clarification of a Fractured Paradigm." *Journal of Communication* 43 (4): 51–58.

Freedman, E. 2009. "When a Democratic Revolution Isn't Democratic or Revolutionary: Press Restraints and Press Freedoms After Kyrgyzstan's Tulip Revolution." *Journalism* 10 (6): 843–61.

Freedman, E. 2011. "Theoretical Foundations for Researching the Roles of the Press in Today's Central Asia." In *After the Czars and Commissars: The Press in Post-Soviet Authoritarian Central Asia*, edited by E. Freedman and R. Shafer. East Lansing, MI: Michigan State University Press.

Freedman, E. 2012. Deepening Shadows: The Eclipse of Press Rights in Kyrgyzstan. *Global Media and Communication* 8 (1): 47–64.

Freedman, E., and R. Shafer. 2014. "Contrasting Regional Portraits of Press Rights on Post-Soviet Terrain: The Baltics vs. The Caucasus and Central Asia."

Paper presented at the International Association for Media & Communication Research Hyderabad, India, July.

Junisbai, B. 2011. "Oligarchs and Ownership: The Role of Financial-Industrial Groups in Controlling Kazakhstan's 'Independent' Media." In *After the Czars and Commissars: The Press in Post-Soviet Authoritarian Central Asia*, edited by E. Freedman and R. Shafer. East Lansing, MI: Michigan State University Press.

Junisbai, B., A. Junisbai, and N. Y. Fry. 2015. "Mass Media Consumption in Post-Soviet Kyrgyzstan and Kazakhstan: The View from Below." *Demokratizatsiya: The Journal of Post-Soviet Democratization* 23 (3): 233–56.

Juraev, A. 2002. "The Uzbek Mass Media Model: Analysis, Opinions, Problems." *Central Asia and the Caucasus* 13 (1): 130–38.

Kulikova, S., and G. Ibraeva. 2002. *The Historical Development and Current Situation of the Mass Media in Kyrgyzstan.* Occasional Paper 1, CIMERA.

Kulikova, S. 2008. New Media in New Democracies: Perceptions of Good Governance Among Traditional and Internet-Based Media Users in Kyrgyzstan. Unpublished doctoral dissertation, Louisiana State University.

Kulikova, S., and D. D. Perlmutter. 2007. "Blogging Down the Dictator? The Kyrgyz Revolution and Samizdat Websites." *International Communication Gazette* 69 (1): 29–50.

Ministry of Information and Communication of the Republic of Kazakhstan. 2017. http://mic.gov.kz/en. Accessed December 18, 2017.

Ministry of Justice of Kyrgyz Republic. 2013. Elektronnaya baza dannykh sredstv massovoi informatsii KR. http://minjust.gov.kg/ru/content/smi. Accessed December 18, 2017.

Nabers, D. 2015. *A Poststructuralist Discourse Theory of Global Politics.* Houndmills and New York: Palgrave Macmillan.

Pietiläinen, J. 2006. "Foreign News and Foreign Trade—What Kind of Relationship?" *The International Communication Gazette* 68 (3): 217–28.

Wu, H. D. 2003. "Homogeneity Around the World? Comparing the Systemic Determinants of International News Flow between Developed and Developing Countries." *Gazette* 65 (1): 9–24.

CHAPTER 9

"Crisis" and Crimean Tatars: Discourses of Self-determination in Flux

Didem Buhari-Gulmez

INTRODUCTION

This study focuses on the crisis and transformation of Crimean Tatar[1] self-determination movement after the Russian annexation of Crimea. Identifying itself as an indigenous population of Crimea, Crimean Tatars were deported by Stalin after the Second World War and started to return to Crimea after the fall of the Soviet Union. On their return, they discovered that Crimean Tatar legacy had been almost "wiped away" from Crimea during their half-a-century exile. Crimean Tatar street names were changed to Russian, their houses were occupied, and the majority of the population consisted of ethnic Russian settlers. Crimean

---

[1] A Muslim indigenous population of Crimea who speaks Turkic language and who faced mass deportation many times since the nineteenth century. Around 250,000 Crimean Tatars returned to Crimea after the dissolution of the Soviet Union (13% of the Crimean population before the Russian annexation). More than two million Crimean Tatars currently live in Turkey.

D. Buhari-Gulmez (✉)
International Relations, İzmir University of Economics, İzmir, Turkey

© The Author(s) 2018
E. Resende et al. (eds.), *Crisis and Change in Post-Cold War Global Politics*, https://doi.org/10.1007/978-3-319-78589-9_9

Tatars faced serious difficulties and constant, multiple "crises" in read-justing to the new conditions in their "homeland" in social, economic, and cultural domains. Yet, the main and most visible "crisis" in Crimea is the Russian annexation which has not only affected the local, national, and regional politics but also global dynamics. While the international community focuses on the Russian–Ukrainian conflict over Crimea and East Ukraine Crimean Tatars fear becoming increasingly "invisible" and neglected. Following Nabers' seminal work establishing the missing conceptual link between crises and transformations, this article seeks to reveal the paradoxical changes in the Crimean Tatar discourses about Crimean Tatar identity (Self), Russian and Ukrainian "Others," and national self-determination.

Overall, it argues that (1) Crimean Tatars tend to represent the Russian annexation of Crimea as "the crisis" referring to the deinsti-tutionalization of Crimean Tatar political agency[2] in Crimea and the increasing "invisibility" of Crimean Tatar self-determination claims due to the ongoing "hegemonic struggles" in Crimea, which overlooks the multiplicity of crises Crimean Tatars have been facing since their return; (2) changes in Crimean Tatar discourses about Self, Other, and national self-determination precede "the crisis" of Russian annexation; and (3) the new discursive shift of emphasis on "the crisis" operates as a "myth" to deal with the inherent divide within the Crimean Tatar political move-ment in terms of identity and self-determination discourses. After laying out the conceptual framework used in the study, the article will provide a general overview of the Crimean Tatar national movement with an emphasis on Naber's assumption that crises are an inherent quality of the social in the global era. Then, it will explore the multiplicity of Crimean Tatar discourses about self-determination, including the Crimean Tatar diaspora in Turkey by benefiting from the review of the literature and ethnographic interviews with Crimean Tatar activists conducted in April 2013 in Crimea and in February–March 2017 in Istanbul.

---

[2] Meyer and Jepperson (2000) defines agency as enacted by a broader social environment through cognitive scripts and collective myths. In line with this definition, political agency of Crimean Tatars is taken here as a social construction rather than an objective fact that exists independently from a social environment. See also Nikolko's chapter in this edited volume.

CONCEPTUAL FRAMEWORK: SELF-DETERMINATION IN CRISIS

National self-determination is a political project on how to shape the relationship between Self and Others. It claims both unity and uniqueness in terms of representing a community that is entitled to determine its own fate. Self-determination may be wrongly compared to divorce, which reduces the multifaceted concept of secession from a parent state. In fact, rather than defining self-determination as a rupture from an existing political system, it is crucial to note that self-determination leads to "a positive good in itself—self-government, realized autonomy" (Philpott 1998: 70).

The global criteria about self-determination are uncertain given the uneven application of the right to self-determination to different communities. While some communities have been granted the right to their own independent state, autonomous region, or decision to annex with another country, other communities' right to self-determination has failed to receive support from the international community (Geldenhuys 2009: 235). During the decolonization era, some former colonies have been transformed into "independent states" without much regard to their capability or will to sustain a nation-state (Fabry 2010: 168; Hironaka 2005).

According to Young (2007), globalization underlying complex interdependencies has led to a redefinition of sovereignty, agency, and self-determination as it has rendered the principle of non-intervention redundant. Instead of "non-interference" model of self-determination which draws clear boundaries between inside and outside, Young suggests a shift toward an emerging "non-domination" approach to self-determination. By redefining self-determination as "non-domination," it is possible to take into account the blurred boundaries between domestic and external and the changing meanings of sovereignty in an era of increasing interconnectedness among societies, groups, and individuals. Hence, the discourses associated with self-determination movements are moving away from state-centrism and the language of rights and resistance (Reid 2011). In other words, self-determining units are not seen as resisting and protecting themselves from external interferences but they are redefined as "open-systems" that have gained an awareness that internal-external dichotomy has become obsolete in the global era (Buhari-Gulmez 2016b). In this context, rather than secession (external self-determination), self-determination claims start to focus on internal self-determination implying democratic and multi-level governance mechanisms that allow shared ruling (Roepstorff 2013).

Another challenge associated with the notion of self-determination in the global era is the difficulty to distinguish between Self and Other (see Neumann 1999; Reinke de Buitrago 2012). Post-westernization scholarship puts a strong emphasis on the changing population and identity dynamics underlying the current mixing of cultures, visions, and political projects. Post-western Europe means that it is no longer possible to distinguish Europe from Asia or overlook "the multiplicity of ethnic, religious, cultural, and political differences that co-exist in Europe, which renders the notion of a singular Western modernity redundant (Delanty 2006; Rumford 2008: 112). For example, given the influence of Confucian and Islamic notions on the continent, Christianity is no more a valid reference point for Europe (Delanty 2006: 1).

The rise of global complexities transforming identity politics cannot be fully grasped without taking into account the relational nature of identity and the tension between universality and particularity (Nabers 2015: 107–9). Identity "can only be established by difference, by drawing a line between something [self] and something else [other]" (Nabers 2015: 107). Accordingly, both Self and Other are social constructs that are reinforced by sedimentary practices that conceal an inherent complexity underlying constant political hegemonic struggles over identity. In times of "crises," the rise of alternative discourses and hegemonic struggles about how to define Self, Other, and the relationship between them become more visible.

When the dominant hegemonic center starts to lose its authority (legitimacy and power), previously marginalized identities and projects start to gain ground. In Friedman's words, "dehegemonization" brings "dehomogenization" challenging the established definitions and institutionalized discourses in a society (Friedman 1994). Alternative discourses that start to move from periphery to the center reflect a duality: They may either seek to re-popularize past traditions experienced in that society (particularity) or they may refer to future-oriented projects that haven't been tested before and which do not necessarily derive from that society (universality). In this framework, the representation of Self and self-determination changes in the context of hegemonic struggles reflecting a tension between particularity and universality. In fact, social change involves the redefinition of the relationship between universalism and particularism and the institutionalization of myths that emphasize both unity and uniqueness (Nabers 2015: 151).

Nabers opposes the prevailing assumption that social change follows a crisis sparked by an external development, if not an "exogenous shock" that "hits" and disrupts an otherwise smoothly operating system. Instead, it is possible to understand crisis as an inherent feature of the social structure which is defined with an "absence of a foundation" or a lack of a uniting element (Nabers 2015: 3). In this sense, the society means constant crises and an "unfinished project" (Nabers 2015: 12). The contingent nature of social structure constituted by a "lack" rather than a single hegemonic project allows alternative political projects to compete with the dominant ones and "leaves the path open for multiple political decisions" (Nabers 2015: 13).

From a post-structuralist perspective, Nabers revolutionizes the relationship between crisis and change. In fact, the emergence of a political project and new political subjectivities invented to deal with the question of how to manage a crisis may precede the recognition of the crisis in question (Nabers 2015: 25). Accordingly, the discourse of "crisis" and "new subjectivities" is constructed in a post hoc manner through the processes of crisis recognition. He criticizes the prevailing agent-centric accounts that suggest focusing on the multiplicity of actor perceptions and interpretations about a "crisis" that exists "out there" overlooking the fact that "meanings themselves are at stake in 'crisis'" and one's crisis may not necessarily be defined as a crisis by others (Nabers 2015: 23).

As "the social per se is in crisis" (Nabers 2015: 12), then the notion of crisis becomes an "empty signifier" in the global era (Nabers 2015: 10). Hence, all discourses of crisis need to be deconstructed to reveal (1) the processes of "structural dislocation" implying the deinstitutionalization of dominant meaning structures and discourses, (2) hegemonic struggles over the representation of Self, and (3) the sedimentary practices that serve to conceal the complex struggles and processes of institutionalization underlying the myths of unity and uniqueness.

CRIMEAN TATAR NATIONAL MOVEMENT IN CRISES

Crimean Tatars faced mass deportations many times in history since the Russian annexation of Crimea in 1783. Before 1783, Crimean Tatars constituted the majority of the Crimean population. As the "offspring" of the Crimean Khanate that was established in the fifteenth century, Crimean Tatars claim that they are an "indigenous" nation of Crimea rejecting the status of minority (OSCE 2013). Due to repressive policies and the Crimean war of the 1850s, many Crimean Tatars were forced to out-migrate from the Crimea. In December 1917, Crimean Tatars established the Crimean People's Republic, which was quickly invaded by Bolshevik forces one month later. In 1921, the Crimean Autonomous Soviet Socialist Republic was established by Veli Ibrahimov, a Crimean Tatar who was executed in 1928 by Stalin (Fisher 1978: 141). The radical processes of Sovietization gradually eliminated Crimean Tatar intelligentsia and undermined Crimean Tatars' economic, social, and political activities, culture, language, and religion (Fisher 1978: 142). Russification and then Sovietization led to systematic repression of Muslim clergy in Crimea, the destruction of mosques and madrassahs, and the resulting decline of Islam (İzmirli 2013b: 1).

The Second World War was an important turning point for Crimean Tatars as the promise of self-rule put forward by Hitler's Germany succeeded to divide them into two camps: those who fought for Stalin against those who joined the ranks of Nazi army. After the War, Stalin ordered the mass deportation of all Crimean Tatars by officially accusing them of "mass treason" (Fisher 1978: 166). Even those who had earned a medal in the Soviet army were deported by force to Central Asia, Uzbekistan in particular. During their exile, Soviet authorities destroyed Tatar cultural and historical monuments, mosques, and graveyards; changed street names; and revised history textbooks in order to delete Crimean Tatars from the Crimean past (Fisher 1978: 171). Crimean Tatars in exile faced serious difficulties in asserting their national and cultural distinctiveness, which implied that the Crimean Tatar youth lacked the institutions to learn Crimean Tatar language and religion (Kırımlı 1989).

In May 1954, Soviets unilaterally decided to annex Crimea to the Ukrainian Soviet Socialist Republic "exporting" the Crimean Tatar question to Ukraine. Crimea was then populated by a Russian majority and Ukrainians perceived the Soviet decision as a plot against the Ukrainian nation-building (Kırımlı 1989). De-Stalinization era allowed many other deported communities such as Chechens, Ingush, Karachays, Balkars, and Kalmyks to return to Crimea but Crimean Tatars who attempted to return to the Crimea were denied official permissions for residence and work or directly sent to prisons. Since individual efforts to return failed at the time, collective Crimean Tatar campaigns involving sending petitions and letters to both Soviet and foreign authorities successfully sought to "internationalize" and render visible the Crimean Tatar cause. The National Movement of Crimean Tatars attracted international attention to the question of Tatar repatriation, especially after the 1987 demonstrations in Moscow. However, the Crimean Tatar nationalist movement was internally divided. Yuri Osmanov and Mustafa Dzhemilev led two different projects. "The Organization of the Crimean Tatar National Movement" established in 1989 by Osmanov followers was accused by Dzhemilev followers of radicalism. After Osmanov was assassinated in 1993, Dzhemilev's movement that is based on the discourse of "non-violence" has become the sole representative of the Crimean Tatar self-determination movement.

Upon their return to the Crimea after the end of the Cold War, Crimean Tatars convened in June 1991 the Crimean Tatar Congress in Simferopol and decided to establish the Crimean Tatar *Mejlis* (representative assembly of the Crimean Tatar People) electing Mustafa Dzhemilev as the President of Crimean Tatar nation. The Mejlis was not officially recognized by Ukraine as an official representative of Crimean Tatars but in 1999, the Ukrainian Presidency founded the "Council of Representatives of Crimean Tatar People" consisting of Mejlis members to serve as an official channel for Crimean Tatar-Ukrainian dialogue (İzmirli 2013a). By the 2001 census in the Crime, around 250,000 Crimean Tatars had returned to their "motherland" and constituted the third big ethnic community in Crimea after ethnic Russians (58%) and Ukrainians (24%). By May 2013, the Crimean Tatars had increased from 12 to 13.7% of the Crimean population (OSCE 2013). Crimean Tatars' repatriation coincided with Ukraine's state-building and suffered from the lack of resources and insufficient political commitment in the Ukrainian and Crimean authorities. The referendum about officializing Crimean autonomous region was met by Crimean Tatar suspicions. They feared that ethnic Russians constituting the majority of the Crimean population would use their privileged position in order to deny cultural, economic, and political rights to Crimean Tatars.

Crimean Tatars faced an important number of problems and crises after their return to Crimea. The most visible crisis was about the land allocation issue. When they returned, they found their houses occupied by Russians and Ukrainians. Their demands for new houses from the Crimean and Ukrainian authorities remained mostly unanswered, and Crimean Tatars started to occupy lands in rural areas and build their own houses. Crimean authorities denounced land squatting as unlawful and destroyed some of the houses built by Crimean Tatars, which led to clashes between Crimean authorities and Crimean Tatars.

Ethnic Russians and Ukrainians also resented Crimean Tatar land squatting policy and started to organize counter-land squatting movements as a response. Crimean Tatar houses which were built illegally have been denied water and electricity by the authorities and their inhabitants live in dire conditions. There were only 15 schools for Crimean Tatar pupils, encouraging Crimean Tatars to learn Russian instead of Crimean Tatar language. Apart from this, Crimean Tatars built a university, museum, library, a TV channel, and several mosques with only limited financial resources deriving from Ukraine and Crimean Tatar diaspora (Muratova 2009: 267). Vandalism against Islamic places and symbols associated with the Crimean Tatar identity and the negative reactions toward Crimean Tatars' commemoration events of their deportation reflected anti-Tatar sentiments in Crimea (İzmirli 2013b: 1, 2013c).

According to Dzhemilev, the number of apologists among ethnic Russians regarding the mass deportation of Crimean Tatars is significant: More than 70% of the Russian-speaking people of Crimea see Stalin's decision of deportation as justified, believing that Crimean Tatars were "traitors" who had collaborated with the enemy (Dzhemilev 2010b). Candidates in the Crimean local elections usually put the emphasis on the necessity to "protect Russian interests" and "prevent the 'Tatarization' of Crimea" (Dzhemilev 2010b: 94). Crimean Tatar political representation in the Crimean and Ukrainian governments remained limited due to the electoral threshold of five percent and the ban on electoral blocs (İzmirli 2013a). Unemployment in general was high among Crimean Tatar youth leading to allegations of anti-Tatar discrimination in the Crimean society. These problems faced by Crimean Tatars on a daily basis since their return demonstrate the fact that crises have always been a constitutive part of Crimean Tatar social reality.

Ukraine's Presidential elections of 2010 were perceived by Dzhemilev followers as the rise of anti-Crimean Tatar people to the Crimean and Ukrainian governments. After being elected as the new Ukrainian President, Viktor Yanukovych adopted a Presidential decree that unilaterally amended the composition of the Council of Representatives of the Crimean Tatar People at the expense of the Crimean Tatar Mejlis which decided in response to boycott the Council (Dzhemilev 2010a: 117). Dzhemilev was already alarmed by pro-Russian activism in Georgia, which also involved the Russian Black Sea fleet deployed in Sevastopol. The Crimean Tatar Mejlis campaigned for the removal of the Russian fleet from Crimea and feared that Russian activism might eventually spread to the Crimea. Dzhemilev and his followers chose to side with the pro-Western forces in Ukraine and Crimea and supported the pro-EU "Euromaidan" protests against the pro-Russian forces who sought closer alliance with Russia. They complained about the rise of radical Islamists in the Crimea who were allowed by the Crimean and Ukrainian authorities to run parallel religious organizations and mosques and organize anti-Western demonstrations and events (Temnenko 2009: 10–13). Crimean Tatar leadership saw this development as a Russian plot to weaken Crimean Tatar self-determination claims and provoke anti-Tatar sentiments in the public (Buhari-Gulmez 2016a).

The Russian annexation of Crimea based on a referendum that aimed to legitimize it in the eyes of the international community has been perceived as "the crisis": Crimean Tatar leaders were either deported or threatened with sanctions under the anti-extremism laws of Russia. The Mejlis was closed down, and the Crimean Tatar mosques and cultural centers have become targets of police raids in search for evidence of extremism. In brief, Crimean Tatars have experienced a plethora of crises since their return to the peninsula. Before the 2014 Russian annexation, the discourse of crisis was mainly shaped around the problems deriving from the 1944 Deportation. Yet, there has been a discursive shift of emphasis away from the 1944 Deportation to the 2014 Annexation. The next section deals with the Crimean Tatar discourses about self-determination after the Russian annexation.

"THE CRISIS" AND POST-CRISIS DISCOURSES ABOUT CRIMEAN TATAR SELF-DETERMINATION

Before the Russian annexation, Crimean Tatars were focusing on the Deportation of 1944 they called "Sürgün" as the main crisis in their history (Aydıngün and Aydıngün 2007). Each year they had to struggle with the authorities in order to commemorate "Sürgün." Around 300,000 Crimean Tatars returned from exile since the late 1980s, but millions of Crimean Tatars still live in different countries, including Turkey, Bulgaria, and Uzbekistan among others. Some Crimean Tatars decided not to return to Crimea because, in the words of a Crimean Tatar repatriate, "their life had already been cut off into two and they did not want to start from zero again" (anonymous interview 2013, quoted in Buhari-Gulmez 2015). Nevertheless, many of those who chose not to return are often actively supporting the revival of Crimean Tatar culture in the Crimea. For instance, the Crimean Tatar diaspora in Turkey currently run more than 50 Crimean Tatar cultural associations that actively host conferences and activities to support the Crimean Tatar national cause throughout Turkey. Commemoration of "Sürgün" (Deportation of 1944) was the most visible "crisis" until 2014. Interviews in Crimea reveal several "myths" about "Sürgün" which has been constitutive of the Crimean Tatar identity such as the "Arabat Tragedy," a myth about the disappearance of a Crimean Tatar village during the Deportation. The Arabat Tragedy is about a village of Crimean fishermen and salt miners who were forgotten by the Soviet soldiers who had already reported to Moscow that they had "cleansed" the Crimea from Tatars. After noticing they had forgotten to deport Arabat villagers, Soviet soldiers put the village inhabitants to a boat and sank it (Altan n.d.). The search for the sunken boat has remained fruitless so far.

An event organized in 2016 by the Crimean Tatar association in Yalova hosted a Crimean Tatar professor of history who emphasized that "a speech on 'the problems of Crimean Tatars after their return' might have been more meaningful before the Russian invasion. But after the Russian annexation, the Crimean Tatar problem has turned into a question of survival." He criticized those who were optimistic about Putin's rhetoric promising to improve the living standards for all minorities, including Crimean Tatars. He argued that even though Crimean Tatars were disappointed with the failure of the Ukrainian authorities to help Crimean Tatar repatriation in an effective manner, "At least we had some hope that things might improve for us in the future. Now we are facing a survival threat [from anti-Tatar authorities]."

The Russian annexation through the March 2014 referendum changed the structural parameters in Crimean politics at the expense of Tatar nation-building. The Crimean Tatar Mejlis and its supporters boycotted the referendum claiming that the choices of the Russian-speaking majority of Crimea did not represent Tatars and announced their intention to organize a referendum on Crimean Tatar's self-determination (Salem 2014; Baczynska 2014). Following the Russian annexation, Dzhemilev's entry to Crimea was de facto banned by the Crimean authorities. Russian anti-extremism laws were used to suspend the activities of the Crimean Tatar Mejlis, media (ATR channel broadcasting in Crimean Tatar), and political circles. Crimean Tatar demonstrations, including the Deportation commemoration, have been disallowed, and those who participated in "illegal" demonstrations have become political prisoners under the risk of deportation (Human Rights Watch 2014).

Crimean Tatar activists often denounced as "provocateurs" in Crimea after the Russian annexation have frequently become targets of threats and abduction (Shapovalova and Burlyuk 2016: 14). Crimean Tatar diaspora's anxiety derives from the new challenges underlying their communication with their fellows in Crimea under Russian authority. It is no longer possible to directly travel to Crimea from Turkey, and there is a new requirement of a visa from the Russian authorities in order to legally enter the peninsula. Visa requirement and the fees for processing visa applications have become serious obstacles against Crimean Tatar diaspora's link with Crimea. They still continue their campaigns to render the Crimean Tatar cause more visible in the international arena by holding the World Crimean Tatar Congress in Turkey and organizing other political and cultural activities in Ukraine.

A March 2017 meeting of the Heads of Crimean Tatar associations in Istanbul sought to develop a common strategy about how to attract more effectively the world's attention to the Crimean Tatar suffering under the Russian government. Crimean Tatar diaspora meeting also revealed an attempt to bridge the existing divides within the Crimean Tatar diasporic community. By putting a strong emphasis on "the crisis" of Russian annexation, Crimean Tatar diaspora leaders openly invited all Crimean Tatars to leave aside the ongoing internal conflicts within the community and unify their forces in a time of "crisis." They state that the Russian "Other" has a privileged position in terms of spreading false rumors about the Crimea in general and Crimean Tatars in particular. The Russian public and the international community are often misinformed about the Crimean Tatar views about self-determination and Russian rule. Crimean Tatar diaspora aims to publish and translate their political opinions and academic research on Crimean Tatar nationalism through their own journals published by their associations in Turkey.

Anti-Tatar discourses include two opposite claims about Crimean Tatar views on self-determination. First, Crimean Tatars are accused of secessionism and threatening the territorial integrity and unity of Crimea. According to the alternative discourse that has also started to gain ground after the Russian annexation, Crimean Tatars are a minority that enjoys better living standards and rights under the Russian rule. Both types of discourses find echo in the Crimean public, and the accusations of extremism and radicalization against Crimean Tatars reinforce the perception that Crimean Tatars might be a risk or threat to the society. Crimean Tatar diaspora puts an emphasis on Dzhemilev's principled opposition to violence in order to respond to the allegations of Crimean

Tatar extremism. By linking the Crimean Tatar cause to extremism and radical Islamism, Russian authorities benefit from the global war on terror and the increasing securitization against the rise of Islamic State in the Middle East. There is no credible evidence about Crimean Tatar support to the IS or other radical Islamist movements but the discourse of radicalization in the media and official circles serves to undermine the legitimacy of the Crimean Tatar nationalism. This type of discourses seeks to reduce Crimean Tatar agency to a threat to be pacified and which may easily be an instrument at the hands of the Russia's rivals. In an opinion piece entitled "A conflict along the lines of Kosovo is brewing in the Crimea," the former Prime Minister of Crimea and former Ukrainian Minister of Internal Affairs blamed Crimean Tatars for provoking tension in the region:

> [A] conflict is brewing in the Crimea; you'd have to be blind not to see it. And it's being artificially provoked by specific forces and using specific funds…Our Slavonic brotherhood is like a thorn in the side of Western civilization…So that the conflict in the Crimea does not subside, it is periodically stimulated, both ideologically and financially. Here the roles are clearly delineated: the "aggrieved" side, the Crimean Tatars headed by the Mejlis; the "oppressors," state authorities and the "occupiers," that is, the rest of the population of the peninsula. (Mogilev quoted in Coynash 2011)

Islam plays a paradoxical role in the Crimean Tatar nation-building (Buhari-Gulmez 2016a: 72). It serves to distinguish the Crimean Tatar Self from other communities of the Crimea. This explains the strong emphasis on the Muslim identity of Crimean Tatar nationalists. Yet, when radical Islamist discourses attempted to raise their clout in the peninsula, Crimean Tatar Mejlis leadership was the first to oppose them and ask for the deportation of radical Islamists from Crimea (İzmirli 2013b: 9; Muratova 2009: 269). Rather than a political project supporting a sharia regime, Islam was a system of values and rituals confined to festivals, ceremonies for birth, marriage, circumcision, and funerals (Yarosh and Brylov 2011: 257). Radical Islamists were seen as a threat to Crimean Tatar nation-building since they discouraged the usage of Crimean Tatar language and reduced the Crimean Tatar cause to an oppression of the Muslim in the hands of non-Muslims (Temnenko 2009: 10–13). Dzhemilev and the Crimean Tatar Mejlis supported a pro-Western and secular Crimean Tatar identity similar to that of Turkey. They accused the Crimean and Ukrainian authorities of failing to prevent the entry of radical Islamists coming from Russia and Uzbekistan disguised as "returning Tatars" (Kuzio 2009). The interviews with Crimean Tatar activists in 2013 revealed the widespread suspicion that pro-Russian separatists were turning a blind eye to the rise of radical Islamic activities on the peninsula in order to use the latter as a pretext to spread anti-Tatar sentiments and show Crimean Tatars as weak and divided (Goble 2013; Wilson 2013). As early as 2004, Dzhemilev stated that:

> Brochures of a provocative nature have appeared which say things like Muslims don't have to obey laws if the head of the state is not a Muslim. So what does that mean? That I should not obey Ukrainian law? That is provocation designed to spark a conflict. Fortunately, we are able to keep such things under control for the moment. (Dzhemilev quoted in Krushelnycky 2013)

Differentiating "Tatar Islam" from "foreign (radical) Islam," Crimean Tatar leadership frequently protested the rise of radical Islamic activities in Crimea:

> Various sects, including extremist and totalitarian ones, those which object to nationality and plan to create a global Islamic caliphate, call democratic values inventions of unbelievers, promote division among the Crimean Tatars, and discredit Islam are not traditional for our people and were introduced to Crimea by outsiders. (Dzhemilev quoted in Buhari-Gulmez 2016a: 76)

Crimean Tatar diaspora's articles preceding the annexation accused radical Islamists of encouraging Crimean Tatars to speak Russian rather than Crimean Tatar. They also claimed that radical Islamist groups were supported by the Russian secret services and pro-Russian forces in the Crimea (Aytar 2009: 10).

> [T]he efforts on splitting our people, both in political and religious context continue and the 'neighboring country' [Russia] supported projects to 'create and support new public and political, religious, youth, female organisations of Crimean Tatars of various directions on condition that they will oppose Mejlis. (Dzhemilev 2011)

The Crimean Tatar discourse about the role of external forces or the neighboring country in Islamic radicalism conceals the constant hegemonic struggles over the definition of Self, including "the power to define what belongs to Islamic tradition and what does not" (Yarosh and Brylov 2011: 252–53). A number of Tatars recruited by a radical Islamist organization Hizb-at Tahrir allegedly joined the jihadist forces in Syria (Al Arabiya News 2013). In addition, terrorist organizations might easily recruit the Crimean Tatar youth who faced serious problems in terms of lack of political representation, socioeconomic problems, and unemployment (Kuzio 2009). Besides, during an interview with Dzhemilev in April 2013, the author asked a question about the Crimean Tatar project of self-determination. Dzhemilev answered the question by emphasizing the Crimean Tatars' will to expand their cultural and political rights by remaining within Ukraine rather than secession. According to Dzhemilev, it was not realistic to support an independent Crimean Tatar Republic given the insufficient number of people and resources to sustain independence. Dzhemilev supported a close alliance of Ukraine with the European Union which, in his opinion, would help the Ukrainian government to expand Crimean Tatar rights within Ukraine.

Following the Russian annexation, the banishment of Dzhemilev from Crimea and the suspension of the Crimean Tatar Mejlis meant the fall of the dominant discourse about who is a Crimean Tatar and paved the way for the rise of alternative hegemonic projects about Crimean Tatar identity. In other words, structural dislocation underlying the deinstitutionalization of the Crimean Tatar political discourses has brought to the fore the preexisting hegemonic struggles over Crimean identity and self-determination and opened the prevailing "myth" of Crimean Tatar unity to debate. Crimean Tatar activists are generally divided between those who support the secessionist model of self-determination and others who prefer to collaborate with Ukraine in order to "take back" Crimea from Russia. The sixth Crimean Tatar Qurultay convened immediately after the declaration of Crimean annexation by Russia. They emphasized the Crimean Tatar people's right to self-determination (Emel 2014).

After the annexation, Ukraine appointed Dzhemilev as the Commissioner of the President of Ukraine on Crimean Tatar People's Affairs and it officially recognized the Crimean Tatars' right to self-determination and their representative assembly, i.e., the Mejlis (Shapovalova and Burlyuk 2016: 32). It also decided in 2017 to take Russia to the European Court of Human Rights for banning the Crimean Tatar Mejlis and persecuting its leaders. Commemoration of the Crimean Tatar Deportation was organized in Kiev, and Ukrainian Parliament recognized in November 2015 the Deportation of 1944 as a "genocide" against Crimean Tatars. Yet, there is some suspicion about Ukraine's support among Crimean Tatar diaspora. It is argued that rather than reinforcing Crimean Tatar agency, Ukraine might attempt to instrumentalize the Crimean Tatar question in order to contest the legitimacy of Russian acts in the eyes of the international community. Crimean Tatar-Ukrainian collaboration has not been immune to problems. The Crimean Tatar battalion assisting the state border guard service of Ukraine since 2015 was confiscated through use of violence by Ukrainian Army after a disagreement they faced in February 2017 (Sabah Daily 2017).

According to the Russian government, Ukraine and the pro-Western media deliberately misinformed the international community about the Crimean Tatar question.

> Thus, after the transfer of Crimea and Sevastopol under the Russian jurisdiction, the human rights aspect of the Crimean Tatar issue has been artificially and wilfully exaggerated by many Ukrainian, European and American officials as well as some Western media. This is just another manifestation of Kiev-propelled campaign to portray the reunification Crimea with Russia as illegitimate.[3]

Russian embassies regularly share the results of sociological studies sponsored by the Russian Federal Agency on Affairs of nationalities (FADH) claiming that Crimean Tatars report their high satisfaction with the Russian rule and there is no support for Crimea's reunification with Ukraine.[4]

> In reality, however, the Russian Government has taken of a number of measures recently aiming to address some concerns of the Crimean Tatar community, such as the rehabilitation of Crimean Tatars (which also implies an increase in pensions of ex-deported people), the building

---

[3] Press release of the Embassy of the Russian Federation in the Republic of Botswana, "On the situation with Crimean Tatars," 1 February 2017. http://www.botswana.mid.ru/press-release_e.html.

[4] The head of FADH Igor Barinov: "According to our recent sociological studies in the Republic of Crimea, aimed specifically at representatives of the Crimean Tatar population, to answer the question: 'If given the opportunity, would you like to move to another area of the Crimea, another region of Russia, to Ukraine, to another country?' 0% of the respondents answered that they would like to move to Ukraine" (TASS 2016).

of a mosque in the Crimean capital Simferopol, and the continuation of the Crimean Tatar curricula in schools. An important change in the legal framework is that Article 10 of the Constitution of the Republic of Crimea, adopted on 11 April 2014, recognizes Crimean Tatar along with Russian and Ukrainian as official languages. The adoption of these measures is positively perceived by the concerned population.[5]

In response, the Ukrainian government claims that Russia is systematically seeking to eliminate non-Russian cultures and identities from the Crimea:

As part of russification policies, the education system in Crimea has been entirely changed over to the Russian language... There is a serious problem around studies of subjects in the Crimean Tatar language. Presently, only 2.76% of schoolchildren in Crimea are learning the Crimean Tatar language. The units in scientific and educational institutions, especially higher institutions which were focused on the study of Crimean Tatar culture, have been shut. As a result, teachers and researchers with long careers of study of this subject lost their jobs.[6]

The 2016 election of a Crimean Tatar muftiah in Ukraine attracted Russian criticisms which stated that "Those people [Crimean Tatar muftiah elected in Ukraine] can never represent Crimean Tatars." Perceiving the Crimean Tatar muftiah in Ukraine as a parallel, rival organization, Russian authorities sought to emphasize that who represents the Crimean Tatar people and identity is open to question (Safarov 2016). Crimean Tatar diaspora argues that Russia aims to emphasize the internal divisions within the Crimean Tatar self-determination movement and support an emerging pro-Russian Crimean Tatar leadership who would suggest remaining within Russia. During the last meeting about the future of Crimean Tatars in Istanbul, a number of Crimean Tatar activists pointed to the rise of pro-Russian press statements given by Crimean Tatars. Reflecting the established discourse of Dzhemilev which has been structurally dislocated in Crimea, the diasporic leadership in Turkey

[5] Press release of the Embassy of the Russian Federation in the Republic of Botswana, "On the situation with Crimean Tatars," 1 February 2017. http://www.botswana.mid.ru/press-release_e.html.

[6] "Statement in Response to the Statement of the Russian Federation on Linguistic Rights of National Minorities in Ukraine," delivered by the Delegation of Ukraine to the 1137th meeting of the OSCE Permanent Council, 16 March 2017. http://www.osce.org/permanent-council/307241?download=true.

tends to overlook the Crimean Tatars who oppose Dzhemilev and adopt a pro-Russian rhetoric. Denounced as "traitors" or "being bought by Russia," their revisionist projects about Crimean Tatar identity and its relationship to Russia remain marginalized by the diaspora. In addition, there is a suspicion against the Russian instrumentalization of the Kazan Tatars who have increased their presence in Crimea after the Russian annexation by emphasizing the "Tatar brotherhood" transcending ethnic differences (Gabidullin and Edwards 2014). According to Hakan Kırımlı, Crimean Tatars should not be confused with Kazan and Volga Tatars, who live in the Russian Semi-autonomous Republic called "Tatarstan." Thus, "Crimean" is not solely a geographical connotation; it is an inseparable part of the Crimean Tatar ethnic identity (Kırımlı 2014).

Concluding Remarks

This study focuses on the Crimean Tatar self-determination movement with a special emphasis on the "crisis" discourses by benefiting from Naber's conceptual framework. In this context, the study emphasized the discursive shift from "Deportation crisis" to "Annexation crisis" in the Crimean Tatar community, including the diaspora. In fact, Crimean Tatars have encountered multiple crises on a constant basis since their return in the 1990s. The emphasis on "the crisis" serves to conceal the hegemonic struggles over who is a Crimean Tatar and what kind of self-determination she/he claims. Several myths and sedimentary practices led by the Crimean Tatar institutions such as the Mejlis represent a dominant discourse based on internal self-determination and non-violence. However, structural dislocation of this discourse which preceded the recognition of the "crisis" implies the opening up of the taken-for-granted foundations of Crimean Tatar subjectivities to debate. Alternative hegemonic projects about Crimean Self and self-determination claims have become much more visible, and a review of the Crimean Tatars' post-crisis discourses reflects the tensions between particularity and universality.

First, the prevailing discourses about self-determination can be divided into two camps: between those who advocate external self-determination, i.e., secession and those who seek internal self-determination of Crimean Tatars within Ukraine (Mejlis and Dzhemilev leadership in particular). The first section of the study lays out the global shift of emphasis from non-interference/secession model of self-determination to non-domination/power-sharing model. Hence, it is possible to claim that

Dzhemilev's discourse about self-determination reflects the universalist approach to Crimean Tatar self-determination whereas secessionists adopt a particularist stance emphasizing the link between a particular territory and parochial identity. As regards the Islam's place in the Crimean Tatar identity, there is a competition between "Tatar Islam" which emphasizes the particularity and the "radical/foreign" Islam that seeks to transcend ethno-national differences (universality). In addition, there is a clash between the universalist discourse of "Tatar brotherhood" put forward by Kazan Tatars and the particularist discourse about the uniqueness of Crimean Tatars. Last but not least, pro-Russian Crimean Tatar discourses have been overlooked as insignificant by the diaspora leadership although the question of "who represents Crimean Tatars" still remains unanswered. By laying out the main traits of the ongoing hegemonic struggles over Crimean Tatar self-determination, this study suggests focusing on the processes of institutionalization and sedimentary practices underlying the negotiation between particularity and universality reflected upon new Crimean Tatar subjectivities.

Overall, since 2014 Crimean Tatars tend to represent the Russian annexation of Crimea as "the crisis" referring to the deinstitutionalization of Crimean Tatar political agency in Crimea and the increasing "invisibility" of Crimean Tatar self-determination claims given the ongoing "hegemonic struggles" over who represents Crimean Tatars. The emphasis on the Crimean annexation as "the crisis" overlooks the multiplicity of constant crises that Crimean Tatars have been experiencing since their return to Crimea in the 1990s. In fact, changes and contestations of the prevailing narratives about the Crimean Tatar Self, Other, and national self-determination did not suddenly appear after "the crisis" of Russian annexation. The discursive shift of emphasis on "the crisis" (Russian annexation) operates as a "myth" to deal with the inherent divide within the Crimean Tatar political movement in terms of identity and self-determination claims. Based on the current tensions between universalist and particularist discourses, the study aims to inspire future studies that will trace the processes through which Crimean Tatar subjectivities are reconstructed. In this context, it is crucial to establish the "missing link" between a constant series of crises underlying the universal principle of self-determination—organizing a subjectivity into autonomous agency—and the selected "crisis" that serves as a myth to unify Crimean Tatars under a particularist hegemonic project.

REFERENCES

Al Arabiya News. 2013. "Islamic Radicals Test Ground in Calm Ukraine." *Al Arabiya News*, July 29. http://english.alarabiya.net/en/perspective/2013/07/29/Islamic-radicals-test-ground-in-calm-Ukraine-.html. Accessed March 28, 2017.

Altan, M. B. n.d. "The Arabat Tragedy: Another Page from the Surgun." International Committee for Crimea. http://www.iccrimea.org/surgun/arabat.htm. Accessed March 28, 2017.

Aydıngün, İ., and A. Aydıngün. 2007. "Crimean Tatars Return Home: Identity and Cultural Revival." *Journal of Ethnic and Migration Studies* 33 (1): 113–28.

Aytar, N. 2009. "5. Kırım Tatar Kurultayının 2. Oturumu" [The second session of the 5th Crimean Tatar Qurultay]. *Kırım Bülteni* 12 (65): 8–10.

Baczynska, G. 2014. "Russia or Ukraine? Crimean Tatars Consider Their Own Vote." Reuters, March 25. http://www.reuters.com/article/2014/03/25/us-ukraine-crisiscrimea-tatars-idUSBREA2O1F320140325. Accessed March 28, 2017.

Buhari-Gulmez, D. 2015. "From 'Sürgün' to Russian Annexation: The Crimean Tatar Question and the Return of the 'Old Demons'." *Research Turkey* IV (6): 82–95. http://researchturkey.org/from-surgun-to-russian-annexation-the-crimean-tatar-question-and-the-return-of-the-old-demons/. Accessed March 28, 2017.

Buhari-Gulmez, D. 2016a. "Religion as Identity Marker: The Dilemma of Crimean Tatars." In *Nation-Building and Identity in the Post-Soviet Space: New Tools and Approaches*, edited by Rico Isaacs and Abel Polese. Farnham: Ashgate. ISBN: 978-1-4724-5476-8.

Buhari-Gulmez, D. 2016b. "Autonomy, Self-Determination and Agency in a Global Context." *ProtoSociology* 33 (1): 149–67.

Coynash, H. 2011. "Volatile Appointment for the Crimea." *KyivPost*, November 9. https://www.kyivpost.com/opinion/op-ed/volatile-appointment-for-the-crimea-116606.html. Accessed March 28, 2017.

Delanty, G. 2006. "The Idea of a 'Postwestern Europe'." In *Europe and Asia Beyond East and West*, edited by Gerard Delanty. London: Routledge.

Dzhemilev, M. 2010a. "Address to the 5th Qurultay of the Crimean Tatar People," August 28, 115–31.

Dzhemilev, M. 2010b. "Crimean Tatars: Problems and Prospects." Speech at the European Parliament, March 17.

Dzhemilev, M. 2011. Speech at Simferopol Qurultay Meeting, May 18.

Emel (Journal of Crimean Tatar Foundation in Istanbul). 2014. "Kırım Tatar Milli Kurultayının tam metni" [Full Text of the Crimean Tatar Qurultay]. *Emel* 84 (246–249): 119–20.

Fabry, M. 2010. *Recognizing States.* Oxford and New York: Oxford University Press.

Fisher, A. W. 1978. *The Crimean Tatars.* Stanford, CA: Hoover Press.

Friedman, J. 1994. *Cultural Identity and Global Process.* London: Sage.

Gabidullin, I., and M. Edwards. 2014. "Crimea Crisis: The Tatarstan Factor: Why Did Politicians from Kazan Pay Frequent Visits to Crimea Recently?" *Al Jazeera*, March 15. http://www.aljazeera.com/indepth/opinion/2014/03/crimea-crisis-tatarstan-factor-2014314143349496558.html. Accessed March 28, 2017.

Geldenhuys, D. 2009. *Contested States in World Politics.* Basingstoke and New York: Palgrave Macmillan.

Goble, P. 2013. "Politicization of Islam in Crimea Threatens Peninsula's Stability." *Eurasia Daily Monitor* 19, May 12. http://www.ukrweekly.com/archive/2013/The_Ukrainian_Weekly_2013-19.pdf. Accessed March 28, 2017.

Hironaka, A. 2005. *Neverending Wars: The International Community, Weak States, and the Perpetuation of Civil War.* Cambridge and London: Harvard University Press.

Human Rights Watch. 2014. "Rights in Retreat: Abuses in Crimea," November 17. https://www.hrw.org/report/2014/11/17/rights-retreat/abuses-crimea. Accessed March 28, 2017.

İzmirli, İ. P. 2013a. "On Revitalization of the Language and Culture of the Crimean Tatars and Other Formerly Deported People in Crimea, Ukraine: Assessment of Needs and Recommendations." OSCE, Martinus Nijhoff Publishers, The Hague, Netherlands. http://papers.ssrn.com/sol3/papers.cfm?abstract_id=2308866. Accessed March 28, 2017.

İzmirli, İ. P. 2013b. "Fragmented Islam and Inter-Ethnic Conflict in Crimea, Ukraine: Assessment of Needs and Recommendations." OSCE, Martinus Nijhoff Publishers, The Hague, Netherlands. http://papers.ssrn.com/sol3/papers.cfm?abstract_id=2309381. Accessed March 28, 2017.

İzmirli, İ. P. 2013c. "Jamestown Foundation: Two Crimean Tatar Mosques Torched in Crimea on the Eve of Major Muslim Holiday." *Eurasia Daily Monitor*, October. http://www.ecoi.net/local_link/261096/387248_de.html. Accessed March 28, 2017.

Kırımlı, H. 1989. "Soviet Educational and Cultural Policies Toward the Crimean Tatars in Exile (1944–1987)." *Central Asian Survey* 8 (1): 69–88.

Kırımlı, H. 2014. "The Ethnogenesis of the Crimean Tatars." http://www.thewildfield.org/2014/04/the-ethnogenesis-of-crimean-tatars.html. Accessed March 28, 2017.

Krushelnycky A. 2013. "Ukraine: Crimea's Tatars—Clearing the Way for Islamic Extremism?" (Part 4). Radio Free Europe/Radio Liberty, August 26. http://www.rferl.org/articleprintview/1054513.html. Accessed March 28, 2017.

Kuzio, T. 2009. "Islamic Terrorist Threat in the Crimea." *Eurasia Daily Monitor* 6 (223), December 4. http://www.jamestown.org/single/?no_cache=1&tx_ttnews%5Btt_news%5D=35807&tx_ttnews%5BbackPid%5D=7&-cHash=6e194dfc8d#.Uu2jqfl_tzs. Accessed March 28, 2017.

Meyer, J. W., and R. Jepperson. 2000. "The 'Actors' of Modern Society: The Cultural Construction of Social Agency." *Sociological Theory* 18 (1): 100–20.

Muratova, E. 2009. "'He Who Pays the Piper Calls the Tune': Muslim Sponsors of Islamic Revival in Crimea." *Religion, State and Society* 37 (3): 263–76.

Nabers, D. 2015. *Poststructuralist Discourse Theory of Global Politics.* Houndsmills and New York: Palgrave Macmillan.

Neumann, I. B. 1999. *Uses of the Other: 'The East' in European Identity Formation.* Minneapolis: University of Minnesota Press.

OSCE. 2013. "The Integration of Formerly Deported People in Crimea, Ukraine: Needs Assessment." The Hague, August 16. http://www.osce.org/hcnm/104309. Accessed March 28, 2017.

Philpott, D. 1998. "Self-determination in Practice." In *National Self-determination and Secession*, edited by M. Moore. Oxford: Oxford University Press.

Reid, K. 2011. "Against the Right of Self-Determination," August 9. http://ssrn.com/abstract=1905257. Accessed March 28, 2017.

Reinke de Buitrago, S. 2012. *Portraying the Other in International Relations: Cases of Othering, Their Dynamics and the Potential for Transformation.* Newcastle upon Tyne: Cambridge Scholars Press.

Roepstorff, K. 2013. *The Politics of Self-determination: Beyond the Decolonisation Process.* Abingdon and New York: Routledge.

Rumford, C. 2008. *Cosmopolitan Spaces: Europe, Globalization, Theory.* New York: Routledge.

Sabah Daily. 2017. "Ukraine Expropriates Crimean Tatar Battalion's Base," Doğan News Agency. February 13. https://www.dailysabah.com/europe/2017/02/13/ukraine-expropriates-crimean-tatar-battalions-base. Accessed March 28, 2017.

Safarov, F. 2016. "Kırım'dan Ukrayna'ya FETÖ tepkisi" [FETO Criticism from Crimea to Ukraine]. Sputnik News, November 20. https://sptnkne.ws/cJZy. Accessed March 28, 2017.

Salem, H. 2014. "Crimea's Tatars Fear the Worst as It Prepares for Referendum." *The Guardian*, March 13. https://www.theguardian.com/world/2014/mar/13/crimea-tatars-fear-worst-prepares-referendum. Accessed March 28, 2017.

Shapovalova, N., and O. Burlyuk. 2016. "The Situation of National Minorities in Crimea Following Its Annexation by Russia." European Parliament's Committee on Human Rights, Belgium. http://www.europarl.europa.eu/RegData/etudes/STUD/2016/578003/EXPO_STU(2016)578003_EN.pdf. Accessed March 28, 2017.

Temnenko, Z. 2009. "Islam and Hizb ut-Tahrir's Activities in Crimea." Ukraine Working Paper #41. CAEI—Centro Argentino de Estudios Internacionales, June 20. https://www.files.ethz.ch/isn/125726/RU_41.pdf. Accessed March 28, 2017.

TASS (Russian News Agency). 2016. "Official Says Most Crimean Tatars Are Against Reunification with Ukraine," August 17. http://special.tass.ru/en/politics/894817. Accessed March 28, 2017.

Wilson, A. 2013. "Ukraine's Crimean Tatars Need EU Attention." EUobserver, September 6. http://euobserver.com/opinion/121351. Accessed March 28, 2017.

Yarosh, O., and D. Brylov. 2011. "Muslim Communities and Islamic Network Institutions in Ukraine: Contesting Authorities in Shaping of Islamic Localities." In *Muslims in Poland and Eastern Europe: Widening the European Discourse on Islam*, edited by Katarzyna Górak-Sosnowska. Warsaw: University of Warsaw Press.

Young, I. M. 2007. *Global Challenges: War, Self-determination and Responsibility for Justice*. Oxford: Polity Press.

CHAPTER 10

The Self/Other Space and Spinning the Net of Ontological Insecurities in Ukraine and Beyond: (Discursive) Reconstructions of Boundaries in the EU Eastern Partnership Countries Vis-à-Vis the EU and Russia

Susanne Szkola

INTRODUCTION

Since the coming-into-existence of the EU's Eastern Partnership (EaP)[1] – as more differentiated (eastern) European Neighborhood Policy (ENP)[2] approach – denominations of Armenia, Azerbaijan, Belarus,

---

[1] The Eastern Partnership (EaP) is a joint initiative involving the EU, its member states and six Eastern European partners: Armenia, Azerbaijan, Belarus, Georgia, Moldova and Ukraine (see Schumacher et al. 2018).

[2] The European Neighborhood Policy (ENP) was launched in 2004 in the light of the European Security Strategy (2003) and the upcoming EU enlargements (2004 and 2007) dealing with the outlook of new neighbours after the enlargements and "stability and prosperity in Wider Europe" (Schumacher et al. 2018).

S. Szkola (✉)
Brussels School of International Studies, University of Kent, Brussels, Belgium

© The Author(s) 2018
E. Resende et al. (eds.), *Crisis and Change in Post-Cold War Global Politics*, https://doi.org/10.1007/978-3-319-78589-9_10

Georgia, Moldova and Ukraine as countries which could be considered "in between" (Danii and Mascauteanu 2011) the EU and Russia, within the "spheres of influence" or the "near abroad," respectively, have featured quite significantly throughout all types of discourses. As the ENP/ EaP was initially designed to avoid "new dividing lines" in Europe and aiming at the creation of a zone of stability, prosperity and security on the European continent, these re-emerging categorizations fit yet again in the emerging debate on a "New Cold War in Europe" within which these signifiers of belonging (Jerez-Mir et al. 2009) to a certain socially constructed and cognitively evaluated group regain immense importance (Weisel and Böhm 2015).

It is exactly within foreign policy discourse that preferences, attitudes and alignments are constituted based on collective identity constructions (Ashmore et al. 2001). In other words, they are constituted on mechanisms of belonging and otherness. These discursive strategies of highlighting belonging to (imagined) communities (Anderson 1996), yet security communities (Deutsch 1957; Adler 1997), could be observed to be the cornerstones of securitization strategies of the EU and Russia vis-à-vis the common neighbourhood – and of the countries of the common neighbourhood vis-à-vis the EU and Russia vice versa. These idealistic and materialistic positionings, making sense of the world and others, are part of an amalgamation of identity politics: of self-constituted and ascribed identities—the latter being supported by processes of socialization and conditionality, labelled "Europeanization" or "Russification," respectively.

In contrast to, but in relation to, the ideas of the debate on a potential new Cold War in Europe, this argument is substantiated by recalling a basic premise of securitization literature (Buzan 1991; McSweeney 1996; Buzan et al. 1998; Buzan and Wæver 2003; Buzan and Hansen 2007; Balzacq 2011, 2015) which has described the situation after the Cold War in Europe as to be defined by the presence of two Regional Security Complexes (RSC): a European RSC and a post-Soviet one centred around Russia, which together built the European Supercomplex (Buzan and Wæver 2003: 437). Especially, the latter RSC has been "structured by two long term patterns: (1) waves of growth and contraction of the Russian Empire and (2) change in degrees of separateness and involvement with other regions, primarily Europe" (Buzan and Wæver 2003: 397).

Arguing that what Buzan and Wæver called "separateness and involvement" could better be modelled as different conceptualizations of otherness/belonging, the model presented here assumes that the bridge between the two regional foreign policies of the EU and Russia could be identified in them being different anchors of belonging, yet otherness, whilst concrete images of amity/enmity co-constitute the situation of collective identities on the ground. This collective identity formation, understood as a function of othering, is then one of the conceptual and categorical boundary drawings—inherently linked to (definitional/normative) power.

Hence, this chapter tries (1) to map this variety of others and varying definitions of otherness and cognitive boundaries within this complex security configuration, (2) to highlight motivations for those conceptualizations and, in doing so, (3) to unpack those (security) relations. It will do so by shifting the attention from the EU and Russia as "framing actors" towards the perceptions of the countries in-between—in order to draw the attention yet again back to their agency. To do so, the chapter proceeds as follows: first, it recapitulates central conceptual underpinnings and discusses focal assumptions of research on identity constitutions, ontological security and securitization theory and connects this with image theory. Second, some methodological issues are raised before discussing in the third section the empirical observations which are divided into two parts: whereas the first tackles the relational identity layer and the net of significant Others, the second zooms into the "Selves" and their ontological security rationales. The chapter concludes with some more general findings on ontological security (seeking) in/for Ukraine and beyond.

Conceptual Underpinnings

The foreign policy-identity and the identity-security nexus are two academic compounds which are vividly debated and tackled from a variety of positions. In this, the terminology referring to identity is multiple: "identification," "attachment," "categorization," "self-understanding," "role conceptualization," "social location or position" or "groupness" are just a few examples (Hagström and Gustafsson 2015: 3). The arising question of continuity and change within this is closely related to the agency vs. structure debate on which much ink has been spilled, not least in International Relations (IR) theory. This paper follows the post-structuralist approach on identity and foreign policy, which postulates a dynamic and mutually constitutive relationship between them. In other words, foreign policies are reliant upon representations of identity, but identities are constituted and reconstructed also through the formulation of foreign policy. In this understanding, material forces and ideas are so interlinked in the discursive practice of foreign policy that the two cannot be separated from each other for they are indeed ontologically inseparable. However, the understanding of this (re-)construction of identity is often under-conceptualized and needs further elaboration.

In accordance with early role theory sociologists, identity is here treated as layered and simultaneously constituted on mutually interacting levels of intersubjective meaning making (Harnisch 2011). These two levels refer to a "domestic (internal) domain" ("I" or "We") and an "international (relational) domain" ("Me" or "Us") of identity construction. A "domestic domain" is, thus, impossible other than in relation to an "international" one. In this context, the fragile and ever-so-to-be-negotiated balancing act between the domestic locus and the international locus of one's identity construction is to be found—in the context of foreign and security policy—in the mechanism of ontological security seeking. This is to say that these points require a rather different concept of identity, a "relational" understanding where demarcations between domestic and international, identity and difference, or self and other, are exactly what constitutes identity (Campbell 1998; Connolly 1985; Neumann 1992).

These notions of spatial, temporal and social power highlight the practice of categorization and its inherent linkage to collective identity constructions via subjective security perceptions by the virtue of defining the Other and the Self. This "categorial power" of defining in-category status cuts across the debate on "normative power(s)" as this very act of defining in-category status could be theorized as an act of labelling something as "normal." However, categorical power is rather the outcome of a much more complex process of identity demarcations and takes into account not only representations of imaginary sets of belonging/otherness but ideological projections of power—of boundaries and borders connected with security discourses through their very implementations as discursive power (could) manifest(s) itself. This socially diffuse production of subjectivity in systems of meaning and signification is, in terms of Barnett and Duvall (2005), productive power. It is, then, a "sequencing" that takes place: only through (internal) discourses, social collective identity meanings and positions are generated which then feed into structural power concerns (external)—as structural power "concerns the structures – or, more precisely, the co-constitutive relations of [social] relative positions" (Barnett and Duvall 2005: 25). Power and (perceptions of) in/securities are then inherently linked—and constitutive of each other—via identity constructions. In other terms, categories (of belonging) are either part of the fundamental self/other ontology and/or securitized.

ONTOLOGICAL SECURITY (SEEKING)

Ontological Security Theory (OST) (Steele 2005, 2008; Mitzen 2006; Delehanty and Steele 2009; Lupovici 2012; Rumelili 2015a, b) as a framework to understand behaviour in realms of security and perceptions of security (on a mostly state-centric level) has featured widely in the recent IR debate and turn on narratives (Huysmans 1998; Alexander et al. 2005; Delehanty and Steele 2009). OST holds that the motivations for behaviour could be found in needs of holding and reconstructing a positive self-identity, a constant and consistent self-reflexive positive narrative of the self. This biographical continuity (of the state/society) in form of narratives and images of the self (in fact, an internal domain identity) and the other is sought to be institutionalized by routinized relationships with those significant Others. Reducing uncertainty about the behaviour of those Others and creating predictability are functions of this institutionalization of reimagined relationships.

However, as Ejdus (2017) quite convincingly argues, whilst some studies have drawn attention to the main argument of OST—that is, that states are ready to compromise their physical security in order to stabilize and defend their ontological security, little attention was paid to these critical situations that render actors ontologically insecure. This ties in with quite some IR and FPA literature engaging in the discussion on how and why change in foreign policy (decision) making is rendered possible, particularly highlighting the notion of critical junctures (Flockhart 2005). Crises, as focal point of this book project, defined by Nabers (2015) as "disruptive processes," are exactly these critical situations in world politics, these "radical disjunctions that challenge the ability of collective actors to go on" (Ejdus 2017). They are, indeed, a re-negotiation of community boundaries and a (re)construction of collective identities. In line with an argument put forward by Chernobrov (2016), this paper suggests that images are instrumentalized within these co-constitutive relationships: as OST assumes security to rest in an ever-so-positive representation of the Self, images of othering and belonging are used as balancing mechanism of those relationships to secure stability in "going on (as usual)." This inherent drive for consistency (Festinger 1962; Lupovici 2012) within this system opens up space for two quite different strategies of dissonance reduction within the aforementioned discourses according to two types of dissonances: cognitive and ontological.[3]

First, consistent with the overall assumption that the aforementioned images of amity and enmity work as cognitive proxies for power configurations, OST puts forward that there's a hierarchy of needs to be achieved by the state: first, securing a positive self-conceptualization, then physical security. This rationale for a positive self-identity thus may lead to foreign policy choices inconsistent with physical security needs. In that scenario, images are strategically used as cognitive bridges between the (physical) security policy and ontological security needs in light of the strategic environment and perceived national security threats (Subotić 2015).[4] Second, otherness and belonging as distinct representations of those instrumentalized balancing methods of states'/societies' drive for ontological security shape intergroup relations (relational domain): they stimulate the construction of security communities and provide incentives to repel outsiders (Subotić 2015). Therefore, the "systemic structure" is a function of otherness, and thus a function of belonging to an in-group vs. an out-group (cf. the English School).

Identity Politics, Securitization and Images

Switching away from the essentialist meaning of friends and foes in the Schmittian sense and their provokingly simple/undercomplex and dehumanizing categorizations of others (Kteily et al. 2016), arguing in line with Mouffe (2005) opens up the discursive space in

---

[3]"[...] ontological dissonance is [...] the clash [that] stems from the perception that the measures required to placate the ontological insecurity of each of the threatened identities are themselves in conflict." (Lupovici 2012: 810).

[4]States, over time, do create "national security cultures"—which are constructed by national mythologies of past events and relationships with historical friends or foes (Katzenstein 1996). It could be argued that the definitions of amity and enmity applied by Buzan and Wæver in the RSCT were meant to refer to that concept.

which images and narratives of enmity and amity are constantly invoked as instruments and methods to mobilize groups and foster in-group cohesion (Alexander et al. 1999). These images and narratives, which provide probabilistic heuristics about the Other's behaviour, are understood as cognitive shortcuts towards reality and are a powerful tool of political discourse (Williams 2003; Chernobrov 2016). Looking at how friends and foes are constructed in political discourse provides a powerful analytical tool for recent developments. Acknowledging this antagonistic constitutive dimension should be understood as admonition of Schmittian reflexes, to "think with Schmitt against Schmitt" (Mouffe 2005). Thus, images of amity and enmity are heuristic categories of (discourse) analysis rather than foundational principles. In this sense, these discourses represent discourses of danger (Stern 2005) which discern the self from the other and "tell [...] what to fear" (Stern 2005: 34). These evaluations construct subjective positions on the boundary of "we" and "them," and they are reproduced through performance (Stryker 2008). This reflex of "to fix where/who we are" is central to the production of in/security where the inside is rendered secure and the outside dangerous (Stern 2005). This assignment of "foreign threat" represents a notion of securitizing the identity of the respective group—inherently linked to OST.

Unpacking those security relations is crucial to deepen the understanding of dynamics of collective identity formation, and about how aspects of othering influence those security relations and perceptions as "who (we say) we are matters in how we conceive of, strive for, and practice security" (Stern 2005: 7). These identity constellations—the nexus of different mutually constructed and constituting identity positions (Stern 2005: 32), or as Buzan and Wæver (2003) put it, self-other conceptualizations as (re-)production of social order—lead to a reframed definition of what foreign and security policy is, namely "[a]ll practices of differentiation, of exclusion (possibly figured as relationships of otherness) which constitute their objects as foreign in the process of dealing with them." (Campbell 1998: 76). Accordingly, collective identity formation is always a product of border formation, an articulation at the boundary of in-group/out-group, thus defined and moderated between "them" and "us" (Korostelina 2007).

Image theory draws the connection between those actors' images of Others and theoretical considerations on approaches to security—and their potential resulting behaviour—as it holds that these images contain information about actors' capabilities, intentions, previous experiences/memories as well as perceptions of threat (Alexander et al. 2005; Gaufman 2017). It is this sense-making and informational value of images, which brings conceptualizations of categorial power back in the model—by virtue of connecting all dots of both identity layers with the narratives about the other and the self. This is the case, because images of other (and the self) can be thought of as a continuum along a function of goal compatibility [1], relative status [2] and relative power [3] (Alexander et al. 2005: 30).[5] Identity positions in turn, then, affect social perceptions and behaviour (Korostelina 2007: 15): in particular, the out-group image which is negatively perceived and stereotyped— relating those reflexive, non-material securitization discourses back to performances, yet again.

METHODOLOGICAL CONSIDERATIONS

For this research, both the relational and internal identity layers were under scrutiny, the latter referring to the self-images at hand, the former as images of the other. As the main interest was to identify notions of othering/belonging in the realms of foreign and security policy, the main (re)sources for this analysis were the main foreign, security and defence policies in place from 2009 to 2016 (in Belarus, Armenia, Azerbaijan, Georgia, Moldova, Ukraine) for and in which frames of the self(s)/other(s) were inductively explored, identified and retrieved in a two-step process of discourse analysis (Hopf and Allan 2016). Conceptual frames (Goffman 1974) are here understood as ways of organizing experience and a way to structure perceptions. Accordingly, a frame designates the core meaning of a statement that might be classified and coded. This was applied here by, first, inductively identifying core notions and elements of othering/belonging and then, second, structuring and relating them to main images. Relating to that, framing is considered as a strategy of addressing an audience in order to promote a particular interpretation of a given issue. Thus, the frames found already represent a certain notion of securitization strategy. This approach, of course, is limited to highlighting policy elite conceptualizations.

---

[5] The taxonomy of these images reads as follows: ally (1: compatible, 2 and 3 equal), enemy (1: incompatible, 2 and 3 equal), dependent (1: incompatible, 2 and 3 lower), barbarian (1: incompatible, 2 lower, 3 higher) and imperialist (1: incompatible, 2 and 3 higher) (Alexander et al. 2005: 30).

Moreover, these findings were contrasted and supplemented by look-ing at societal identity conceptualizations within the same time frame (Abdelal 2009; Hopf and Allan 2016).

However, it is up to further research to explore comparable notions within society and other fluid identity groups to gain better understand-ing of converging or even diverging collective identity notions—bearing within high potential for further fragmentation of different layers of group identities. One advantage of looking at images here is that they are relatively more durable, stable evaluating indicators and patterns of social information on amity/enmity—floating signifiers so to say (Finlay et al. 1967; Alexander et al. 2005; Finley 2010).[6]

"THE (SIGNIFICANT) OTHERS" AND THE RELATIONAL IDENTITY LAYER: OTHERING IN EU–RUSSIA RELATIONS AS COMMON DENOMINATOR?

Rushing from one initiative to the other without having a signifi-cant outcome, EU–Russia relations have suffered from being under-defined (Freire and Kanet 2012; Allison 2013). The Partnership and Cooperation Agreement with Russia signed in 1994 was framed by long and difficult negotiations with Russia pressing for a better deal and the EU as shaper of norms insisting on conditionality and norms conver-gence. "Looking back at the history of EU–Russia relations since 1991 it is possible to observe a gradual increase in Russia's identification of the EU's position as a power politics actor in its immediate neighborhood" (Made and Sekarev 2011).

However, strategic interaction has been fairly limited under the impression of the first Chechen War and the Russian debt crisis. Despite this, the EU's Common Strategy on Russia in June 1999 reaffirmed the importance of Russia and post-sovereign principles (Haukkala 2010). Russia's mid-term EU strategy 2000–2010 can be regarded as a direct answer to that, already opposing the mentioned principles emphasizing sovereignty and interest-based cooperation (Freire and Kanet 2012). Trying to establish EU–Russia relations in the first place, various aspects

---

[6]Inspired by attribution theory, these images are, basically, a probability judgement within which, however, the principle of fundamental attribution error may occur.

of common duty in the neighbourhood were neglected in the policy documents, leaving behind fundamentally different interpretations of security and the way of implementing them—economic aspects always played a major role in this relationship.

Putin's presidencies initially including a "European Choice" and Russia's cooperative role in the post-9/11 developments in combination with first signs of domestic liberalization boosted the cooperation and emphasized equality in interstate relations (Hopf 2008) but eventually just contributed to a more fuzzy constellation of EU–Russia relations with only virtual progress: the Four Common Spaces (2005) in the light of the Big-Bang enlargement and Russia's rejection of the ENP, the EU–Russia Permanent Partnership Council because of Russia's insistence of a special strategic partnership, not ranking it amongst the other eastern countries, and the Modernization Partnerships (2009/2010) in the light of the Caucasus crisis and thus the necessity to re-establish relations.

"Cooperation on security issues between Brussels and Moscow has been rather limited," argue Freire and Kanet (2012). Indeed, despite all efforts, the implementation of a partnership has been slow and inconsistent: the external security pillar was under constant contestation without being able to find consensus on a denomination for the "common neighborhood," thus revealing again fundamental differences and abstention from cooperation in security issues (Whitman and Wolff 2010). At the same time, Russian leaders consider that NATO enlargement has reinforced "old dividing lines," despite cooperation under the NATO-Russia Council (Allison 2013).

Moreover, the 2008 war in Georgia was a turning point for EU–Russian security relations (Freire and Kanet 2012): both Russia and Georgia were blamed for having been the aggressor with the EU trying to mediate; at the same time, NATO enlargement was off the table with the European Union Monitoring Mission in Georgia as a freezing exercise (Haukkala 2010), having in mind the failed proposal of a New Security Treaty for Europe by Medvedev. Hence: "A cooperative security approach can only emerge when the EU and Russia would share a meaningful set of views and interests" (Freire and Kanet 2012). This could not be observed so far in EU–Russia relations persisting of fundamentally different interpretations of (security) actorness and different modes of cooperation deduced from them.

Russian and European policies imposed on the neighbourhood have been fairly competitive regarding all these aspects in the last years, fostering the fear of alienation of CIS countries from Russia (Made and Sekarev 2011) exemplified by Lavrov's assessment of the EaP as an attempt to extend the EU's sphere of influence which opposes Russian interests (Freire and Kanet 2012) and the fact that both actors have not been able to find a common denomination for these countries. Approaches to design complementary policies—as seen above—have been rather limited in scope, coherence and support. The deepening constitution of the ENP in form of the EaP and Association Agreements, thus, exactly constitutes what has manifested to have been a pivotal point for EU–Russia relations: a strong input of EU identity projection, of a redefinition of in-group belonging and, thus, a rather strong othering of the Russian position and vice versa (Korosteleva 2017; Tocci 2017) (Table 10.1).

A clear split within the patterns of international institutional belonging can be observed: Russian-led integrationist projects (CIS, EurAsEC, CU, CSTO) have different members than regional and international institutions (in)formed by the EU.[7] This belonging can be interpreted in two terms: first, as seeking respective security alignments and communities in the light of a perceived arms race and an insecure material environment[8]— even so exacerbated by those military expenditures interpreted through amity/enmity lenses—second, as a strategy to underline ideational belongings even further, to progress and continue in the same direction and to foster these commonalities as a function of identity convergence.

---

[7] This correlates with the intensity and form of NATO cooperation too.

[8] As figures on the respective military expenditures from 2009 to 2014 show (SIPRI 2016; at constant 2011 prices and exchange rates), the military spending levels in terms of % GDP are around 3–4% for Armenia, Azerbaijan, Georgia and Russia with slightly lower levels for Belarus($\sim$1.4%) and Ukraine ($\sim$2%) whilst Moldova invests only around 0.3%. In terms of military expenditure as percentages of government spending, again, Russia ($\sim$10.7%), Armenia ($\sim$16.5%), Azerbaijan ($\sim$11.6%) and Georgia ($\sim$11%), on average, show significantly higher levels than Belarus ($\sim$3.2%), Moldova ($\sim$0.9%) or Ukraine($\sim$5.5%). Although the aggregated spending level of all those countries together (from US\$ 72 billion in 2009 to US\$ 102.1 billion in 2014) remains very low in contrast to, for example, NATO (from US\$ 1095 billion in 2009 to US\$ 911 billion in 2014), or the aggregated spending of all EU countries (not on an EU level, from US\$ 190 billion in 2009 to US\$ 264 billion in 2014), the trend is opposing: whilst the military expenditure of NATO is decreasing, aggregated spending of all EU countries and the countries under scrutiny are increasing—observing a particular stark increase in expenditure in the latter countries. These figures showcase the dynamics of a security spiral with military build-ups.

Table 10.1 Patterns of international institutional belonging (up to 2015)

	CIS	EurAsEC	CU	CSTO	GUAM	BSEC	NATO	ENP	BSS	TRACECA	INOGATE
Russia	x	x	x	x			NRC	#	x		#
Armenia	x	#	x	x		x	IPAP	x	x	x	x
Azerbaijan	x			#	x	x	IPAP	x	x	x	x
Georgia	#			#	x	x	NGC	x	x	x	x
Belarus	x	x	x	x				x	x		x
Moldova	x	#			x	x	IPAP	x	x	x	#
Ukraine	#	#			x	x	NUC	x	x	x	x

CIS: Commonwealth of Independent States, EurAsEC: Eurasian Economic Community, CU: Customs Union, CSTO: Collective Security Treaty Organization, GUAM (Georgia–Ukraine–Azerbaijan–Moldova): Organization for Democracy and Economic Development, BSEC: Organization of the Black Sea Economic Cooperation, NATO: North Atlantic Treaty Organization, ENP: European Neighborhood Policy, BSS: Black Sea Synergy, TRACECA: (EU) Transport Corridor Europe-Caucasus-Asia, INOGATE: (EU) Interstate Oil and Gas Transport to Europe

"THE SELVES" AND ONTOLOGICAL SECURITY NOTIONS: SPINNING A NET OF INSECURITIES

As Edjus (2017) has shown insightfully for the case of Serbia and the unilateral declaration of independence of Kosovo, developments which question already existing understandings of collective identities lead to significant re-negotiations of understandings of those boundaries and highlight the fundamental struggle for different discursive meaning by all parties involved—where it is not possible anymore to continue with the same entity ontology anymore.

As such, the Ukraine crisis fundamentally highlights another case of ontological insecurity, where the (narrated) existence and autobiography of Ukraine—in the light of at least elite policy discourses as scope of this paper—are challenged and reconfigured. From this ontological insecurity due to the developments in Eastern Ukraine and Crimea, a very specific net of ontologies, captured in enemy/amity images, emerges—in particular, when looking at a set of countries, where a litany of "frozen conflicts" is to be found.

Looking at images of amity and enmity of and in the countries of the Eastern Partnership, a very fragmented, yet polarized picture of relationships and related security outcomes emerges. This conundrum depicts a situation where ideational self-conceptualizations are based on sovereign national identities and their preservation and enhancement, which often contradict aspirations of neighbouring countries and regional structures. Moreover, there is a litany of (significant) others and institutions to be found with the involvement of the EU and Russia significantly shaping patterns of belonging and foreign policy orientations.

It is exactly within the scope and logic of ontological security seeking how and why the frames of othering/belonging found in the elite policy discourses of the EaP countries are constituted and articulated. Although all countries are part of the Eastern Partnership initiative, two geographically defined country sets have to be distinguished: one, the countries north of the Black Sea—Belarus, Ukraine and Moldova—and two, the countries east of the Black Sea—Georgia, Azerbaijan and Armenia. One can identify within those two differentiated country sets—regional security sub-complexes—particular intergroup comparison processes. However, these particular comparisons have broader implications as these lead to spillovers of similar image constitutions and alignments to the other regional sub-complex, thus fostering the interconnectedness of those two subsets.

This, in particular, can be observed when looking at images of amity and enmity in Ukraine and Georgia: both countries perceive Russia as an imperialist power whose actions range from active war promotion, violating territorial integrity and creating de facto occupied territories to limiting policy options and questioning state sovereignty. Both self-conceptualizations are coherently linked to "following a European way," so that Russia's actions are in particular seen as provocations and violations of the very self-concept—territorial integrity and sovereignty. As those actions go to the core of ontological security, having experienced conflicts with Russia in the recent past (Georgia in 2008, Ukraine recently) and its arms build-up contribute very negatively to its imperialist image—in both ideational and material terms. In this context, it is interesting to observe that it is also through this identical identification of Russia as being barbarian that one can observe a convergence of very friendly images of Georgia and Ukraine vis-à-vis the other.

These images exist within the foreign and security policy elites of those countries, not necessarily within the broader public—leaving quite significant space for re-interpretations and identity leverages (Szkola 2017)—or regions which are not under direct control of those elites. There, the "ontics," the politics of ontological security rationales and their seeking, could differ quite significantly as feelings of belonging are recalibrated —often with external impetus within that undertaking. This applies in both cases just discussed: within Ukraine, the identity topographies are far from being coherent or homogeneous (Chatham House 2017; Korostelina 2003, 2014) as it is also true for Georgia (Coene 2016). Parts of Eastern Ukraine as well as especially Abkhazia and South Ossetia along with Transnistria (also known as Transdniester) are fitting examples where the ontics of a central elite are not shared or adhered to and where boundaries of belonging are redrawn, actively and/or passively, intentionally and/or inadvertently.

Moreover, another layer of identity complexity as just highlighted shows that far from being coherent sub-complexes in terms of self-conceptualizations themselves, both feature very distinctive interpretations of their social context and otherness and belonging. Whereas Belarus is still very much focused on its Union State with Russia—and derives from that that nearly all neighbouring states are not friendly to

Table 10.2 Images of amity and enmity in the foreign and security policies in the EaP countries

Armenia	Azerbaijan	Georgia	Belarus	Moldova	Ukraine
Azerbaijan: imperialist/ barbarian	**Armenia:** barbarian	**Russia:** imperialist	**Russia:** "natural" ally	**Romania:** ally	**Armenia:** dependent
Turkey: imperialist	**Georgia:** strategic ally	**Turkey:** ally	**USA:** imperialist	**Russia:** imperialist	**Georgia:** ally
Russia: most important ally	**Iran:** important ally	**Ukraine:** ally	**CSTO/ CIS/ EurAsEC:** institutional ally	**Ukraine:** ally	**Russia:** imperialist
CSTO/CIS: institutional ally	**Turkey:** strategic ally	**EU:** strong, "natural" ally	**EU:** very selective ally	**EU:** ally	**EU:** most important ally
USA/ NATO: strategic/very selective ally	**Russia:** strategic ally	**NATO:** strong ally		**NATO:** ally	**NATO:** most important ally
EU: strategic, very selective ally	**EU/NATO:** strategic, selective ally				

that extent that only solutions within a post-Soviet integration will be beneficial, e.g. with Russia and Kazakhstan—it is interesting to see that within a situative materialistic context cognitive evaluations of the EU feature quite positively on its agenda—amidst its "balanced multi-vector foreign policy" (White and Feklyunina 2014). This can be highlighted as an example of a situational co-constitution of friendly images and a reorientation of self-conceptualizations.[9] Moldova, on the other hand, also identifies Russia as imperialist other and, derived from that, views Ukraine, Georgia and Romania as very friendly and allied others.

When looking at the second sub-complex, even more complex, mutually exclusive self-conceptualizations emerge—with profound implications for the co-constitutions of images of amity and enmity.

---

[9] See footnote 5 for a taxonomy and description of the images mentioned on the Table 10.2.

At the basis of this lies the Nagorno-Karabakh conflict[10] which features as most important issue in both Armenia's and Azerbaijan's self-identifications, as both interpret Nagorno-Karabakh and its population as being integral part of its sovereignty, territorial integrity and national identity. It is not surprising that a conflict which is integrated into the very self-definition constitutes very negative perceptions of the involved other. Thus, both Armenia and Azerbaijan hold images of each other varying from barbarian to imperialist. It is within this context, that a net of other significant others is constructed through those lenses, in particular with a focus on national identity ties as military build-ups (see footnote 4). Georgia is the only neighbour who is accepted as (selective) ally by both states—from that, perceptions of amity and enmity draw clear distinctions of (un)friendly others given their perceived material and ideational positioning on self-conceptualization issues. Whereas Armenia sees Russia as most important ally and together with that the CSTO and CIS as institutional allies, Azerbaijan and Turkey are depicted as archenemies. Coming from that, the EU and NATO are only seen as strategic and very selective allies. Vice versa, perceptions of security follow the same logic in Azerbaijan: Armenia is perceived as the barbarian other with Turkey, Georgia and in particular Iran being strategic allies. It is noteworthy that also Russia is seen a strategic ally with the EU and NATO only featuring in situational identifications.

PUBLIC PERCEPTIONS OF THE IN-BETWEEN IN THE IN-BETWEEN: POLARIZATIONS AND SOLIDARITIES

[10]The Nagorno-Karabakh conflict is a territorial and ethnic conflict between Armenia and Azerbaijan over the disputed region of Nagorno-Karabakh and seven surrounding districts, which are de facto controlled by the self-declared Nagorno-Karabakh Republic, but are internationally recognized as de jure part of Azerbaijan (CFR 2017).

Table 10.3 Layers of identification: internal/relational. All WVS Wave 6 2010–2014[a] (except Moldova WVS Wave 5 2005–2009[b])

[in %]	Strongly	Agree	Disagree	Strongly	No answer	Dk
I see myself as part of the local community						
Belarus	5.9	14.7	39.9	37.5	-	1.9
Moldova	46.0	47.6	5.1	0.4	-	0.7
Ukraine	22.3	30.1	26.1	21.5	-	-
Armenia	67.8	29.4	2.2	0.4	-	0.2
Azerbaijan	14.2	25.4	34.4	26.0	-	-
Georgia	66.1	28.5	3.8	1.2	-	0.2
I see myself as part of the [country's nationality] nation						
Belarus	60.4	28.9	6.3	3.8	-	0.6
Moldova	51.7	44.5	3.1	0.3	-	0.1
Ukraine	59.0	27.5	8.7	4.8	-	-
Armenia	74.6	23.3	1.4	0.5	-	0.2
Azerbaijan	77.8	17.3	2.8	2.1	-	-
Georgia	81.9	16.9	1.0	-	0.1	0.1
I see myself as part of the [Belarus, Ukraine, Azerbaijan: CIS] [Armenia: EU | CIS], [Georgia: EU]						
Belarus	19.6	30.6	31.9	16.5	-	1.4
Moldova	-	-	-	-	-	-
Ukraine	23.7	28.2	26.1	21.9	-	-
Armenia						
EU	21.5	31.3	25.0	12.1	-	10.0
CIS	25.3	34.6	18.4	11.1	0.2	10.4
Azerbaijan	3.9	16.5	39.6	40.0	-	-
Georgia	16.0	23.5	28.5	30.2	0.2	1.5

[a]It is interesting to note that there are already vectors of belonging implicitly inherent within these questions as only the officially institutionalized foreign policy direction at that time for the country under scrutiny was given as option for seeing oneself as part of
[b]See Hopf and Allan (2016) on this approach

UKRAINIANS, MOLDOVANS AND BELARUSIANS

This first set delves into the perceptions of Ukrainians, Moldovans and Belarusians to explore their articulations of belonging/otherness and how these interact, overlap and/or differ from present elite images and threat assignments through the processes and acts of labelling. The point of departure for this analysis is the Ukraine crisis as the critical juncture of (assigned) re-narrating, re-negotiation and reorientation of practices, perceptions, boundaries and identities—having profound reverberations not only for Ukraine, but also for "the Others." It is in particular interesting to trace whom of those "others" spin the net of ontological in/security according to what rationales—recreating nets of belonging/otherness by re-narrating and remembering the commonness/differences of experiences (Mälksoo 2015).

The conflict in Ukraine has had a profound impact on the constitution of positive/negative boundary drawings and formations: whereas Russia was seen negatively only by 10% of Ukrainians in 2012, from 2013 onwards one can observe a steady intensification until late 2014 where, with 78%, the peak of polarization of negative sentiments was reached (IRI 2017b). However, these negative perceptions persist on a slightly lower level until today (around 68%). Russia's ontological questioning of the status of Crimea and later Eastern Ukraine could be observed to have reversed the formerly relatively stable image of Russia as a positive, friendly other completely (60% in 2012). At the same time, this also led to a re-evaluation of the EU and the USA—perceived as opposing blocks to Russia which also brings back and has the tendency to mobilize the idea of distinct blocks of belonging/otherness as present during the Cold War. Especially, this peak of Russian enmity perceived by Ukrainians led to a rather strengthened positive image of the USA (from 25% in 2012 to 40% in 2014)—with the tendency of the conflict to be prolonged and new conflict areas and issues to be at stake this is increasing ever so slightly. The same tendency can be observed when looking at the positive image of the EU in Ukraine—however, on a slightly higher level: 40% in 2012 to 50% in 2017. A more nuanced look at these figures reveals an interesting net of friendly and unfriendly others being spun (KIIS 2017).

Poland is perceived as a very friendly country by 58% of Ukrainians, Belarus by 56%, followed by, very interestingly, Canada with 47% and Georgia with 46%. In contrast, Moldova and Turkey are rather perceived as unfriendly (61 and 67%). These images coherently translate into orientations towards the EU and the Eurasian Union as (potential) anchors of institutional belonging: whereas these orientations were still equal in 2011/2012 (42% EU, 40% EEAU), accordingly a polarization of those anchors manifested towards 53% (EU) and 18% (EEAU), respectively, othering the EEAU strongly and underlining perceived belonging to the EU even more so. The same reverse tendency applies to processes of othering in perceptions towards NATO: 34% of Ukrainians were in favour of joining in 2014 in contrast to 43% who "othered" this outlook—in 2017, 46% do hold a positive image of NATO and would join, whereas 27% would not (IRI 2017b).

As this is all connected to the pinnacle experience of the initial re-drawing of Crimean boundaries of belonging/otherness, the same ontological importance is assigned to the so-called Donetsk and Luhansk People's Republics as repetition of the hurtful experience of ontological insecurity: 75% of Ukrainians see these as fundamental part of Ukraine—only 3% see them as part of Russia, another 3% see them as an independent country. However, this picture changes when looking at the self-assignments of those alleged republics, however, with a striking tendency—from 2015, when 32% articulated a preference for these territories to belong to Ukraine "as before," in 2017 this share is 47% (with 31% instead of former 43% perceiving a need for some sort of decentralization and special status within Ukraine)—with also the share of vectors of belonging towards Russia declining from 7 to 2%. These figures could be interpreted as a recalibration of incentives for breaches to ontological security and a movement towards the formerly institutionalized autobiographical narrative of those territories.

These (re-)productions of demarcations of difference and sameness in ontological security seeking rationales can also be traced in Moldova: there, Transnistria is a core category of ontological politics—in elite as well as in popular discourse (IRI 2017a). In contrast to Eastern Ukraine and Crimea as ontics in Ukraine, the assignments of belonging were, however, relatively stable over time (2011–2017) with around 60% of Moldovans delineating Transnistria as an ordinary region of Moldova, 15–20% as a region with a certain autonomy but nevertheless an essential part of the republic and only a small share of around 6% drew it as a part of Russia. Subsequently, a relatively balanced net of enmity/amity vectors as perceived situatedness emerges: the EU is seen as friendly by 66%, Romania by 65%, Ukraine by 56% and the USA by 53%—Russia features within this group with 58%. This is remarkable as this does not replicate the negative image trend of Russia by neighbouring countries (except Belarus and, to some extent, Hungary and Bulgaria). As such, these vectors of belonging then also find articulation in the international orientation: nearly equal shares of around 43% each support the integration into the EU or the Eurasian Union (from 2013 to 2017) with a slight tendency towards the latter. Moreover, NATO membership is rejected as an option by 30/45% (2014/2017) of the population whilst 19/27% (2014/2017) value it. This replicates the implicit perception of NATO/Russia dichotomy (IRI 2017a).

As such, Moldovans situate themselves on the "middle ground" between the polarizing/polarized anchors of belonging/otherness of Ukraine and Belarus (IRI 2017a). As already elaborated, the former has developed a strict enemy image of Russia and amity images of the EU and the USA whereas the latter holds inverse images. Belarusians' images are highly stable with Russia featuring as best friend, followed by China and Kazakhstan, and the USA as main enemy (interestingly, Germany as second) in the whole time period under scrutiny. As such, these views significantly overlap with those of Russia(ns), but also differ in crucial dimensions such as Germany's role but also as Ukraine and Poland feature as friends—not as enemies. Spinning the net broader, also Azerbaijan and Italy are seen in a friendly light. This more nuanced development also reflects the multi-vector orientation of Belarus(ians) (IISEPS 2016).

ARMENIANS, AZERIS AND GEORGIANS

These identifications and evaluations, as approximations for identities through articulations of perceived othering, spill over from Ukraine—and back—also to its wider neighbourhood, namely the South Caucasus as second set under scrutiny. As one main anchor of belonging and therefore source for constituting otherness vis-à-vis the others, the EU holds a particular role in the South Caucasus (CRRC 2013).

A sense of belonging to the EU is perceived very strongly in Georgia (65%) with rates of "equal support/do not support" only at 17%—there is merely a share of population rejecting the idea of belonging to the EU (only 8%). Nevertheless, from 2012 to 2013, mentions of belonging fell from 72% and undecided accounts as well as othering positions rose from 13 to 3%, respectively. This tendency, even more prominent, is also observable in Azerbaijan: the share of population undecided whether they support belonging to the EU or not nearly equalled the share of supporters (34%) with 32%. This is partly a result of rising support of the forth (up from 23% in 2012) and partly a significant fall of feeling of belonging to the EU (this number fell from 49%). Simultaneously, othering in terms of not wanting to belong to the EU rose from 12 to 18%.

These findings are consistent with observations for Armenia: there, the share of people rejecting the idea of belonging to the EU rose 10–23% within one year and now constitutes the highest figure of rejection in the South Caucasus. In line with this, perceptions of belonging decreased sharply from 54 to 41%; 25% are between the stools of those two positions. Not that surprising, membership aspirations for NATO are still the highest within the Georgian population: "fully support" and "rather support" account there for 58% of all replies. However, the share of (rather) non-supporters accounts for 12%—up from 6% the year before. In addition, rather indifferent views ("equally support and do not support") gain more and more shares: in 2013, they represented 19% (in contrast to 14% in 2012).

These rather indifferent attachments also constitute the majority of replies by Azeri respondents: the number rose from 23% in 2012 to 32% in 2013. This change is in line with falling support rates—these went down in the same time frame from 45 to 31% and are now less than the indifferent ones—and rising non-attachment moves: these numbers went up from 14 to 18%. The same tendency is observable in Armenia: indifferent, yet undecided accounts represent the majority with 30% in 2013 (up from 26%). However, the share not supporting in any form of NATO membership now is higher than the share rather feeling attached to it: 28% (2012:23%) compared to 26% (2012:33%). The common denominator for perceptions of NATO attachment, thus, is rather a drifting away of the countries of the South Caucasus represented by falling numbers of support and rising numbers of undecidedness and rejection (CRRC 2013).

It is necessary to put the beforementioned figures of belonging/ otherness into the complete neighbourhood context—to contrast them with perceptions of belonging/otherness to the Eurasian Economic Community. Unfortunately, the available CRRC 2013 data set did not include this question for Azerbaijan so that only Georgian and Armenian perspectives can be displayed and compared consistently. Although with 30.9% being the half of the share of feeling attached to the EU, a sense of positive alignment with the EEC is definitively acknowledged in Georgia. At the same time, othering of this perspective is the highest (22.4%) in comparison with other positions within Georgian society. Moreover, 16.5% are yet undecided and a significant share of 29.8% does not know whether to differentiate or to belong to the EEC.

The fragmentation of the South Caucasus in terms of belonging/otherness is rendered visible in particular by a comparison of those Georgian figures with those of Armenia: whereas only 12.6% reject an idea of attachment with the EEC, over the half of the population (52.4%) perceives this as desirable. This figure, thus, is approximately 13% higher than for the EU and even double when compared to orientations towards NATO. Only 13.8% do not know what to answer when being confronted with this question (see also EBD 2013–2017).

Public Othering and Threat Evaluations in the Eastern Partnership

One outcome of this function of belonging/otherness is also reflected in threat associations as indicator of amity and enmity, eventually. The results of these cognitive evaluations fit into the hypotheses of optimal distinctiveness as well as of in-group narcissism and collective out-group hate. Armenians name Azerbaijan with 60% as biggest threat, Azerbaijan identifies Armenia as such with 64%. Georgia does so with Russia (48%), whereas the latter labels the USA as biggest threat (64%). Moreover, these findings fit also for Belarus, Ukraine and Moldova—where they are in line with the cognitive spillovers of ontological boundary drawing as described above as well. With 44% Belarusians see the USA as biggest threat, whereas it is Russia for both Moldovans and Ukrainians (16 and 52%, respectively). Nevertheless, the Gallup Survey (2015) also finds that threats from non-state actors such as ISIS in particular are increasingly valued as high risks—for example, in Georgia, Azerbaijan and Moldova. These threat assessments could be seen to be mobilized within securitized political elite discourses—they mutually resonate in the chosen cases amplifying each other.

It is only within those images of the others that military inputs are cognitively evaluated and reshaped. Thus, Russia's build-up is perceived as providing security guarantees by Belarus and to a certain extent by Azerbaijan and Armenia, whereas Ukraine and Georgia—and to a certain extent Moldova—perceive this as fundamental challenge to their self-conceptualizations. Finding a balance between inputs of the EU and Russia as (non-)regional others and all other significant others in the region whilst navigating between upholding and re-constituting codified behaviour and conceptualizations is an immense task for all countries under scrutiny. For example, momentums of that can be identified in Armenia's and Azerbaijan's sketchy evaluations of Russia and the EU whilst holding contradicting images of each other. There, it is to see whether a potentially converging Russian-led integration project would reconcile or foster those contradictions. Moreover, with Georgia and Ukraine identifying themselves as fundamentally European, it is to see how this further fragmentation and recalibration of the sub-complexes will shape perceptions of otherness and how and if so these conceptualizations of otherness will contribute to friendly or unfriendly images vis-à-vis even further material inputs, perceptions of insecurity and, thus, a potential resort to old patterns.

Concluding Remarks

One basic premise of Buzan and Wæver's work was that there were two RSCs to be found after the Cold War in Europe: a European RSC and a post-Soviet one centred around Russia, which together built the European supercomplex. Especially the latter RSC has been "structured by two long term patterns: (1) waves of growth and contraction of the Russian Empire and (2) change in degrees of separateness and involvement with other regions, primarily Europe" (Buzan and Wæver 2003: 397). This paper has argued that what Buzan and Wæver called "separateness and involvement" could better be modelled as different conceptualizations of otherness with concrete images and narratives of amity and enmity informing and co-constituting the situation on the ground. According to this model, the bridge between the two regional foreign policies of the EU and Russia could be identified in them being different anchors of belonging, yet otherness, diffusing potentially mutually exclusive sets of ideational and material factors. Within this complex, relational factors in form of self-conceptualizations and their co-constitutive motivations in form of contextual ideational and situational material factors play an important role as they inform images and narratives of amity and enmity vis-à-vis the others. It is important to note that only when those positive self-conceptualizations meet negative evaluations of those present others, that these images and narratives will be activated to constitute negative perceptions of security, of "out-group hate."

Policies of the EU and Russia have both structured the region of the EU Eastern Partnership countries to a large extent and influenced and changed the structures fundamentally—whilst approaches to explain these observations have included thoughts on sovereign and post-sovereign institutionalism and geopolitical considerations, less attention has been devoted to potential issues related to identity constructions. However, especially since 2008 and the coming-into-existence of the EU Eastern Partnership as a differentiated approach towards Belarus, Armenia, Azerbaijan, Georgia, Moldova and Ukraine within the ENP, the overlap of the EU's and Russia's foreign policies there could be understood as different, polarizing anchors of belonging and otherness, creating a distinct set of motivations for the EaP countries to adhere to one of those groups in this complex setting—cutting across the dimensions of values and interests.

These de facto contradicting images of allies vs. imperialist/barbarian others there have an impact on those others, too: they, vice versa, mutually constitute images and narratives of otherness and belonging, which, in turn, amplifies the images of enmity and amity of those countries in-between, given ever so more distinctive patterns of alignment/ alienation of those providing incentives. Within this complex, applying a twofold concept of identity—relational and internal—supplements the analysis strongly—as they inform images and narratives of amity and enmity vis-à-vis ontological security seeking mechanisms.

Ontological security approaches provide understandings of (broader) situations based on behaviour, which fundamentally is constituted by an actor's need of "securing" a certain self-conceptualization. However, these social identities are rather exogenous to the system itself—which, in turn, leaves the question open why these specific self-conceptualizations are evoked. Here, applying mechanisms of othering/belonging understood as inter- and intragroup dynamics showed the underlying mechanisms supporting those constitutions quite insightfully. On the other hand, it was possible to dig deeper into the outcomes, the performances, of discourses of security/insecurity as those discourses were framed by broader group dynamics, e.g. to move beyond the reflexive space.

Thus, conceptualizing and embedding ontological security seeking as balancing mechanism between those two identity arenas seems to strengthen significantly the meaning of this otherwise rather generic mechanism and to make sense of how to understand critical junctures. Critical junctures are then to be found in the questioning of ontological self-and-other assumptions and understandings, in the re-negotiation of community boundaries and a (re)construction of collective identities. In this way, it was possible to see a limited trickle-down effect of security dialogues from elites to people as elites—as creators of the main policy documents—have much more ontologically fest positions. A drifting apart of positions of othering/belonging between elites and societies could be observed: leaving room for manoeuvre for other anchors to leverage those in terms of applied identity politics.

Summarizing all those factors, the security situation for the countries under scrutiny is discouraging. They have witnessed a strong commitment to self-conceptualizations which are mutually exclusive. From that, securing these ontological standpoints has led to portraying the (not only) surrounding others as imperialist or even barbarian, as major security threats to the very own existence. Within this existential reasoning, even little changes in comparative (military) advantages constitute heightened perceptions of insecurity as those enmity lenses bundle negative out-group perceptions. It is within this existentialized context that intergroup boundaries are very clearly defined so that it is very difficult to overcome inherited patterns of contradicting self-conceptualizations and, thus, of negative intergroup evaluations. Seeing those factors as endogenous to a co-constitutive environment, changes to this setting could only be realized due to the diffusion of material and ideational factors as well as to expectations of significant others. In this context, it is to see whether the diverse inputs of the EU and Russia are evaluated as being reasonably intense and (bene)fitting for the respective country as to implement these momentums into its self-conceptualization and whether this would constitute a significant change in who is perceived as amicable or inimical other.

In the light of yet again rising populism and nationalism combined with abstract, undercomplex and openly aggressive reasoning, it is of utmost importance to decode these ontological security rationales and existentialized categorizations—around yet eerily familiar lines—to make sense of how and why these countries conceive of their surroundings as they do and what spaces for political manoeuvres emerge given these struggles for and of belonging.

The crisis in Ukraine not only let to a substantial refortification of already existing images of the self(s) and other(s), but reflects a situation where, through mutual constitutions of collective identity, of othering/belonging, not only one actor (Ukraine) was rendered ontologically insecure, but in particular Georgia as well. In this realm, balancing images of (the) significant other(s) were observed a discursive strategy of rendering one ontologically secure again. It is exactly this outlined mobilizing effect of images that led to a spillover of ontological insecurities and securitizations of specific identities from "Ukraine to beyond." The EaP "beyond," in turn, will have further ramifications to face—also, if, in ontological terms, it will still be the Eastern Partnership in years to come.

References

Abdelal, R. 2009. *Measuring Identity.* Cambridge: Cambridge University Press.

Adler, E. 1997. "Imagined (Security) Communities: Cognitive Regions in International Relations." *Millennium—Journal of International Studies* 26 (2): 249–77.

Alexander, M. G., M. B. Brewer, and R. K. Hermann. 1999. "Images and Affect: A Functional Analysis of Out-Group Stereotypes." *Journal of Personality and Social Psychology* 77 (1): 78–93.

Alexander, M. G., S. Levin, and P. J. Henry. 2005. "Image Theory, Social Identity, and Social Dominance: Structural Characteristics and Individual Motives Underlying International Images." *Political Psychology* 26 (1): 27–45.

Allison, R. 2013. *Russia, the West, and Military Intervention.* Oxford: Oxford University Press.

Anderson, B. R. 1996. *Imagined Communities: Reflections on the Origin and Spread of Nationalism.* London: Verso.

Ashmore, R. D., Lee J. Jussim, and D. Wilder. 2001. *Social Identity, Intergroup Conflict, and Conflict Reduction.* Oxford: Oxford University Press.

Balzacq, T. 2011. *Securitization Theory: How Security Problems Emerge and Dissolve.* PRIO New Security Studies. Milton Park, Abingdon, Oxon: Routledge.

Balzacq, T. 2015. "The 'Essence' of Securitization: Theory, Ideal Type, and a Sociological Science of Security." *International Relations* 29 (1): 103–13.

Barnett, M., and R. Duvall. 2005. "Power in International Politics." *International Organization* 59 (01): 39–75.

Buzan, B. 1991. *People, States, and Fear: An Agenda for International Security Studies in the Post-Cold War Era*, 2nd ed. New York: Harvester Wheatsheaf.

Buzan, B., and L. Hansen. 2007. *International Security.* Los Angeles: Sage.

Buzan, B., and O. Wæver. 2003. *Regions and Powers: The Structure of International Security.* Cambridge: Cambridge University Press.

Buzan, B., Ole Wæver, and J. d. Wilde. 1998. *Security: A New Framework for Analysis.* Boulder: Lynne Rienner Publications.

Campbell, D. 1998. *Writing Security: United States Foreign Policy and the Politics of Identity.* Minneapolis: University of Minnesota Press.

Caucasus Research Resource Centers. 2013. "Caucasus Barometer": Caucasus Barometer 2013 Regional Dataset. http://www.crrccenters.org/caucasusbarometer. Accessed January 28, 2018.

Chatham House. 2017. The Struggle for Ukraine. https://www.chathamhouse.
org/sites/files/chathamhouse/publications/research/2017-10-18-struggle-
for-ukraine-ash-gunn-lough-lutsevych-nixey-sherr-wolczukV5.pdf. Accessed
January 28, 2018.
Chernobrov, D. 2016. "Ontological Security and Public (Mis)Recognition of
International Crises: Uncertainty, Political Imagining, and the Self." *Political
Psychology* 37 (5): 581–96.
Coene, F. 2016. *Euro-Atlantic Discourse in Georgia: The Making of Georgian
Foreign and Domestic Policy After the Rose Revolution.* Oxon: Ashgate.
Connolly, W. E. 1985. "Taylor, Foucault, and Otherness." *Political Theory*
13 (3): 365–76.
Council on Foreign Relations (CFR). 2017. Global Conflict Tracker: Nagorno-
Karabakh Conflict. https://www.cfr.org/interactives/global-conflict-tracker#!/
conflict/nagorno-karabakh-conflict. Accessed January 28, 2018.
Danii, O., and M. Mascauteanu. 2011. "Moldova Under the European
Neighbourhood Policy: 'Falling Between Stools'." *Journal of Communist
Studies and Transition Politics* 27 (1): 99–119.
Delehanty, W. K., and B. J. Steele. 2009. "Engaging the Narrative in Ontological
(In)Security Theory: Insights from Feminist IR." *Cambridge Review of
International Affairs* 22 (3): 523–40.
Deutsch, K. W. 1957. *Political Community and the North Atlantic Area:
International Organization in the Light of Historical Experience.* Princeton,
NJ: Princeton University Press.
Ejdus, F. 2017. "Critical Situations, Fundamental Questions and Ontological
Insecurity in World Politics." *Journal of International Relations and
Development.* https://doi.org/10.1057/s41268-017-0083-3. Accessed
January 28, 2018.
Festinger, L. 1962. *A Theory of Cognitive Dissonance.* Stanford, CA: Stanford
University Press.
Finlay, D. J., O. R. Holsti, and R. R. Fagen. 1967. *Enemies in Politics.* Chicago:
Rand McNally.
Finley, Simon A. 2010. "An Identity-Based Understanding of Intergroup
Conflict." *Contemporary Justice Review* 13 (4): 425–41.
Flockhart, T. 2005. "Critical Junctures and Social Identity Theory: Explaining
the Gap Between Danish Mass and Elite Attitudes to Europeanization."
Journal of Common Market Studies 43 (2): 251–71.
Freire, M. R., and R. E. Kanet. 2012. *Russia and Its Near Neighbours: Identity,
Interests and Foreign Policy.* Houndmills, Basingstoke, and Hampshire:
Palgrave Macmillan.
Gallup Survey. 2015. Eastern Europeans, CIS Residents See Russia, U.S. as Threats.
http://news.gallup.com/poll/190415/eastern-europeans-cis-residents-
russia-threats.aspx. Accessed January 28, 2018.

Gaufman, E. 2017. *Security Threats and Public Perception*. Cham: Springer International Publishing.

Goffman, E. 1974. *Frame Analysis: An Essay on the Organization of Experience*. Cambridge, MA: Harvard University Press.

Hagström, L., and K. Gustafsson. 2015. "Japan and Identity Change: Why It Matters in International Relations." *The Pacific Review* 28 (1): 1–22.

Harnisch, S. 2011. *Role Theory in International Relations: Approaches and Analyses*. London: Routledge.

Haukkala, H. 2010. *The EU–Russia Strategic Partnership: The Limits of Post-sovereignty in International Relations*. London: Routledge.

Hopf, T. 2008. *Russia's European Choice*, 1st ed. New York, NY: Palgrave Macmillan.

Hopf, T., and B. B. Allan. 2016. *Making Identity Count*. New York: Oxford University Press.

Huysmans, J. 1998. "Security! What Do You Mean? From Concept to Thick Signifier". *European Journal of International Relations* 4 (2): 226–55.

Independent Institute of Socio-Economic and Political Studies (IISEPS). 2016. Friends and Foes of Belarus, June. http://www.iiseps.org/?p=4793& lang=en. Accessed January 28, 2018.

International Republican Institute (IRI). 2017a. Public Opinion Survey Residents of Moldova. http://www.iri.org/sites/default/files/iri_moldova_poll_march_2017.pdf. Accessed January 28, 2018.

International Republican Institute (IRI). 2017b. Public Opinion Survey of Residents of Ukraine. http://www.iri.org/sites/default/files/2013%20July% 2017%20Survey%20of%20Ukainian%20Public%20Opinion%2C%20May%20 14-28%2C%202013.pdf and http://www.iri.org/sites/default/files/2017-may-survey-of-residents-of-ukraine_en.pdf. Accessed January 28, 2018.

Jerez-Mir, M., J. Real-Dato, and R. Vázquez-García. 2009. "Identity and Representation in the Perceptions of Political Elites and Public Opinion: A Comparison Between Southern and Post-communist Central-Eastern Europe." *Europe-Asia Studies* 61 (6): 943–66.

Katzenstein, P. J. 1996. *The Culture of National Security: Norms and Identity in World Politics*. New York: Columbia University Press.

Kiev International Institute of Sociology (KIIS). 2017. Changes in the Attitude of the Population of Ukraine Toward Russia and of the Population of Russian Toward Ukraine. http://www.kiis.com.ua/?lang=eng&cat=re-ports&id=680&page=2. Accessed January 28, 2018.

Korosteleva, E. 2017. "Putting the EU Global Security Strategy to Test: 'Cooperative Orders' and Othering in EU–Russia Relations." *International Politics*. https://doi.org/10.1057/s41311-017-0128-7. Accessed January 28, 2018.

Korostelina, K. V. 2003. "The Multiethnic State-Building Dilemma. National and Ethnic Minorities' Identities in the Crimea." *National Identities* 5 (2): 141–59.

Korostelina, K. V. 2007. *Social Identity and Conflict: Structures, Dynamics, and Implications*, 1st ed. New York: Palgrave Macmillan.

Korostelina, K. V. 2014. *Constructing the Narratives of Identity and Power: Self-imagination in a Young Ukrainian Nation*. Lanham: Lexington Books.

Kteily, N., G. Hodson, and E. Bruneau. 2016. "They See Us as Less than Human: Metadehumanization Predicts Intergroup Conflict via Reciprocal Dehumanization." *Journal of Personality and Social Psychology* 110 (3): 343–70.

Lupovici, A. 2012. "Ontological Dissonance, Clashing Identities, and Israel's Unilateral Steps Towards the Palestinians." *Review of International Studies* 38 (4): 809–33.

Made, V., and A. Sekarev. 2011. *The European Neighbourhood After August 2008*. Dordrecht: Republic of Letters.

McSweeney, B. 1996. "Identity and Security: Buzan and the Copenhagen School." *Review of International Studies* 22 (1): 81–93.

Mitzen, J. 2006. "Ontological Security in World Politics: State Identity and the Security Dilemma." *European Journal of International Relations* 12 (3): 341–70.

Mouffe, C. 2005. *On the Political. Thinking in Action*. London: Routledge.

Mälksoo, M. 2015. "'Memory Must Be Defended': Beyond the Politics of Mnemonical Security." *Security Dialogue* 46 (3): 221–37.

Nabers, D. 2015. *A Poststructuralist Discourse Theory of Global Politics*. Houndsmills and New York: Palgrave Macmillan.

Neumann, I. B. 1992. "Identity and Security." *Journal of Peace Research* 29 (2): 221–26.

Rumelili, B. 2015a. *Conflict Resolution and Ontological Security*. Oxon: Routledge.

Rumelili, B. 2015b. "Identity and Desecuritisation: The Pitfalls of Conflating Ontological and Physical Security." *Journal of International Relations and Development* 18 (1): 52–74.

SIPRI. 2016. SIPRI Military Expenditure Database. https://www.sipri.org/databases/milex. Accessed January 28, 2018.

Schumacher, T., A. Marchetti, and T. Demmelhuber. 2018. *The Routledge Handbook on the European Neighbourhood Policy*. Oxon: Routledge.

Steele, B. J. 2005. "Ontological Security and the Power of Self-identity: British Neutrality and the American Civil War." *Review of International Studies* 31 (3): 519–40.

Steele, B. J. 2008. *Ontological Security in International Relations: Self-identity and the IR State*. London: Routledge.

Stern, M. 2005. *Naming Security—Constructing Identity: "Mayan women" in Guatemala on the Eve of "Peace".* Manchester, UK: Manchester University Press.

Stryker, S. 2008. "From Mead to a Structural Symbolic Interactionism and Beyond." *Annual Review of Sociology* 34 (1): 15–31.

Subotić, J. 2015. "Narrative, Ontological Security, and Foreign Policy Change." *Foreign Policy Analysis* 12 (4): 610–27.

Szkola, S. 2017. "Discursive Reconstructions of Boundaries in the South Caucasus Countries vis-à-vis the EU and Russia and the Crux of Securitization." UPTAKE Working Paper No. 5. Available at: http://www.uptake.ut.ee/wp-content/uploads/2017/06/05_szkola.pdf.

Tocci, N. 2017. "A Crisis of Perception and Reality in EU–Russia Relations." http://valdaiclub.com/a/highlights/crisis-of-perception-and-reality/. Accessed January 28, 2018.

Weisel, O., and R. Böhm. 2015. "'Ingroup Love' and 'Outgroup Hate' in Intergroup Conflict Between Natural Groups." *Journal of Experimental Social Psychology* 60 (1): 110–20.

White, S., and V. Feklyunina. 2014. *Identities and Foreign Policies in Russia, Ukraine and Belarus: The Other Europes.* London and New York: Palgrave Macmillan.

Whitman, R. G., and S. Wolff, eds. 2010. *The European Neighbourhood Policy in Perspective: Context, Implementation and Impact.* Basingstoke: Palgrave Macmillan.

Williams, M. C. 2003. "Words, Images, Enemies: Securitization and International Politics." *International Studies Quarterly* 47 (4): 511–31.

World Values Survey. Wave 5, 2005–2009 Official Aggregate v.20140429. www.worldvaluessurvey.org. Accessed January 28, 2018.

World Values Survey Association. Wave 6, 2010–2014 Official Aggregate v.20150418. www.worldvaluessurvey.org. Accessed January 28, 2018.

INDEX

© The Editor(s) (if applicable) and The Author(s),
under exclusive license to Springer International Publishing AG,
part of Springer Nature 2018
E. Resende et al. (eds.), *Crisis and Change in Post-Cold War
Global Politics*, https://doi.org/10.1007/978-3-319-78589-9

CPSIA information can be obtained
at www.ICGtesting.com
Printed in the USA
LVHW07*1049130518
577031LV00013B/704/P